KT-175-492

THE
PAUL HAMLYN
LIBRARY

DONATED BY
THE PAUL HAMLYN
FOUNDATION
TO THE
BRITISH MUSEUM

opened December 2000

WITHDRAWN

To

PETER HENDRIE (1917-1968)
Founder Member of the Socialist
Labour League whose dedicated
labours made this edition of
Trotsky's work possible. His work
was always characterized by dogged
tenacity, meticulous attention to
detail and a profound respect for the
scientific heritage of Marxism, which
will assure the successful establishment of socialism in Britain.

Leon Trotsky

Problems of the Chinese Revolution

With Appendices by Zinoviev, Vuyovitch, Nassunov and Others

NEW PARK PUBLICATIONS
London 1969

Published by New Park Publications Ltd., 186a Clapham High Street,
London, S.W.4.

MAY 1969

Translated by Max Shachtman

Printed by Plough Press Ltd. (TU), r/o 180 Clapham High Street,
London, S.W.4.

Contents

Introduction

The tempestuous events which have transformed China and the world situation in the past 40 years and the tasks with which Marxist revolutionaries are confronted today have enhanced the importance of the articles, speeches and documents brought together in this book.

That the particular questions at issue relate to the Second Chinese Revolution of 1925-1927 and the reasons for its defeat should lead no one to believe that this is simply a book about China for historians or specialists. On the contrary, while this volume is invaluable for the light which it sheds on a crucial and tragic episode in the history of the Chinese working class and peasantry its principal concern is with the tactics and strategy of world revolution. In that respect it forms part of a continuous struggle for theory waged by Trotsky and the Left Opposition which began in the early 1920s and is continued today by the International Committee of the Fourth International.

The main items in this collection consist of articles and speeches by Leon Trotsky beginning with a full-scale attack on Stalin's justification for the policy imposed upon the Chinese Communist Party and concluding with a balance sheet of the disaster to which it led written some three years later. The period covered was a decisive one in the history of the international communist movement. These years, dominated by the struggle in China, also marked the intensification of the attack on the Left Opposition in Russia which ended with defeat and the dispersal and exile of its leading members. As will be seen, the dateline moves from Moscow, first to Trotsky's place of exile in Alma Ata and then, after his expulsion from the Soviet Union, to Prinkipo in Turkey.

The defeat of the Left Opposition was a necessary stage in the consolidation of the ascendancy of the Stalinist bureaucracy. In fact, however, even before the revolutionary events in China had begun, the possibilities left open for the Opposition to express itself had been greatly reduced. It is true that some semblance of a debate still took place in the Comintern, but the great majority of party members only heard the case of the Opposition as it was presented in distorted form in the official press organs. The items published here were not made freely available to members of the party so that they could draw their own conclusions. In fact they were only given limited circulation or were not known at all outside narrow circles of the Opposition itself or of a few party functionaries. Even the reports from supporters of the official line who had seen on the spot the disasters to which it led were similarly suppressed, as in the case of the Letter from Shanghai printed in the Appendix.

Like many of the classics of Marxism, then, this book is the result of a polemic, but one which had to be conducted under very disadvantageous conditions. It was part of a struggle against the revision of Marxism by the bureaucratic caste which had assumed power in the first workers' state. It provides an example of the Marxist method applied to concrete problems of revolutionary tactics and strategy in an extremely complex and rapidly changing situation. It stands on the ground of the Permanent Revolution as tested and confirmed in the three Russian Revolutions and strengthened by the experience gained in Germany and other countries since 1917. It thus re-asserts and enriches fundamental Marxist theoretical principles in the light of the specific experiences of the Chinese Revolution, that is to say of a revolutionary struggle in a semi-colonial country subordinate to the imperialist powers.

When revolutionary events began to erupt in China the political line which flowed from the theory of 'socialism in one country' propounded for the first time by Stalin in 1924 began to be put to the test. Stalin's Theses rested on three points: that the Chinese Revolution was a national liberation struggle, that the bourgeoisie was weak and that the Chinese Communists could utilize the experience and would have the support of the Soviet Union. Already Chiang Kai-shek, the leading military figure in the bourgeois national movement, the Kuomintang, had been made an honorary member of the Executive Committee of the Comintern and Chinese Communists had been instructed to join the KMT as individual members. This support for a bourgeois nationalist movement, the Canton government and the army of Chiang Kai-shek— built up and strengthened with Russian advisers and assistance—

rested on a false estimation of the relationship of forces in China and thus on the nature of the coming revolution.

It was not accidental that former Mensheviks, such as Martinov, were entrusted with the task of elaborating and defending Comintern policy in China. Stalin's line depended on a theory of 'revolution by stages' not unlike that put forward by the Mensheviks in Russia. As Trotsky shows, their press abroad spoke with approval of the support given to the KMT. This perspective required that the proletariat and peasantry should accept in practice the leadership of the bourgeoisie. Stalin supposed that there was in China a class conflict between feudal landowners and an urban bourgeoisie and petty bourgeoisie. In fact most of the land was owned by bourgeois landowners who rented it to a mass of poverty-stricken peasants who at the same time were exploited by village usurers, also part of the bourgeoisie. The support for the KMT, especially the cadre of its army, came in large part from this bourgeoisie, closely bound up with the exploitation of the peasantry and thus unable to tolerate an agrarian revolution which was the object of the peasant movement. A further contradiction existed in the towns where the 'national bourgeoisie', although it had its differences with imperialism, made common cause with it in keeping down the working class, suppressing strikes and smashing working-class organizations. When Chiang Kai-shek took power in Canton in March, 1926, and went on to take measures against the working class, he continued nevertheless to enjoy the full support of the Comintern.

To grasp the intricacies of the situation and the fundamental differences between the line of Trotsky and that of Stalin-Bukharin-Martinov it is necessary, of course, to study carefully the items brought together in this book. There can be no doubt, on the basis of such a study, that support for the Kuomintang marked a flagrant breach with all the principles of Bolshevism and flew in the face of the Theses on the National and Colonial Question drawn up by Lenin and approved by the Comintern only a few years before. Instead of fighting for its independent line, which was meeting with a ready reception from the small but strategically placed working class, the Chinese Communist Party was obliged to dissolve itself into the KMT and become political coolies for Chiang Kai-shek. Instead of being able to call for the expropriation of the landlords, Chinese Communists, in the nationalist armies, had to take their orders from officers drawn from the bourgeois land-owning class. Not only were the Chinese Communists disarmed politically as well as militarily under instructions from the Comintern, but every disaster to which this led was glossed over and explained away to preserve the illusion of the blamelessness and infallibility of the leadership in Moscow. Necessarily, at the same time, this was accompanied by a vicious campaign against all critics of the line which effectively prevented them from making their voices heard.

Looked at historically, with the documents open for inspection and in the light of the actual course followed by events in China the case against Stalin and his supporters appears completely damning. Even those who thought that it might succeed could hardly fail to admit that the result was bloody and disastrous defeat. The effort to redeem the situation by launching the ill-fated Canton insurrection was in keeping with the irresponsibility of the whole China policy and opened the way for the further adventures of the 'third period'. Those who in one way or another continue to apologize for Stalin, not least of all the Maoists, have a difficult job to explain away his role in bringing about the defeat of the Second Chinese Revolution. But these events were not isolated, nor were the policies which led to these defeats a temporary course applied only to China. On the contrary, the self-same policies had been applied in Germany and were being carried on in relation to the TUC in Britain. It is impossible to cut out and forget the Chinese episode when dealing with Stalinism as being in some way exceptional. Furthermore, critics of Trotskyism generally forget China because it is also difficult to fit into some of the arguments which they have brought against the theory of permanent revolution and Trotsky's struggle for Marxism against the revisionism comprised in the theory of 'socialism in one country'.

In fact, Trotsky's writings on China form a piece with his whole theoretical work: his critique of the Draft Programme of the Communist International, his urgent warnings about the disasters awaiting the German proletariat before 1933, his analysis of the Popular Front policies in France and Spain. They form part of the development of the science of revolution elaborated by Marx and Engels, enriched by the experience of Bolshevism, geared to the epoch of imperialism by Lenin and carried on in the period of defeats during the 1930s by Trotsky, continued today by the Fourth International.

In relation to China, as in the other episodes mentioned, it was not a case of Trotsky being wise after the event. Especially in the case of China he warned about errors which could have been corrected, about dangers which could have been averted. His critics may say, armed with the benefit of hindsight, that he should have done or said this rather than that, that he made mistakes (which he admitted) or bow down before the accomplished fact in the shape of the Soviet bureaucracy and Maoism. It is necessary, therefore, to examine two or three points which may give rise to misunderstanding about Trotsky's position on the Chinese question.

Now, as it had done all along, after the bloody defeat of the Chinese workers and peasants the Stalinist leadership of the Comintern looked around for scapegoats. Where could they be found more easily than among the leaders of the Chinese Communist Party who had for a number of years obediently followed the political line imposed by the Comintern? The majority of the Chinese leadership were youthful and enthusiastic. They accepted the discipline of the Comintern, based as it was upon the enormous prestige of Bolshevism and the Russian Revolution. To blame them for their adherence to instructions is hardly helpful; in any case they did not know that the Opposition was putting forward an alternative. Chen Du-Siu, who later joined the Left Opposition, then declared that all along he had had serious doubts about the policy imposed on the party, of which he was leader, by the Comintern advisers acting under Stalin's direction. At the most the Comintern would only be justified in criticizing the Chinese for the way in which they carried out the line—and they did not hesitate to excuse themselves by doing this. But the real point is that the line itself was a suicidal one which condemned the Chinese Communist Party to defeat. There is no way in which Stalin's responsibility can be evaded. Had the Chinese Communist leadership been more experienced in applying the tactical line they would still have been bound by a strategy which exposed their whole membership and their supporters in the working class to Chiang Kai-shek's reign of terror when that honorary member of the Comintern, sponsored by Stalin, did what his class position imposed upon him.

Of course, it may be said that in his first statements on the Chinese situation Trotsky did not oppose explicitly the entry of Communists into the Kuomintang. The reason for this is not obscure and, though it may have been a mistake in retrospect, it flowed from particular tactical considerations. Involved here was the alliance between Trotsky and his supporters and the Zinovievites. As is well known, in the controversy over Trotsky's 'Lessons of October' Trotsky and Zinoviev were on opposite sides. Moreover, the basis upon which Zinoviev opposed Stalin's policy in China was different from that of Trotsky. These differences may be summarized as follows: Trotsky applied to China the theory of the permanent revolution, Zinoviev was guided by Lenin's slogan of 'the democratic dictatorship of the proletariat and the peasantry', the pre-February line of the Bolsheviks. Trotsky was convinced that this slogan would have an even shorter life in China than in Russia and admitted that he made what was, indeed, an accommodation to the incorrect Zinovievite position for tactical reasons. In the same way the alliance with Zinoviev also meant that in public statements the question of the Chinese Communist Party leaving the Kuomintang at once could not be raised. In a letter written to Max Shachtman in 1930 quoted in the Introduction to the original English-language edition of the present work (1932) Trotsky made clear that he had opposed entry to the KMT from the beginning and that constant conflicts arose with his Zinovievite allies on the issue during the short period in which they worked together. To ask Trotsky to have raised the question in the first part of 1926 would no doubt have meant throwing the Zinovievites more quickly into the arms of the Stalinists and would have reduced still further the possibility of redressing in time the disastrous course pursued in China under Comintern instructions.

After the defeat of the Second Chinese Revolution, Trotsky assumed that there would be a period of reflux in which the bourgeoisie would be strengthened temporarily on the basis of a certain economic revival. Under such conditions, with a new influx of foreign capital and some industrial development, account had to be taken of the possibility of a constitutional development and the establishment of some form of parliamentary government. Within such a context it would have been correct for the Chinese Communist Party to re-group its forces and prepare for the Third Revolution by fighting for democratic tasks, including through parliamentary struggle. Trotsky added that this seemed, in 1928, only a probable and not an inevitable development and that 'a new disintegration of the country, as well as external causes, may prevent its realization'.

Events were soon to show that there was to be no opportunity for a smooth and stable course of parliamentary development in Chinese history. The onset of the World Economic Depression rapidly changed the relationship of the Chinese bourgeoisie to imperialism, weakening and dividing it. The Japanese invasion threatened China with direct colonization and challenged the older imperialist interests on warlike terms. The depression destroyed any possibility of the Western imperialist countries providing the large-scale capital investment needed to open up the Chinese market in competition with the Japanese. The nationalist regime under Chiang Kai-shek thus remained of a militarist Bonapartist type with only some formal gestures to parliamentary government. Meanwhile the disintegration of China went on apace. The bourgeoisie became increasingly demoralized and discredited, virtually abandoned by its Western backers. The burdens on the masses, particularly on the peasantry, thus became more intolerable.

The ability of the Maoist policy to succeed arose from a successful and empirical adaptation to the conditions in China brought about by the decay of world capitalism. It included a shift in the focus of Communist Party activity from the cities—where the militant workers had been decimated in 1926-1927 and a good deal of suspicion of communist policy remained—to the rural areas where peasant discontent was mounting. It was based on the building of peasant armies in the so-called 'Soviet' areas. It adopted the slogan of 'new democracy' which was essentially no different from the 'bloc of four classes' and the revolution by stages which the Stalinist leadership had imposed in the Second Revolution. All this was freely salted with nationalism and the unity of all patriotic classes against the Japanese (and later the Americans) and sprinkled with the mild phrases of the Popular Front period.

It is true that the line proposed by Stalin carried these tendencies to their logical conclusion: an alliance with the Kuomintang and an indefinite period of bourgeois parliamentary rule. The Maoist leadership rejected these suggestions and went its own way. In a sense Stalin had taken over Trotsky's 1928 prognosis—after it had long since been made obsolete by world developments. Nothing less than an abject capitulation would have been required from the Chinese Communist Party to realize Stalin's policy, capitulation to a Kuomintang regime which was dying from internal decay. There was no longer any basis for the rule of the national bourgeoisie short of the re-conquest of the country by foreign imperialism. Such a possibility was excluded in the 1940s. The Chinese peasant armies, recruited and directed by the Maoist Communist Party, thus led the successful Third Revolution which culminated in 1949. The military forces of the KMT melted away in the closing stages of the civil war and no significant section of the population was any longer prepared to fight on its behalf. The armies of Mao Tse-tung thus marched in to fill the power vacuum with comparatively little difficulty.

The tasks which the new regime assumed remained those of 'socialism in one country', a country which, moreover, was still more backward than Russia in 1917. The stormy history of China since 1949 is a product of this situation. The victory in China, which could have decisively changed the whole history of the world in 1926, was certainly important in 1949 but its immediate impact must not be over-estimated. In Europe the betrayals of Stalinism and social democracy had killed the post-war revolutionary upsurge and the Chinese Revolution did not revive it. While the colonial liberation movement received some encouragement from the Communist victory in China it must not be forgotten that for many years, as expressed at Bandung and elsewhere, the Peking leadership pursued a conciliatory policy towards the national bourgeoisie which was not without an echo of the disastrous errors of the 1926 period. In fact, in Indonesia, under the leadership of Aidit and supported by Peking, history repeated itself in tragic form. Moreover, Mao's policy did not shake the hold of Stalinism, which, as the many theoretical documents issued during the height of the dispute with Moscow show, it completely failed to understand. Rather, in moving to the left, despite the fact that he had disregarded the prescriptions of Stalin for China, Mao continued to assert his fidelity to Stalin. It was only when the 'Khrushchevite revisionists' coupled their 'de-Stalinization' with a conciliatory policy towards world imperialism which threatened Chinese national interests that the break with Moscow became irrevocable. This left the Maoists as the only open admirers and defenders of the Stalin line, albeit one which had cost the lives of thousands of Chinese communists and which, if pursued in the nineteen-forties, would have prevented the victory of the Third Chinese Revolution.

Had the victory of the Chinese Revolution been assured in

1926-1927 there can be no doubt that the course of world history would have been fundamentally changed. The consequences of Stalin's policy in China were thus profound and tragic. It meant the continued isolation of the first workers' state which, with the smashing of the Opposition, continued on its course of bureaucratic degeneration. Nowhere were the results of this more evident than in the policy imposed in the next years on the Communist International which led directly to the defeat of the powerful and highly-organized German working class and the victory of Hitler in 1933. The plague of fascism decended on large sections of the European working class and the way was prepared for the Second Imperialist War with all it meant in bloodshed and misery. The same agonizing picture is presented in China and the Far East. The victory of Chiang Kai-shek opened the way for Japanese imperialism in China because of his regime's inability to solve the national democratic tasks imposed in a semi-colonial country. A Communist China, in the thirties, would, on the other hand, been the spearhead for the revolutionary advance of the workers and peasants of Asia in which the Japanese militarists and imperialists would have been among the first victims.

It is unrealistic, clearly, to pursue such exercises in what might have been. But these remarks may serve to show what was really at stake in China: the tempo of the world revolution, the fate of the international working class, the future of humanity. Trotsky surely wrote with this broad historical perspective constantly in his mind, as the whole body of his theoretical writings shows. In other words, his articles and speeches on the Chinese question are not to be seen as merely a polemic about tactics in which what was at stake was only the revolution in China. Far more fundamental theoretical questions were involved. Stalin and his supporters, in their China policies, reflected the narrow interests of the ascending bureaucratic caste in Russia. Their viewpoint was based upon a short-run perspective and a summary estimation of the Chinese situation largely in isolation from the world context. They hoped for quick and easy victories in China and banked on Chiang Kai-shek, and then on the so-called 'Left' Kuomintang, as safe and faithful allies, at least for a period. An essentially narrow-minded and empirical appreciation of national struggles was a direct consequence of the theory of 'socialism in one country'. It was not at this stage that the bureaucracy was consciously counter-revolutionary : it wanted the revolution in China to succeed, but in the form of a bourgeois democratic revolution of a sort which was already an historical archaism.

In the controversy over the Chinese Revolution, therefore, it can be said that on every score, despite some mistakes or doubtful tactical moves which could only have been averted with hindsight, Trotsky, and those members of the Opposition who remained unshaken and unintimidated, have been vindicated all along the line. Those who continue the struggle of Trotsky for the construction of the Fourth International will find this book an invaluable guide to and educator in the Marxist method. What is more, Trotsky's analysis of the 1926-1927 debacle provides an unshakeable foundation to the struggle against the insidious revisionism of the Pabloite group which split the Fourth International in 1953 and who now, under the leadership of Ernest Mandel, challenge every basic principle of Marxism, and and particular, the theory of the Permanent Revolution which Trotsky defends so ably and exhaustively in his polemic with the revisionists of another era. It is in this sense, and still more as a major contribution to Marxism, that this book should be read and worked over today.

February 1969   TOM KEMP

The Chinese Revolution and the Theses of Comrade Stalin

THE THESES of comrade Stalin entitled *Problems of the Chinese Revolution* were published in *Pravda* on April 21, 1927, a few days after the close of the plenary session of the Central Committee,* to which these theses were never presented and at which they were never discussed (although all the members of the plenum were still in Moscow).

Moreover, the theses of comrade Stalin are erroneous to such a point, they turn the matter upside down to such a degree, they are so permeated with the spirit of *khvostism,*† they are so inclined to perpetuate the mistakes already made, that to remain silent about them would be a positive crime.

---

* The theses of comrade Stalin are published in the name of the Central Committee. This does not change the fact that the theses were not examined by the plenum of the Central Committee. The Political Bureau charged three of its members, comrades Stalin, Bukharin and Molotov, to look over the theses of comrade Stalin and in case of agreement, to publish them in the name of the Central Committee. Naturally, it is not a question of the formal side of the matter, which nobody raises. But it is quite clear that such a 'simplified' method of deciding questions of world importance, after the mistakes made and the heavy defeats, in no wise serves the interests of the party and of the Chinese revolution.

† A popular Russian expression which is difficult to translate in a word. It signifies the policy of dragging behind the tail of events. From the Russian word *khvost,* or tail.—Tr.

THE LESSONS OF THE CHINESE EVENTS MUST BE DRAWN

1. The prohibition of an open discussion of the theoretical and tactical problems of the Chinese revolution has been motivated of late by the fact that such a discussion would delight the enemies of the USSR. Naturally it would be quite impermissible to make public facts that could be seized upon by enemies, who, incidentally, do not shrink from the direct invention of 'facts' and 'documents'. But there is no need at all for such a discussion. It is only a question of determining the driving forces of the Chinese revolution and of estimating the basic line of its political direction. In other words, it is a question of discussing *the same questions to which the theses of comrade Stalin are devoted.* If these theses can be published, then why cannot a criticism of them be published?

It is an unheard-of mistake to contend that a discussion of the problems of the Chinese revolution can injure our state interests. If this were so, then not only the Communist Party of the Soviet Union but every other party of the Communist International, including the Chinese, would have to abstain from any discussion. But the interests of the Chinese revolution, as well as the interests of the education of all the Communist parties in the world, demand an open, energetic, exhaustive discussion of all the problems of the Chinese revolution, especially those in dispute. It is not true that the interests of the Communist International conflict with the state interests of the USSR. The renunciation of discussion of the mistakes is not dictated by the interests of a workers' state, but by a false 'apparatus-like', bureaucratic attitude towards the Chinese revolution as well as towards the interests of the USSR.

2. The April defeat of the Chinese revolution is not only a defeat for the opportunist line but also a defeat for the bureaucratic methods of the leadership, through which the party is confronted with every decision as an accomplished fact: the

decision, it is explained, does not justify criticism until facts demonstrate its annulment, whereupon it is just as automatically, that is, behind the back of the party, replaced by a decision which is frequently more erroneous, like the present theses of Stalin. Such a method, which, in and by itself, is incompatible with the development of a revolutionary party, becomes an especially heavy obstacle to young parties that can and should learn independently from the experiences of defeats and mistakes.

The theses of comrade Stalin are published. At least within the limits of these theses, the questions of the Chinese revolution can and must be discussed openly and from every angle.

THE YOKE OF IMPERIALISM AND THE CLASS STRUGGLE

3. The peculiarity of the Chinese revolution—in comparison, for example, with our revolution of 1905—lies above all in the semi-colonial position in China. A policy that disregarded the powerful pressure of imperialism on the internal life of China would be radically false. But a policy that proceeded from an abstract conception of national oppression without its class refraction and reflection would be no less false. The main source of the mistakes in the theses of comrade Stalin, as in the whole leading line in general, is the false conception of the role of imperialism and its influence on the class relationships of China.

The imperialist yoke is supposed to serve as a justification for the policy of the 'bloc of four classes'. The yoke of imperialism leads allegedly to the fact that 'all' (!) the classes of China look upon the Canton government as the 'national government of the whole of China in the same way' (!). (Speech of comrade Kalinin, *Izvestia,* March 6.) This is essentially the position of the Right Kuomintang man, Dai Tshi Tao, who pretends that the laws of the class struggle do not exist for China—because of imperialist pressure.

China is an oppressed semi-colonial country. The development of the productive forces of China, which is proceeding in capitalist forms, demands the shaking off of the imperialist yoke. The war of China for its national independence is a progressive war, because it flows from the necessities of the economic and cultural development of China itself, as well as because it facilitates the development of the revolution of the British proletariat and that of the whole world proletariat.

But this by no means signifies that the imperialist yoke is a mechanical one, subjugating 'all' the classes of China in the 'same' way. The powerful role of foreign capital in the life of China has caused very strong sections of the Chinese bourgeoisie, the bureaucracy and the military to join their destiny with that of imperialism. Without this tie, the enormous role of the so-called 'militarists' in the life of modern China would be inconceivable.

It would further be profound *naïveté* to believe that an abyss lies between the so-called comprador bourgeoisie, that is, the economic and political agency of foreign capital in China, and the so-called 'national' bourgeoisie. No, these two sections stand incomparably closer to each other than the bourgeoisie and the masses of workers and peasants. The bourgeoisie participated in the national war as an internal brake, looking upon the worker and peasant masses with growing hostility, and becoming ever readier to conclude a compromise with imperialism.

Installed within the Kuomintang and its leadership, the national bourgeoisie has been essentially an instrument of the compradors and imperialism. It can remain in the camp of the national war only because of the weakness of the worker and peasant masses, the lack of development of the class struggle, the docility of the Kuomintang in the hands of the bourgeoisie. the lack of independence of the Chinese Communist Party and **the docility of the Kuomintang in the hands of the bourgeoisie.**

It is a gross mistake to think that imperialism mechanically welds together all the classes of China from without. That is the position of the Chinese Cadet, Dai Tshi Tao, but in no wise ours. The revolutionary struggle against imperialism does not weaken, but rather strengthens the political differentiation of the classes. Imperialism is a highly powerful force in the internal relationships of China. The main source of this force is not the warships in the waters of the Yangtse Kiang—they are only auxiliaries—but the economic and political bond between foreign capital and the native bourgeoisie. The struggle against imperialism, precisely because of its economic and military power, demands a powerful exertion of forces from the very depths of the Chinese people. To really arouse the workers and peasants against imperialism is possible only by connecting their basic and most profound life interests with the cause of the country's liberation. A workers' strike—small or large—an agrarian rebellion, an uprising of the oppressed sections in city and country against the usurer, against the bureaucracy, against the local military satraps, all that arouses the multitudes, that welds them together, that educates, steels, is a real step forward on the road to the revolutionary and social liberation of the Chinese people. Without that, the military successes and failures of the Right, semi-Right or semi-Left generals will remain foam on the surface of the ocean. But everything that brings the oppressed and exploited masses of the toilers to their feet inevitably pushes the national bourgeoisie into an open bloc with the imperialists. The class struggle between the bourgeoisie and the masses of workers and peasants is not weakened, but, on the contrary, is sharpened by imperialist oppression, to the point of bloody civil war at every serious conflict. The Chinese bourgeoisie always has a solid rearguard behind it in imperialism, which will always help it with money, goods and shells against the workers and peasants.

Only wretched philistines and sycophants, who hope in their

hearts to obtain freedom for China as an imperialist bounty
for the good behaviour of the masses, can believe that the
national liberation of China can be achieved by moderating the
class struggle, by curbing strikes and agrarian uprisings, by
abandoning the arming of the masses, etc. When comrade
Martinov proposes that strikes and the struggle on the land
be replaced by a solution of the questions through the medium
of governmental arbitration, then he differs in no way from Dai
Tshi Tao, the philosophical inspirer of Chiang Kai-shek's policy.

Democratic or Socialist Revolution?

4. The senseless contention is attributed to the Opposition
that China now stands on the eve of a socialist dictatorship of
the proletariat. There is nothing original in this 'criticism'.
On the eve of 1905 and later on, the Mensheviks frequently
declared that Lenin's tactic would be correct if Russia were
directly on the eve of the socialist revolution. Lenin, however,
explained to them that his tactic was the only road to the radical
victory of the democratic revolution which, under favourable
conditions, would begin to grow over into a socialist revolution.

The question of the 'non-capitalist' path of development of
China was posed in a conditional form by Lenin, for whom,
as for us, it was and is ABC wisdom that the Chinese
revolution, left to its own forces, that is, *without the direct
support of the victorious proletariat of the USSR and the
working class of all advanced countries,* could end only with
the conquest of the broadest possibilities for the capitalist development of the country, with more favourable conditions for
the labour movement.

5. No less basically false is the contention that the
question as to whether the Chinese proletariat needs an independent party; whether this party needs a bloc with the Kuo-

mintang or must subordinate itself to it; whether Soviets are necessary, etc., must be solved in accordance with how we conceive the course and the tempo of the *further* stages of the Chinese revolution. It is quite possible that China will have to pass through a relatively prolonged stage of parliamentarism, beginning with a Constituent Assembly. This demand is inscribed on the banner of the Communist party. If the bourgeois democratic revolution does not grow into a socialist revolution in the near future, then in all probability the workers' and peasants' Soviets will pass from the scene for a definite stage and give way to a bourgeois regime, which, depending on the progress of the world revolution, will in turn give way, at a new historical stage, to the dictatorship of the proletariat.

6. But first of all, the inevitability of the capitalist path has by no means been proved; and secondly—this argument is now incomparably more timely for us—the bourgeois tasks can be solved in various ways. The slogan of the Constituent Assembly becomes an empty abstraction, often simple charlatanry, if one does not add who will convoke it and with what programme. Chiang Kai-shek can raise the slogan of a Constituent Assembly against us even tomorrow, just as he has now raised his 'workers' and peasants' programme' against us. We want a Constituent Assembly convoked not by Chiang Kai-shek but by the executive committee of the workers' and peasants' Soviets. That is the only serious and sure road.

7. Basically untenable is the endeavour of comrade Bukharin to justify the opportunist and compromising line by referring to the allegedly predominant role of the 'remnants of feudalism' in Chinese economy. Even if comrade Bukharin's estimation of Chinese economy rested on an economic analysis and not on scholastic definitions, the 'remnants of feudalism' would still be unable to justify the policy which so manifestly facilitated the April *coup d'état.*

The Chinese revolution has a national bourgeois character principally because the development of the productive forces of Chinese capitalism collides with its governmental customs dependence upon the countries of imperialism. The obstruction of the development of Chinese industry and the throttling of the internal market involve the conservation and rebirth of the most backward forms of production in agriculture, of the most parasitic forms of exploitation, of the most barbaric forms of oppression and violence, the growth of surplus population, as well as the persistence and aggravation of pauperism and all sorts of slavery.

No matter how great the specific weight of the typically 'feudal' elements in Chinese economy may be they can be swept away only in a revolutionary way, and consequently not in alliance with the bourgeoisie but in direct struggle against it.

The more complicated and tortuous is the interlacing of feudal and capitalist relations, the less the agrarian question can be solved by legislation from above, the more indispensable is the revolutionary initiative of the peasant masses in close union with the workers and the poor population of the cities, the falser is the policy that clings convulsively to the alliance with the bourgeoisie and the large landowner and subordinates its work among the masses to this alliance. The policy of the 'bloc of four classes' not only prepared the bloc of the bourgeoisie with imperialism, but also meant the preservation of all the survivals of barbarism in administration and in economy.

To invoke the bourgeois character of the Chinese revolution, in particular against the Soviets, is simply to renounce the experiences of our bourgeois revolutions of 1905 and February 1917. In these revolutions, the immediate and essential objective was the abolition of the autocratic and feudal regime. This aim did not exclude, but demanded the arming of the workers and the formation of Soviets. Here is how Lenin treated the subject after the February revolution:

For an effective struggle against the tsarist monarchy, for a real assurance of liberty not only in words, not in elegant promises of the rhetoricians of liberalism, the workers must not support the new government, but the government must 'support' the workers. For the only guarantee of freedom and of the final destruction of tsarism is *the arming of the proletariat,* the consolidation, the extension, the development of the role, the significance, and the power of the workers' and soldiers' Soviets. Everything else is phrases and lies of the politicians in the liberal and radical camps who are deceiving themselves. Support the arming of the workers or at least do not obstruct this process, and freedom in Russia will be invincible, the monarchy irretrievable, the republic assured. Otherwise the people will be deceived. Promises are cheap. They cost nothing. All the bourgeois politicians in *all* the bourgeois revolutions have 'fed' the people with promises and stupefied the workers. Our revolution is a bourgeois revolution, *therefore* the workers must support the bourgeoisie; that is what the worthless politicians from the camp of the liquidators say. Our revolution is a bourgeois revolution, say we, the Marxists; *therefore* the workers must open the eyes of the people to the deception of the bourgeois politicians, must teach it to put no trust in words, to rely upon *its own* forces, *its own* organisation, *its own* unity, *its own* arms. (Lenin, Vol XIV, part 1, pages 10-11, *Pravda,* March 21, 1917.)

The Chinese revolutionist who casts the over-cunning resolutions and comments on the bloc of four classes out of his head, will firmly grasp the sense of these simple words of Lenin, will be sure not to go astray and will attain the goal.

THE SCHOOL OF MARTINOV IN THE CHINESE QUESTION

8. The official leadership of the Chinese revolution has been oriented all this time on a 'general national united front' or on the 'bloc of four classes' (*c.f.* the report of Bukharin; the leader in the *Communist International,* No. 11; the unpublished speech by Stalin to the Moscow functionaries on April 5, 1927; the article by Martinov in *Pravda* on April 10; the leader in *Pravda* of March 16; the speech by comrade Kalinin in *Izvestia* of March 6, 1927; the speech by comrade Rudzutak in *Pravda*

of March 9, 1927; etc., etc.). Matters had gone so far on this track, that on the eve of Chiang Kai-shek's *coup d'état*, *Pravda*, in order to expose the Opposition, proclaimed that revolutionary China was not being ruled by a bourgeois government but by a 'government of the bloc of four classes'.

The philosophy of Martinov, which has the sorry courage to carry all the mistakes of Stalin and Bukharin in the questions of Chinese policy to their logical conclusion, does not meet a trace of objection. Yet it is tantamount to trampling under foot the fundamental principles of Marxism. It reproduces the crudest features of Russian and international Menshevism, applied to the conditions of the Chinese revolution. Not for nothing does the present leader of the Mensheviks, Dan, write in the last number of *Sotsialistichesky Vestnik** :

> 'In principle' the Bolsheviks were also for retaining the 'united front' in the Chinese revolution up to the completion of the task of national liberation. On April 10, Martinov, in *Pravda*, most effectively and despite the obligatory abuse of the social democrats, in a quite 'Menshevik manner' showed the 'Left' Oppositionist Radek the correctness of the *official* position which insists on the necessity of retaining the 'bloc of four classes', on not hastening to overthrow the coalition government in which the workers sit side by side with the big bourgeoisie, not to impose 'socialist tasks' upon it prematurely. (No. 8, April 23, 1927, page 4.)

Everyone who knows the history of the struggle of Bolshevism against Menshevism, particularly in the question of relations to the liberal bourgeoisie, must acknowledge that Dan's approval of the 'rational principles' of the Martinov school is not accidental, but follows with perfect legitimacy. It is only unnatural that this school should raise its voice with impunity in the ranks of the Comintern.

The old Menshevik tactic of 1905 to 1917, which was crushed under foot by the march of events, is now transferred

---

* 'The Socialist Herald', a journal published in Berlin by the Foreign Bureau of the Russian Menshevik party.—Tr.

to China by the Martinov school, much the same as capitalist trade dumps its most inferior merchandise, which finds no market in the mother country, into the colonies. The merchandise has not even been renovated. The arguments are the same, letter for letter, as they were twenty years ago. Only, where formerly the word *autocracy* stood, the word *imperialism* has been substituted for it in the text. Naturally, British imperialism is different from autocracy. But the Menshevik reference to it does not differ in the slightest from its reference to autocracy. The struggle against foreign imperialism is as much a class struggle as the struggle against autocracy. That it cannot be exorcised by the idea of the national united front, is far too eloquently proved by the bloody April events, a direct consequence of the policy of the bloc of four classes.

WHAT THE 'LINE' LOOKED LIKE IN PRACTICE

9. On the past period, which terminated with the April *coup d'état*, the theses of comrade Stalin announce:

'The line adopted was the only correct line.'

What did it look like in practice? An eloquent reply is supplied by Tang Ping Shan, the Communist minister of agriculture, in his report at the Seventh Plenum of the ECCI in December 1926*.

---

* Tang was at that time one of the leaders of the Chinese Communist Party and the official reporter on the Chinese question at the Seventh Plenum of the ECCI. A vehement adversary of 'Trotskyism', he entered the bourgeois government of Wang Chin Wei at Hankow with the portfolio of minister of agriculture. In that capacity he appears to have taken seriously Stalin's instructions on the need of restraining the agrarian movement. As Communist minister of agriculture, he took command of an armed detachment. He subsequently deserted the Communist party entirely and his last known political act was contained in the announcement of his efforts to create an anti-Communist party under his own leadership.—Tr.

Since the establishment of the national government in Canton last July, which is nominally a government of the Left wing, *the power has actually been in the hands of the Right wing.* . . . The movement of the workers and peasants cannot develop to its full breadth as a result of various obstacles. After the March putsch a *military dictatorship of the Centre* [that is, Chiang Kai-shek] was established, while the political power remained as before in the hands of the Right wing. The whole political power, which should properly [!] have belonged to the Left wing, is finally lost.

So: the Left 'should have' had the power, but finally lost it; the state power belonged to the Right, the military authority, which is incomparably more powerful, and was entirely in the hands of the 'Centre' of Chiang Kai-shek, which became the centre of the conspiracy. Under such conditions, it is not difficult to understand why 'the movement of the workers and peasants' could not develop as it should have.

Tang Ping Shan gives an even more precise characterisation of what the 'only correct line' looked like in reality:

. . . *We sacrificed the interests of the workers and peasants in practice.* . . . After lengthy negotiations with us, the government did not as much as promulgate a trade union law. . . . The government did not accept the demands of the peasantry, which we presented to it in the name of various social organisations. When conflicts arose between the large landowners and the poor peasants, the government always took the side of the former.

How could all this happen? Tang Ping Shan cautiously names two reasons:

(a) 'The Left leaders are not capable of consolidating and extending their influence by means of political power';

(b) The Right wing 'won the possibility to act, partly *as a result of our wrong tactic'.*

10. Such are the political relations that received the pompous title of the 'bloc of four classes'. Such 'blocs' abound in the revolutionary as well as the parliamentary history of bourgeois countries: the big bourgeoisie leads the petty-bourgeois

democrats, the phrasemongers of the national united front, behind it, and the latter, in turn, confuse the workers and drag them along behind the bourgeoisie. When the proletarian 'tail', despite the efforts of the petty bourgeois phrasemongers, begins to stir too violently, the bourgeoisie orders its generals to stamp on it. Then the opportunists observe with an air of profundity that the bourgeoisie has 'betrayed' the national cause.

11. But did not the Chinese bourgeoisie 'nevertheless' fight against imperialism? This argument too is an empty commonplace. The compromisers of every country, in similar cases, have always assured the workers that the liberal bourgeoisie is fighting against reaction. The Chinese bourgeoisie utilised the petty bourgeois democracy only in order to conclude an alliance with imperialism against the workers. The Northern expedition only served to strengthen the bourgeoisie and weaken the workers. A tactic that prepared such a result is a false tactic. 'We sacrificed the interests of the workers and peasants in practice,' says Tang Ping Shan. What for? To support the bloc of four classes. And the results? A colossal success of the bourgeois counter-revolution, the consolidation of shattered imperialism, the weakening of the USSR. Such a policy is criminal. Unless it is mercilessly condemned, we cannot take a step forward.

The Theses Justify a Line for Which There Is No Justification

12. The theses endeavour even now to justify the policy which united the party of the proletariat with the big bourgeoisie within the framework of one organisation, the Kuomintang, where the whole leadership was in the hands of the bourgeoisie. The theses declare: 'This was the line . . . for the utilisation of the Rights, their connections and experiences, in

so far as they submitted [!] to the discipline of the Kuomin-tang.' Now we know very well how the bourgeoisie submitted to 'discipline' and how the proletariat utilised the Rights, that is, the big and middle bourgeoisie, their 'connections' (with the imperialists) and their 'experiences' (in strangling and shooting the workers). The story of this 'utilisation' is written in the book of the Chinese revolution with letters of blood. But this does not prevent the theses from saying: 'The subsequent events fully confirmed the correctness of this line.' Further than this no one can go!

From an enormous counter-revolutionary *coup d'état*, the theses of Stalin draw the positively miserable conclusion that the policy of 'isolating the Right' within the united Kuomin-tang must be 'replaced' by a policy of 'determined struggle' against the Right. All this after the Right-wing 'comrades' have begun to speak in the language of machine-guns.

13.   The theses refer, to be sure, to a 'previous prediction' on the inevitability of the bourgeoisie's withdrawal from the revolution. But are such prophecies by themselves sufficient for a Bolshevik policy? The prediction that the bourgeoisie will quit is an empty commonplace unless definite political conclusions are drawn from it. In the already quoted article, which approves the semi-official line of Martinov, Dan writes: 'In a movement that embraces such antagonistic classes, *the united front cannot of course last forever.*' (*Sotsialistichesky Vestnik,* April 23, 1927, page 3.) So Dan also acknowledges the 'inevitability of the bourgeoisie's withdrawal'. In practice, however, the policy of Menshevism in the revolution consists of retaining the united front at any cost, as long as possible, at the price of adapting its own policy to the policy of the bour-geoisie, at the price of cutting down the slogans and the activity of the masses, and even, as in China, at the price of the organisational subordination of the workers' party to the political

apparatus of the bourgeoisie. The Bolshevik way, however, consists of an unconditional political and organisational demarcation from the bourgeoisie, of a relentless exposure of the bourgeoisie from the very first steps of the revolution, of a destruction of all petty-bourgeois illusions about the united front with the bourgeoisie, of tireless struggle with the bourgeoisie for the leadership of the masses, of the merciless expulsion from the Communist party of all those elements who sow vain hopes in the bourgeoisie or idealise them.

Two Paths and the Mistakes of the Past

14. The theses of comrade Stalin, to be sure, seek to oppose to each other the two paths of development of the Chinese revolution: one under the leadership of the bourgeoisie, with its suppression of the proletariat and an inevitable alliance with foreign imperialism; the other under the leadership of the proletariat against the bourgeoisie.

But in order that this second prospect of the bourgeois-democratic revolution should not remain an empty phrase, it must be said openly and plainly that the whole leadership of the Chinese revolution up to now has been in irreconcilable contradiction to it. The Opposition has been and is subjected to a rabid criticism precisely because, from the very beginning, it brought to the fore the Leninist manner of putting the question, that is, the path of the struggle of the proletariat against the bourgeoisie for the leadership of the oppressed masses of city and country within the framework and on the foundation of the national-democratic revolution.

15. From the theses of Stalin it follows that the proletariat can separate itself from the bourgeoisie only after the latter has tossed it aside, disarmed it, beheaded it and crushed it under foot. But this is precisely the way the abortive revolution of 1848 developed, where the proletariat had no banner of its own,

but followed at the heels of the petty-bourgeois democracy, which in turn trotted behind the liberal bourgeoisie and led the workers under the sabre of Cavaignac. Great though the real peculiarities of the Chinese situation may be, the fundamentals that characterised the development of the 1848 revolution have been repeated in the Chinese revolution with such deadly precision as though neither the lessons of 1848, 1871, 1905 and 1917 nor those of the Communist Party of the Soviet Union and the Comintern had ever existed.

That Chiang Kai-shek played the role of a republican-liberal Cavaignac has already become a commonplace. The theses of Stalin, following the Opposition, recognise this analogy. But the analogy must be supplemented. Cavaignac would have been impossible without the Ledru-Rollins, the Louis Blancs and the other phrasemongers of the all-inclusive national front. And who played these roles in China? Not only Wang Chin Wei, but also the leaders of the Chinese Communist Party, above all their inspirers of the ECCI. Unless this is stated openly, explained and deeply impressed, the philosophy of the two paths of development will only serve to screen opportunism *á la* Louis Blanc and Martinov, that is, to prepare a repetition of the April tragedy at a new stage of the Chinese revolution.

THE POSITION OF THE CHINESE COMMUNIST PARTY

16.   In order to have the right to speak about the struggle for the Bolshevik path of the democratic revolution, one must possess the principal instrument of proletarian policy; *an independent proletarian party* which fights under its own banner and never permits its policy and organisation to be dissolved in the policy and organisation of other classes. Without assuring the complete theoretical, political and organisational independence of the Communist party, all talk about 'two paths' is a mockery of Bolshevism. The Chinese Communist Party,

in this whole period, has not been *in alliance* with the revolutionary petty-bourgeois section of the Kuomintang, but
in subordination to the whole Kuomintang, led in reality by
the bourgeoisie which had the army and the power in its hands.
The Communist party submitted to the political discipline of
Chiang Kai-shek. The Communist party signed the obligation
not to criticise Sun-Yat-Senism, a petty-bourgeois theory which
is directed not only against imperialism, but also against the
class struggle. The Communist party did not have its own press,
that is, it lacked the principal weapon of an independent party.
Under such conditions, to speak of the struggle of the proletariat
for hegemony means to deceive oneself and others.

17. By what is the submissive, indistinct, and politically
unworthy position of the Communist party in Chiang Kai-shek's
Kuomintang to be explained? By the insistence upon the
unity of the national front under the actual leadership of the
bourgeoisie which allegedly 'could not' withdraw from the revolution (the school of Martinov), that is, the rejection in practice
of the second, Bolshevik path of which the theses of Stalin
speak as an afterthought, solely for camouflage purposes.

To justify such a policy by the necessity for an alliance
of the workers and peasants, is to reduce this alliance itself to
a phrase, to a screen for the commanding role of the bourgeoisie.
The dependence of the Communist party, an inevitable result
of the 'bloc of the four classes', was the main obstacle in the
path of the workers' and peasants' movement, and therefore
also of the real alliance between the proletariat and the peasantry, without which the victory of the Chinese revolution cannot
even be thought of.

18. What should the Communist party do in the future?
In the theses, there is only a single sentence on this, but one
capable of sowing the greatest confusion and causing irreparable
harm. ' . . . While fighting in the ranks of the revolutionary

Kuomintang,' say Stalin's theses, 'the Communist party must *preserve its independence* more than ever before.' Preserve? But to this day the Communist party has had no such independence. Precisely its lack of independence is the source of all the evils and all the mistakes. In this fundamental question, the theses, instead of making an end once and for all to the practice of yesterday, propose to retain it 'more than ever before'. But this means that they want to retain the ideological, political and organisational dependence of the proletarian party upon a petty-bourgeois party, which is inevitably converted into an instrument of the big bourgeoisie.

In order to justify a false policy, one is forced to call dependence independence, and to demand the preservation of what ought to be buried for all time.

19. Chinese Bolshevism can rise only under a merciless self-criticism by the best elements of the Communist party. To support them in this is our direct duty. The attempt to cover up the mistakes of the past by artificially curbing a discussion of them, will cause enormous harm, primarily to the Chinese Communist Party. If we do not help it to purge itself, in the shortest period, from Menshevism and the Mensheviks, it will enter a prolonged crisis, with splits, desertions and an embittered struggle of various groups. What is more, the heavy defeats of opportunism may clear a road to anarcho-syndicalist influences.

If, in spite of a workers' mass movement, in spite of the powerful rise of the trade unions, in spite of the revolutionary agrarian movement on the land, the Communist party should remain as before an integral appendage to a bourgeois party, and what is more, should it enter the national government created by this bourgeois party, it would be better to say frankly: the time has not yet come for a Communist party in China. It is better not to constitute any Communist party at all than to discredit it so cruelly at the time of a revolution, that is, just at the time when the party is being joined to the working masses with bonds of blood and when great traditions are being created that are destined to live for decades.

WHO WAS MISTAKEN ON THE TEMPO?

20. In Stalin's theses there is of course a whole section devoted to the 'mistakes of the Opposition'. Instead of hitting out at the Right, that is, at the mistakes of Stalin himself, the theses are intent upon striking at the Left, thereby deepening the mistakes, piling up confusion, making the way out more difficult, and driving the line of the leadership down into the swamp of compromise.

21. The main accusation: the Opposition 'does not understand that the revolution in China cannot develop at a rapid tempo'. For some reason or other, the theses drag in here the tempo of the October revolution. If the question of tempo is raised, it must not be measured with the external yardstick of the October revolution, but with the internal class relationships of the Chinese revolution itself. The Chinese bourgeoisie, as is known, paid no attention to the precepts about a slow tempo. In April 1927, it considered it quite opportune to throw off the mask of the united front which had served it so well, in order to open an attack upon the revolution with all its strength. The Communist party, the proletariat, as well as the Left Kuomintang people, showed themselves completely unprepared for this blow. Why? Because the leadership counted upon a slower tempo, because it remained hopelessly behindhand, because it was infected with *khvostism*.

On April 23, that is, after the *coup d'état* by Chiang Kaishek, the Central Committee of the Kuomintang, together

with the 'Left' Wuhan government, published a manifesto,
which said:

> *It only remains for us to regret* [!] *that we did not act when there
> was still time.* For that we apologise [!] sincerely. (*Pravda*, April
> 23, 1927.)

In these doleful and whining avowals lies, against the will
of their authors, a pitiless refutation of the Stalinist philosophy
on the 'tempo' of the Chinese revolution.

22.   We continued to maintain the bloc with the bourgeoisie
at a time when the working masses were driving towards
independent struggle. We attempted to utilise the experiences
of the 'Rights' and became playthings in their hands. We carried
on an ostrich policy in the press, by suppressing and concealing
from our own party the first *coup d'état* by Chiang Kai-shek
in March 1926, the shootings of workers and peasants, and in
general all the facts that marked the counter-revolutionary
character of the Kuomintang leadership.   We neglected to
look after the independence of our own party. We founded no
newspaper for it. 'We sacrificed the interests of the workers
and peasants in practice' (Tang Ping Shan). We did not take
a single serious step to win over the soldiers. We allowed
the Chiang Kai-shek band to establish a 'military dictatorship
of the Centre', that is, a dictatorship of the bourgeois counter
revolution.   On the very eve of the *coup d'état* we blew the
trumpets for Chiang Kai-shek. We declared that he had 'submitted to discipline', and that we had succeeded 'by a skilful
tactical manoeuvre in forestalling an abrupt turn to the Right
that threatened the Chinese revolution' (Raskolnikov's foreword
to the pamphlet by Tang Ping Shan). We remained behind the
events all along the line. At every step we lost in tempo to the
benefit of the bourgeoisie. In this way we prepared the most
favourable conditions for the bourgeois counter-revolution. The
Left Kuomintang at least offers us its 'sincere apology'.   The
theses of Stalin, on the contrary, draw from this whole chain

of truly unparalleled *khvostist* mistakes the remarkable conclusion that the Opposition demands . . . a too rapid tempo.

23. Ever more frequently one hears accusations at our party meetings against the 'ultra-left' Shanghaiers and in general against the Chinese workers for having provoked Chiang Kai-shek by their 'excesses'. No one cites any examples; and what would they prove, anyway? Not a single real people's revolution, drawing millions into its vortex, proceeds without so-called 'excesses'. A policy which seeks to prescribe for the masses just awakening a line of march that will not disturb the bourgeois 'order' is a policy of incurable philistines. It will always break its head against the logic of civil war when, while pronouncing belated curses upon the Cavaignacs and Kornilovs, it denounces at the same time the alleged 'excesses' of the Left.

The 'mistake' of the Chinese workers lies in the fact that the critical moment of the revolution found them unprepared, unorganised and unarmed. But that is not their mistake, it is their misfortune. The responsibility for it falls entirely upon a bad leadership, which let every interval pass.

Does a New Revolutionary Centre Already Exist or Must One First Be Created?

24. On the present state of the Chinese revolution, the theses proclaim: 'Chiang Kai-shek's *coup d'état* means that there will now be two camps, two governments, two armies, two centres in the South: a revolutionary centre in Wuhan and a counter-revolutionary centre in Nanking.' What an inexact, superficial, vulgar characterisation! It is not simply a question of two halves of the Kuomintang but of a new grouping of class forces. To believe that the Wuhan government is already a finished centre, which will simply continue the revolution from the point where it was brought to a stop and beaten to

the ground by Chiang Kai-shek, is to regard the counter-revolutionary *coup d'état* in April as a personal 'desertion', an 'episode'; in a word, it is to understand nothing.

The workers were not simply crushed. They were crushed by those who led them. Can one believe that the masses will now follow the Left Kuomintang with the same confidence that they accorded the whole Kuomintang yesterday? From now on the struggle must be conducted not only against the former militarists allied with imperialism, but also against the 'national' bourgeoisie which, as a result of our radically incorrect policy, has captured the military apparatus and considerable sections of the army.

For the struggle on a new, higher stage of the revolution, the deceived masses must above all be inspired with confidence in themselves, and the not yet awakened masses must be aroused. For this, it must first of all be demonstrated that not a trace has been left of that disgraceful policy which 'sacrificed the interests of the workers and peasants' (*cf.* Tang Ping Shan) in order to support the bloc of the four classes. Any one who will lean in the direction of this policy must be mercilessly driven out of the Chinese Communist Party.

The miserably superficial and bureaucratic idea must be thrown aside that now, after the sanguinary experiences, millions of workers and peasants can be set in motion and led if only the 'banner' of the Kuomintang is waved around in the air a little. (We will surrender the blue banner of the Kuomintang to nobody! cries Bukharin.)

No, the masses need a revolutionary programme and a fighting organisation which grows out of their own ranks and contains within itself the guarantee of contact with the masses and of loyalty to them. The Wuhan authorities are not enough for this: workers', peasants' and soldiers' Soviets are needed for this, Soviets of the toilers.

SOVIETS AND THE ARMING OF THE WORKERS AND PEASANTS

25. After rejecting the vital and indispensable slogan of Soviets, the theses of comrade Stalin declare somewhat unexpectedly that the principal 'antidote [?] to the counter-revolution is the arming of the workers and peasants'. The arming of the workers is undoubtedly a necessary thing. We will have no differences at all on this point. But how are we to explain why it was considered correct up to now to arm the workers to a 'minimum' extent for the welfare of the revolution? that the representatives of the Comintern actually *opposed* the arming of the workers? (*cf.* the letter of the four comrades to the delegation of the CPSU in the Comintern*); that in spite of the full possibility of arming themselves the workers found themselves unarmed at the moment of the *coup d'état*? All this is to be explained by the desire not to break with Chiang Kai-shek, not to offend Chiang Kai-shek, not to push him to the Right. The marvellous 'antidote' was lacking precisely on the day when it was most needed. Today the workers are not arming themselves in Wuhan either—so as 'not to drive away' Wang Chin Wei.

26. The arming of the workers and peasants is an excellent thing. But one must be logical. In Southern China there are already armed peasants; they are the so-called National armies. Yet, far from being an 'antidote to the counter-revolution', they have been its tool. Why? Because the political leadership, instead of embracing the masses of the army through soldiers' Soviets has contented itself with a purely external copy of our political departments and commissars, which, without an independent revolutionary party and without soldiers' Soviets, have been transformed into an empty camouflage for bourgeois militarism.

---

* This instructive document will be found at the back of the present volume among the appendices.—Tr.

27. The theses of Stalin reject the slogan of Soviets with the argument that it would be a 'slogan of struggle against the government of the revolutionary Kuomintang'. But in that case, what is the meaning of the words: 'The principal antidote to the counter-revolution is the arming of the workers and peasants'? Against whom will the workers and peasants arm themselves? Will it not be against the governmental authority of the revolutionary Kuomintang?

The slogan of arming the workers and peasants, if it is not a phrase, a subterfuge, a masquerade, but a call to action, is not less sharp in character than the slogan of workers' and peasants' Soviets. Is it likely that the armed masses will tolerate at their side or over them the governmental authority of a bureaucracy alien and hostile to them? The real arming of the workers and peasants under present circumstances inevitably involves the formation of Soviets.

28. Further: Who will arm the masses? Who will direct the armed men?

So long as the National armies marched forward and the Northern armies yielded ground, the arming of the workers could proceed with relative ease. The timely organisation of workers', peasants' and soldiers' Soviets would have meant a real 'antidote' to the counter-revolution. Unfortunately, the mistakes of the past are irreparable. The whole situation has now taken a sharp turn for the worse. The few weapons seized spontaneously by the workers (are not these the 'excesses' that are spoken of?) have been torn from them. The advance to the North has been suspended. Under these conditions the arming of the workers and peasants is a laborious and difficult task. To declare that the time for the Soviets has not yet arrived and at the same time to launch the slogan for arming the workers and peasants, is to sow confusion. Only the Soviets, at a further development of the revolution, can become the organs capable of really conducting the arming of the workers and of directing these armed masses.

WHY IS IT IMPOSSIBLE TO FORM SOVIETS?

29. To this, the theses reply: 'In the first place Soviets cannot be created at any convenient moment, they are created only in the period of a special rise of the revolutionary wave.' If these words have any sense at all, it is this: We let pass the favourable moment when we did not call upon the masses to create Soviets at the beginning of the last period of powerful revolutionary rise. Once again: the mistakes of the past are irreparable. If we are of the opinion that the Chinese revolution has been crushed for a long time, then the slogan of Soviets will naturally find no echo in the masses. But all the more unfounded then is the slogan of the arming of the workers and peasants. We do not believe, however, that the consequences of the false policy pursued are so heavy and profound. There are many facts that speak for the possibility and the likelihood of a new revolutionary rise in the near future. Among other things, it is indicated by the fact that Chiang Kai-shek is forced to flirt with the masses, to promise the workers the eight-hour day, and all sorts of relief to the peasants, etc. In the event of a further extension of the agrarian movement and a turning of the petty-bourgeois masses of the city against Chiang Kai-shek as an open agent of imperialism, more favourable conditions can arise in the near future under which the now battered proletarian vanguard will re-assemble the ranks of the toilers for a new offensive. Whether this will take place a month sooner or later is of no concern; in any case we must prepare for it now with our own programme and our own organisations. In other words: *the slogan of Soviets will henceforth accompany the whole further course of the Chinese revolution and reflect its destinies.*

30. 'In the second place,' say the theses, 'Soviets are not formed for chattering; they are created primarily as organs of struggle against the existing state power, and for the conquest of power.' That Soviets are not created for chattering is perhaps the only correct point in the theses. But a revolutionist does not propose the arming of the workers and peasants for chattering either. Whoever says here: at the present stage only chatter can be the result of Soviets, but on the contrary, something serious will come out of the arming of the workers and peasants, is either making fun of himself or of others.

31. A third argument: since there is now a series of Left Kuomintang organisations in Wuhan, which in their solemn manifesto of April 23 apologised for having overslept the *coup d'état* of Chiang Kai-shek, the theses draw the conclusion: the creation of Soviets would mean an insurrection against the Left Kuomintang, 'for there is no other governmental authority in this region at present than that of the revolutionary Kuomintang'.

These words fairly reek with the apparatus-like, bureaucratic conception of revolutionary authority. The government is not regarded as the expression and consolidation of the developing struggle of the classes, but as the self-sufficient expression of the will of the Kuomintang. The classes come and go but the continuity of the Kuomintang goes on for ever. But it is not enough to call Wuhan the centre of the revolution for it really to be that. The provincial Kuomintang of Chiang Kai-shek had an old, reactionary, mercenary bureaucracy at its disposal. What has the Left Kuomintang? For the time being, nothing or almost nothing. The slogan of Soviets is a call for the creation of real organs of the new state power right through the transitional regime of a dual government.

32. And what will be the attitude of the Soviets to the

'government of the revolutionary Kuomintang', allegedly the
'only' governmental authority 'in this region'? A truly classic
question! The attitude of the Soviets to the revolutionary Kuomintang will correspond to the attitude of the revolutionary
Kuomintang to the Soviets. In other words: to the extent
that the Soviets arise, arm themselves, consolidate themselves,
they will tolerate over them only such a government as bases
itself upon the armed workers and peasants. What makes the
Soviet system valuable is the fact that, especially in directly
revolutionary epochs, it furnishes the best means of guaranteeing
agreement between the central and local government authorities.

33. Comrade Stalin, as far back as 1925, called the Kuomintang a 'workers' and peasants' party' (!?) (*Problems of
Leninism,* page 264). This definition has nothing in common
with Marxism. But it is clear that with this incorrect formulation comrade Stalin wanted to express the idea that the basis
of the Kuomintang is an anti-bourgeois alliance of the
workers and peasants. This was absolutely false for the period
in which it was said: the workers and peasants, it is true, did
follow the Kuomintang, but they were led by the bourgeoisie
and we know where it led them. Such a party is called bourgeois, and not workers' and peasants'. After the 'withdrawal'
of the bourgeoisie (that is, after it massacred the unarmed and
unprepared proletariat), the revolution, according to Stalin,
passes over to a new stage, in which it is to be led by the Left
Kuomintang, that is, by one, at least so we are to assume,
that will finally realise the Stalinist idea of the 'workers' and
peasants' party'. The question arises: why then will the
creation of workers' and peasants' Soviets mean a war against
the authority of the workers' and peasants' Kuomintang?

34. Another argument: To call for the creation of Soviets
'means to hand the enemies of the Chinese people a new weapon
to combat the revolution, to manufacture new legends and to

pretend that there is no national revolution in China, but an artificial transplanting of Moscow Sovietisation'.

This stupefying argument means that if we develop, extend and deepen the revolutionary movement of the masses, the enemies of the Chinese people will redouble their efforts to calumniate it. This argument has no other sense. Therefore it has no sense at all.

Perhaps the theses have not in mind the enemies of the Chinese people, but the fear of the popular masses themselves of a Moscow Sovietisation? But on what is such a consideration based? It is well known that all the varieties of the 'national' bourgeoisie, Right, Centre and Left, zealously smear themselves with a protective Muscovite colouration in all their political work: they create commissars, political army posts, political departments, plenums of the central committee, control commissions, etc. The Chinese bourgeoisie is not at all afraid of transplanting Muscovite forms, which it carefully debases to serve its own class aims. But why do they apply them? Not out of love for Moscow, but rather because they are popular with the masses of the people. The Chinese peasant knows that the Soviets gave the land to the Russian peasant, and whoever does not know this ought to learn it. The Chinese workers know that the Soviets guaranteed the liberty of the Russian proletariat. The experience of the counter-revolution of Chiang Kai-shek must have made the advanced workers understand that without an independent organisation embracing the whole proletariat and assuring its collaboration with the oppressed masses in the city and on the land, the revolution cannot triumph. The creation of Soviets follows for the Chinese masses from their own experience, and is far from being an 'artificially transplanted Sovietisation' for them. A policy that is afraid to call things by their right name is a false policy. One must be guided by the revolutionary masses and by the objective needs of the revolution, but not by what the enemy will say.

35. It is said: The Hankow government is nevertheless a fact. Feng Yu-hsiang is a fact, Tan Shen Shi is a fact, and they have armed forces at their disposal; neither the Wuhan government nor Feng Yu-hsiang, nor Tan Shen Shi wants Soviets. To create Soviets would mean to break with these allies. Although this argument is not openly formulated in the theses, it is nevertheless decisive for many comrades. We have already heard from Stalin on the Hankow government: the 'revolutionary centre', the 'only governmental authority'. At the same time an advertising campaign is launched for Feng Yu-hsiang in our party meetings: 'a former worker', 'a faithful revolutionist', 'a reliable man', etc. All this is a repetition of the past mistakes under circumstances in which these mistakes can become even more disastrous. The Hankow government and the army command can be against the Soviets only because they will have nothing to do with a radical agrarian programme, with a real break with the large landowners and the bourgeoisie, because they secretly cherish the thought of a compromise with the Right. But then it becomes all the more important to form Soviets. This is the only way to push the revolutionary elements of Hankow to the Left and force the counterrevolutionists to retire.

36. But even if the Soviets do not carry on a war with the 'only' government of Hankow, will they not still bring with them the elements of dual power? Without a doubt. Whoever is really for the course towards a workers' and peasants' government, not only in words but in deeds, must understand that this course leads through a certain period of dual power. How long this period will last, what concrete forms it will assume, will depend upon how the 'only' government in Hankow conducts itself, upon the independence and initiative of the Communist party, upon how rapidly the Soviets develop, etc. It will be our task, in any case, to strengthen the element of the workers and peasants in the dual power and by that provide the genuine

workers' and peasants' Soviet government with a fully developed democratic programme.

37. But dozens of foreign warships are anchored in the Yangtse river which can sweep away Shanghai, Hankow, etc. Is it not insanity to form Soviets under such conditions? This argument too is, of course, not formulated in Stalin's theses, but it is paraded around everywhere in party meetings (Martinov, Yaroslavsky and others). The school of Martinov would like to kill the idea of the Soviets with fear of the British naval artillery. This artifice is not a new one. In 1917, the Social Revolutionists and the Mensheviks sought to frighten us by declaring that the seizure of power by the Soviets would mean the occupation of Kronstadt and Petrograd by the Allies. We answered: only the deepening of the revolution can save it. Foreign imperialism will only reconcile itself to such a 'revolution' as strengthens its own positions in China at the price of a few concessions to the Chinese bourgeoisie. Every real people's revolution that undermines the colonial foundation of imperialism will inevitably meet with the latter's furious resistance. We did try to stop halfway, but this 'only correct line' protected Nanking from the cannon of imperialism as little as it did the Chinese workers from the machine-guns of Chiang Kai-shek. Only the transition of the Chinese revolution to the phase of real mass action, only the formation of workers', peasants' and soldiers' Soviets, only the deepening of the social programme of the revolution, are capable, as our own experiences prove, of bringing confusion into the ranks of the foreign armed forces by arousing their sympathy for the Soviets and thus really protecting the revolution from blows from without.

WHAT DO THE THESES OF STALIN PROPOSE IN PLACE OF SOVIETS?

38. The creation of 'revolutionary peasant committees, workers' trade unions, and other mass organisations as pre-

paratory elements for the Soviets of the future'. What should be the course of these organisations? We do not find a single word on this in the theses. The phrase that these are 'preparatory elements for the Soviets of the future' is only a phrase and nothing more. What will these organisations do now? They will have to conduct strikes, boycotts, break the backbone of the bureaucratic apparatus, annihilate the counter-revolutionary military bands, drive out the large landowners, disarm the detachments of the usurers and the rich peasants, arm the workers and peasants, in a word, solve all the problems of the democratic and agrarian revolution that are on the order of the day, and in this way raise themselves to the position of local organs of power. But then they will be Soviets, only of a kind that are badly suited to their tasks. The theses therefore propose, if these proposals are to be taken seriously at all, to create substitutes for Soviets, instead of Soviets themselves.

39. During all the preceding mass movements, the trade unions were compelled to fulfil functions closely approaching the functions of Soviets (Hong Kong, Shanghai, and elsewhere). But these were precisely the functions for which the trade unions were entirely insufficient. They embrace a too small number of workers. They do not at all embrace the petty-bourgeois masses in the city that incline towards the proletariat. But such tasks as the carrying through of strikes with the least possible losses to the poorer population of the city, the distribution of provisions, participation in tax policy, participation in the formation of armed forces, to say nothing of carrying through the agrarian revolution in the provinces, can be accomplished with the necessary sweep only when the directing organisation embraces not only all the sections of the proletariat, but connects them intimately in the course of its activities with the poor population in the city and country. One would at least think that the military *coup d'état* of Chiang Kai-shek had finally

hammered into the mind of every revolutionist the fact that trade unions separated from the army are one thing, and united workers' and soldiers' Soviets, on the other hand, are quite another thing. Revolutionary trade unions and peasants' committees can arouse the hatred of the enemy no less than Soviets. But they are far less capable than Soviets of warding off its blows.

If we are to speak seriously of the alliance of the proletariat with the oppressed masses in the city and country—not of an 'alliance' between the leaders, a semi-adulterated alliance through dubious representatives, but of a real fighting alliance built and steeled in the struggles of the masses against the enemy—then such an alliance can have no other organisational form than that of Soviets. This can be denied only by those who rely more upon compromising leaders than upon the revolutionary masses below.

SHOULD WE BREAK WITH THE LEFT KUOMINTANG?

From the foregoing remarks may be seen how ill-founded are the whispers about a break of the Communist party with the Kuomintang. 'This is tantamount,' say the theses, 'to deserting the field of struggle and leaving our allies in the Kuomintang in the lurch to the delight of the enemies of the revolution.' These pathetic lines are quite out of place. It is not a question of a break but of preparing a bloc, not on the basis of subordination but on the basis of a genuine equality of rights. A revolutionary Kuomintang has yet to be formed. We are in favour of the Communists working inside the Kuomintang and patiently drawing the workers and peasants over to their side. The Communist party can gain a petty-bourgeois ally, not by prostrating itself before the Kuomintang at every one of its vacillations, but only if it appeals to the workers openly and directly, in its own name, under its own banner, organises them around it and shows the Kuomintang by example and by deed what a party of the masses is, by supporting every forward step of the Kuomintang, by relentlessly unmasking every vacillation, every step backward, and by creating a real revolutionary foundation for a bloc with the Kuomintang in the form of workers', peasants' and soldiers' Soviets.

40. It is absurd to assert that the Opposition stands for the 'political isolation' of the Communist party. This assertion contains just as much truth as the one that the Opposition stood for withdrawing from the British trade unions. Both accusations have only served to mask the bloc with the Right Kuomintang and with the traitorous General Council. The Opposition is energetically in favour of strengthening and developing the bloc with the revolutionary elements of the Kuomintang, for a compact fighting alliance of the workers with the poor population of the city and country, for the course towards the revolutionary dictatorship of the workers, peasants and the urban petty-bourgeoisie.

For this it is necessary:

(a) to recognise as disastrous such forms of the bloc in which the Communist party sacrifices the interests of the workers and peasants to the utopian aim of holding the bourgeoisie in the camp of the national revolution;

(b) to reject categorically such forms of the bloc in which the Communist party hauls down its banner and sacrifices the growth of its own influence and its own authority in the interest of its allies;

(c) to approve a bloc with clearly formulated common tasks, but not to base it upon misunderstanding, diplomatic manoeuvres, sycophancy and hypocrisy;

(d) to lay down the conditions and limits of the bloc with thorough precision and let them be known to all;

(e) for the Communist party to retain full freedom of criticism, and to watch over its allies with no less vigilance than over an enemy, without forgetting for a moment that an ally who bases himself upon other classes or depends upon other classes is only a temporary confederate who can be transformed by the force of circumstances into an opponent and an enemy;

(f) to set the connection with the petty-bourgeois masses higher than a connection with their party leaders;

(g) finally, to rely only upon ourselves, upon our own organisation, arms and power.

Only by observing these conditions will a really revolutionary bloc of the Communist party with the Kuomintang become possible, not a bloc of the leaders, which vacillates and is subject to contingencies, but a bloc based upon all the oppressed masses of the city and country under the political hegemony of the proletarian vanguard.

THE PROBLEMS OF THE CHINESE REVOLUTION AND THE ANGLO-RUSSIAN COMMITTEE

41. In the direction of the Chinese revolution we are confronted not by tactical errors, but by a radically false line. This follows clearly from everything that has been presented above. It becomes still clearer when the policy in China is compared with our policy towards the Anglo-Russian Committee. In the latter case the inconsistency of the opportunistic line did not express itself so tragically as in China, but no less completely and convincingly.

42. In England, as in China, the line was directed towards a rapprochement with the 'solid' leaders, based on personal relations, on diplomatic combinations, while renouncing in practice the deepening of the abyss between the revolutionary

or Leftward-developing masses and the traitorous leaders. We ran after Chiang Kai-shek and thereby drove the Chinese Communists to accept the dictatorial conditions put by Chiang Kai-shek to the Communist party. In so far as the representatives of the All-Russian Central Council of Trade Unions ran after Purcell, Hicks, Citrine and Company and adopted in principle the position of neutrality in the trade union movement,* they recognised the General Council as the only representative of the British proletariat and obligated themselves not to interfere in the affairs of the British labour movement.

43. The decisions of the Berlin Conference of the Anglo-Russian Committee mean our renunciation of support in the future to strikers against the will of avowed strikebreakers. They are tantamount to a condemnation and a flat betrayal of the trade union minority, all of whose activity is directed against the traitors whom we have recognised as the sole representatives of the English working class. Finally, the solemn proclamation of 'non-interference' signifies our capitulation in principle to the national narrowness of the labour movement in its most backward and most conservative form.

44. Chiang Kai-shek accuses us of interfering in the internal affairs of China just as Citrine accuses us of interfering in the internal affairs of the trade unions. Both accusations are only transcriptions of the accusation of world imperialism against a workers' state which dares to interest itself in the fate of the

---

* At the April 1927 meeting of the Anglo-Russian Unity Committee in Berlin, which took place after the betrayal of the British strikes by the British section of the Committee, Tomsky and the other representatives of the Russian trade unions not only proclaimed the 'hearty accord' and 'unanimity' of the Committee, but in the resolution adopted they acknowledged the General Council of the Trade Unions as the 'only representative' of the British workers and pledged themselves to 'non-interference' in the affairs of the British trade union movement.—Tr.

oppressed masses of the whole world. In this case as in others, Chiang Kai-shek, like Citrine, under different conditions and at different posts, remain the agents of imperialism despite temporary conflicts with it. If we chase after collaboration with such 'leaders', we are forced ever more to restrict, to limit and to emasculate our methods of revolutionary mobilisation.

45. Through our false policy we not only helped the General Council to maintain its tottering positions after the strike betrayal, but, what is more, we furnished it with all the necessary weapons for putting impudent demands to us which we meekly accepted. Under the tinkling of phrases about 'hegemony', we acted in the Chinese revolution and the British labour movement as if we were morally vanquished, and by that we prepared our material defeat. An opportunist deviation is always accompanied by a loss of faith in one's own line.

46. The businessmen of the General Council, having received a guarantee of non-interference from the All-Russian Central Council of Trade Unions, are undoubtedly persuading Chamberlain that their method of struggle against Bolshevik propaganda is far more effective than ultimatums and threats. Chamberlain, however, prefers the combined method and combines the diplomacy of the General Council with the violence of British imperialism.

47. If it is alleged against the Opposition that Baldwin or Chamberlain 'also' wants the dissolution of the Anglo-Russian Committee, then one understands nothing at all of the political mechanics of the bourgeoisie. Baldwin justly feared and still fears the harmful influence of the Soviet trade unions upon the Leftward-developing labour movement of Britain. The British bourgeoisie set its pressure upon the General Council against the pressure of the All-Russian Central Council of Trade Unions

upon the traitorous leaders of the trade unions, and on this field the bourgeoisie triumphed all along the line. The General Council refused to accept money from the Soviet trade unions and to confer with them on the question of aid for the mine workers. In exercising its pressure upon the General Council, the British bourgeoisie, through it, exerted pressure upon the All-Russian Central Council of Trade Unions and at the Berlin Conference obtained from the latter's representatives an unprecedented capitulation on the fundamental questions of the class struggle. An Anglo-Russian Committee *of this kind* only serves the British bourgeoisie (*c.f.* the declaration of *The Times*). This will not hinder it from continuing its pressure in the future upon the General Council, and demanding of it a break with the All-Russian Central Council of Trade Unions, for by such a policy of pressure and blackmail the British bourgeoisie wins everything we lose by our senseless and unprincipled conduct.

48. The insinuations that Chiang Kai-shek is 'in solidarity' with the Opposition, because he wants to drive the Communists out of the Kuomintang, have the same value. A remark by Chiang Kai-shek is being circulated in which he is supposed to have said to another general that he agrees with the Opposition in the CPSU on this point. In the text of the document from which this 'quotation' was picked out, the words of Chiang Kai-shek are not adduced as an expression of his views, but as a manifestation of his readiness and aptitude to deceit, to falsehood, and even to disguise himself for a few days as a 'Left Communist' in order to be better able to stab us in the back. Still more, the document in question is one long indictment against the line and the work of the Comintern's representatives in China. Instead of picking quotations out of the document and giving them a sense contrary to that contained in the text, it would be better to make the document itself known

to the Comintern.* Leave aside, however, the misuse of alleged 'quotations' and there remains the 'coincidence' that Chiang Kai-shek has always been against a bloc with the Communists, while we are against a bloc with Chiang Kai-shek. The school of Martinov draws from this the conclusion that the policy of the Opposition 'generally' serves the reaction. This accusation is not new either. The whole development of Bolshevism in Russia proceeded under the accompaniment of Menshevik accusations that the Bolsheviks were playing the game of the reaction, that they were aiding the monarchy against the Cadets, the Cadets against the SRs and Mensheviks, and so on without end. Renaudel accuses the French Communists of rendering aid to Poincaré when they attack the bloc of the radicals and the socialists. The German social democrats have more than once pretended that our refusal to enter the League of Nations plays the game of the extreme imperialists, etc., etc.

The fact that the big bourgeoisie, represented by Chiang Kai-shek, needs to break with the proletariat, and the revolutionary proletariat on the other hand needs to break with bourgeoisie, is not an evidence of their solidarity, but of the irreconcilable class antagonism between them. The hopeless compromisers stand between the bourgeoisie and the proletariat and accuse both the 'extreme' wings of disrupting the national front and rendering assistance to the reaction. To accuse the Opposition of playing the game of Chamberlain, Thomas or Chiang Kai-shek is to show a narrow-minded opportunism, and at the same time to recognise involuntarily the proletarian and revolutionary character of our political line.

49. The Berlin Conference of the Anglo-Russian Committee which coincided with the beginning of British intervention

---

* This document was never made public by the official channels of the Communist International. It will be found reprinted in full among the appendices to this work.—Tr.

in China, did not even dare to allude to the question of effective measures to take against the hangman's work of British imperialism in the Far East. Could a more striking proof be found that the Anglo-Russian Committee is incapable of moving as much as a finger towards really preventing war? But it is not simply useless. It has brought immeasurable harm to the revolutionary movement, like every illusion and hypocrisy. By referring to its collaboration with the All-Russian Central Council of Trade Unions in the 'struggle for peace', the General Council is able to soothe and lull the consciousness of the British proletariat, stirred by the danger of war. The All-Russian Central Council of Trade Unions now appears before the British working class and the working class of the whole world as a sort of guarantor for the international policy of the traitors of the General Council. The criticism directed by the revolutionary elements in Britain against the General Council thereby becomes weakened and blunted. Thanks to Purcell, Hicks and Company, the MacDonalds and Thomases get the possibility of keeping the working masses in a stupor up to the threshold of war itself, in order to call upon them then for the defence of the democratic fatherland. When comrade Tomsky, in his last interview (*Pravda,* May 8), criticised the Thomases, Havelock Wilsons and the other hirelings of the Stock Exchange, he did not mention by a single word the subversive, disintegrating, lulling, and therefore much more pernicious work of Purcell, Hicks and Company. These 'allies' are not mentioned by name in the interview as though they do not even exist. Then why a bloc with them? But they do exist. Without them Thomas does not exist politically. Without Thomas there exists no Baldwin, that is, the capitalist regime in England. Contrary to our best intentions, our support of the bloc with Purcell is actually support of the whole British régime and the facilitation of its work in China. After all that has happened, this is clear to every revolutionist who has gone through the school of Lenin. In a like manner, our collaboration with Chiang Kai-shek blunted the class vigilance of the Chinese proletariat, and thereby facilitated the April *coup d'état*.

The Theory of Stages and the Theory of Socialism in One Country

50. The *khvostist* theory of 'stages' or 'steps' repeatedly proclaimed by Stalin in recent times, has served as the motivation in principle for the opportunist tactic. If the complete organisational and political independence of the Chinese Communist Party is demanded, it means that steps are being skipped over. If Soviet organisations are demanded for drawing the worker and peasant masses into the civil war, it means that 'stages' are being skipped over. If the dissolution of the political bloc with the traitors of the General Council, who are now carrying on the basest work, is demanded, it means that stages are being skipped over. The conservative bourgeois-national Kuomintang government, the military command of Chiang Kai-shek, the General Council—in a word, any one of the institutions created by the pressure of the possessing and ruling classes, and constituting a barrier for the revolutionary class movement, becomes, according to this theory, a great historical stage, to which one's policy must be adapted until 'the masses themselves' pass through it. Once we set out on this road, our policy must be inevitably transformed from a revolutionary factor into a conservative one. The course of the Chinese revolution and the fate of the Anglo-Russian Committee are an imminent warning in this regard.

51. Such facts as the defeat of the great strikes of the British proletariat last year, as the Chinese revolution this year, cannot go by without consequences for the international labour movement, just as the defeat of the German proletariat in the autumn of 1923 did not pass without leaving its traces. An

unavoidable temporary weakening of the revolutionary positions is in itself a great evil. It can become irreparable for a long time if the orientation is wrong, if the strategic line is false. Precisely now, in the period of a temporary revolutionary ebb, the struggle against all manifestations of opportunism and national limitedness and for the line of revolutionary internationalism is more necessary than ever.

By recognising the principle of non-interference, our delegation, regardless of its intentions, promotes the most conservative, most defeatist tendencies in the working class. There is nothing perplexing in the fact that the most backward and weariest sections of the workers of the USSR consider interference in the British strike struggle or the Chinese revolution a mistake. Ever more frequently they argue: 'Are we not taught that we can build up socialism in our country, even without the victory of the revolution in other countries, if only there no intervention? Then we must carry on such a policy as does not provoke intervention. Our interference in British and Chinese affairs is a mistake, because without yielding positive results it drives the world bourgeoisie on to the road of military intervention and thus threatens the construction of socialism in our country.'

There is no doubt and there can be none that now, after the new defeats of the international revolutionary movement, the theory of socialism in one country will serve, independent of the will of its creators, to justify, to motivate and to sanctify all the tendencies directed towards restricting the revolutionary objectives, towards quenching the ardour of the struggle, towards a national and conservative narrowness.

The slightest digression towards the side of 'non-interference', whether covered or not with the theory of socialism in one country, only increases the imperialist danger instead of diminishing it.

It is perfectly clear and incontestable with regard to the Chinese revolution that only a deeper mass impulsion, a more radical social programme, the slogan of the workers' and peasants' Soviets, can seriously shield the revolution from a military attack from without. Only a revolution on whose banner the toilers and oppressed write plainly their own demands is capable of gripping the feelings not only of the international proletariat but also of the soldiers of capital. We know this well enough from our own experiences. We saw and proved it in the years of the civil war at Archangel, Odessa and elsewhere. The compromising and traitorous leadership did not protect Nanking from destruction. It facilitated the penetration of the enemy ships into the Yangtse. A revolutionary leadership, with a powerful social movement, can make the waters of the Yangtse too hot for the ships of Lloyd George, Chamberlain and MacDonald. In any case, this is the only way and the only hope of defence.

The extension of the Soviet front is simultaneously the best defence of the USSR. Under the present circumstances, the talk that our international position has become worse, or can in any way become worse, as a result of some kind of 'Left' mistake, sounds absurd. If our position has grown worse, it is a result of the defeat of the Chinese revolution, a historical and international event, regardless of whether or not we interfere in it. Were we not to interfere in the intervention of imperialism, we would only facilitate its work—against China, and against ourselves as well. But there is a difference between interference and interference. The falsest and most dangerous interference consists of the endeavour to halt the development of the revolution half-way. The struggle for peace occupies the centre of our international policy. But even the most extreme representative of the Martinov school would never dare to contend that our policy of peace can be in contradiction to the development of the Chinese revolution, or inversely, that its development can be in contradiction to our policy of peace. The one supplements the other. The best way to defend the USSR is to vanquish the Chiang Kai-shek counter-revolution and to raise the movement to a higher stage. Whoever rejects Soviets for China under such conditions, disarms the Chinese revolution. Whoever proclaims the principle of non-interference in the relations of the European proletariat weakens its revolutionary vanguard. Both weaken the position of the USSR, the principal fortress of the international proletariat.

Thus we see how one mistake is heaped upon the others and together produce a line which digresses ever more from the line of Bolshevism. Critical voices and warnings are regarded as obstructions. The shifting of the official line towards the Right is supplemented by blows at the Left. To continue on this path would involve the greatest dangers for the Soviet state as well as for the Comintern. Were we to conceal these dangers from the international proletarian vanguard, we would be betraying the banner of Communism.

*　　　*　　　*

We do not doubt for a moment that the mistakes can be repaired, the deviations overcome, and the line rectified without violent crises and convulsions. The language of facts is all too eloquent, the lessons of experience all too plain. It is only necessary that our party, of the Soviet Union as well as of the International, obtains the full possibility to weigh the facts and draw the proper conclusions from them. We firmly believe that they will draw these conclusions in the spirit of revolutionary unity.

May 7, 1927

The Speech of Comrade Chen Du-Siu on the Tasks
of the Chinese Communist Party
EPILOGUE

52. What purpose does Marxism serve in politics? To understand that which is and to foresee that which will be. Foresight must be the foundation of action. We already know what has happened to the predictions of comrade Stalin: one week before the *coup d'état* of Chiang Kai-shek, he defended him and blew the trumpet for him by calling for the utilization of the Right wing, its experiences, its connections (speech to the Moscow functionaries on April 5). In the theses analysed by us, Stalin gives another example of foresight which has also been tested by life. The central question of our criticism of Stalin's theses was formulated by us above as follows: 'Does there already exist a new centre of the revolution or must one first be created?' Stalin contended that after the *coup d'état* of Chiang Kai-shek there were '*two governments, two armies, two centres: the revolutionary centre in Wuhan and the counter-revolutionary centre in Nanking*'. Stalin contended that no Soviets can be built because that would signify an uprising against the Wuhan centre. against the '*only government*' in Southern China. We called this characterisation of the situation 'false, superficial, vulgar'. We called this so-called Wuhan government the '*leaders of Wuhan*' and showed that in Southern China, after the abrupt veering of the civil war to another class line, there is no government as yet, that one must be first created.

In *Pravda* of May 15 the speech of comrade Chen Du-Siu at the convention of the Chinese Communist Party (April 29) is reprinted.

Neither Stalin nor we had this speech when Stalin wrote his theses and we wrote a criticism of them. Chen Du-Siu characterises the situation not on the basis of a general analysis of the circumstances but on the basis of his direct observations. Now, what does Chen Du-Siu say of the new revolutionary movement? He declares plainly that 'it would be a mistake' to consider the Wuhan government an organ of the revolutionary democratic dictatorship: 'It is *not yet a government of the worker and peasant masses but solely a bloc of leaders'*. But is this not word for word what we said against Stalin?

Stalin wrote: 'There is now no other governmental power than the government of the revolutionary Kuomintang.' We answered him on that: 'These words fairly reek with the apparatus-like and bureaucratic conception of revolutionary authority . . . the classes come and go but the continuity of the Kuomintang government goes on forever [allegedly]. But it is not enough to call Wuhan the centre of the revolution for it really to be that' (*cf.* above). Instead of making it clear to the Chinese revolutionists, to the Communists primarily, that the Wuhan government will break its head against a wall if it imagines that it is itself already the only government in China; instead of turning relentlessly against the decorative hypocrisy of the petty-bourgeois revolutionists who have already destroyed so many revolutions; instead of shouting right into the ear of the uncertain, faltering, vacillating centre of Wuhan: 'Do not be misled by outward appearances, do not be dazzled by the glitter of our own titles and manifestos, begin to perform the hard daily work, set masses in motion, build up workers', soldiers' and peasants' Soviets, build up a revolutionary governmental power'—instead of all this, Stalin hurls himself against the slogan of the Soviets and supports the worst, the most provincial and bureaucratic prejudices and superstitious views of those ill-fated revolutionists who fear people's Soviets, and instead have faith in the sacred ink-blots on the pote-paper of the Kuomintang.

53. Comrade Chen Du-Siu characterises the situation on

the basis of his own observations with exactly the same words
with which we characterised the situation on the basis of
theoretical consideration. No revolutionary government but
only a bloc of leaders. But this does not at all mean that
comrade Chen Du-Siu himself draws correct conclusions from
the circumstances correctly characterised by him. Since he is
bound hand and foot by false directives, Chen Du-Siu draws
conclusions which radically contradict his own analysis. He
says: 'We have before us the task of beginning to build up a
genuinely revolutionary and democratic government *as soon as
the situation in the sphere of the national government has
changed and the threat of foreign intervention and the offensive
of the militarists have disappeared.*'

Here we must say directly and openly: put the question
this way and you adopt the surest and shortest road to ruin.
The creation of a genuinely revolutionary government basing
itself on the popular masses is relegated to the moment when
the dangers have disappeared. But the central danger consists precisely of the fact that instead of a revolutionary government in Southern China, there is for the time being only a bloc
of leaders. Through this principal evil, all the other dangers
are increased tenfold, including also the military danger. If we
are to be guarded to the highest possible degree against the
foreign and our 'own' militarist bands, we must become strong,
consolidate ourselves, organise, and arm ourselves. There are
no other roads. We should not stick our heads in the sand.
No artifice will help us here. The enthusiasm of the masses
must be aroused, their readiness to fight and to die for their
own cause. But for this the masses must be gripped as deeply
as possible, politically and organisationally. Without losing
even an hour, they must be given a revolutionary programme
of action and the organisational form of the Soviets. There
are no other roads. Postpone the creation of a revolutionary
government until somebody has eliminated the danger of

war in some way or other, and you take the surest and shortest road to ruin.

54. With regard to the agrarian movement, comrade Chen Du-Siu admits honestly that the agrarian programme of the party (reduction of rent payments) is completely insufficient. The peasant movement, he says, 'is being transformed into the struggle for land. The peasantry arises spontaneously and wants to settle the land question itself.' Further on, comrade Chen Du-Siu declares openly: *'We followed a too pacific policy.* Now it is necessary to confiscate the large estates. . . .' If the content of these words is developed in a Marxian manner, it constitutes the harshest condemnation of the whole past line of the Communist Party of China, and the Comintern as well, in the agrarian question of the Chinese revolution. Instead of anticipating the course of the agrarian movement, of establishing the slogans in time and throwing them among the peasant masses through the workers, the revolutionary soldiers and the advanced peasants, the Chinese Communist Party remained a vast distance behind the spontaneous agrarian movement. Can there be a more monstrous form of *khvostism*? *'We followed a too pacific policy.'* But what does a pacific policy of a revolutionary party mean in the period of a spontaneous agrarian revolution? It signifies the most grievous historical mistake that a party of the proletariat can possibly commit. A pacific policy (the reduction of rent payments), while the peasant is already fighting spontaneously for land, is not a policy of Menshevik compromise but of liberal compromise. Only a philistine corrupted by alleged statecraft can fail to understand this, but never a revolutionist.

55. But from his correct, and therefore deadly, characterisation of the relations of the party to the agrarian movement, comrade Chen Du-Siu draws not only false, but positively disastrous conclusions. 'It is now necessary,' he says, 'to confiscate

the large estates, but at the same time to make concessions to the small landowners who must be reckoned with.' In principle, such a way of posing the question cannot be assailed. It must be clearly determined who and in what part of China is to be considered a small landowner, how and to what limits he must be reckoned with. But Chen Du-Siu says further:

> Nevertheless, it is necessary to await *the further development of the military actions* even for the confiscation of the large estates. The only correct decision at the present moment is the principle of deepening the revolution *only after its extension*.

This road is the surest, the most positive, the shortest road to ruin. The peasant has already risen to seize the property of the large landowners. Our party, in monstrous contradiction to its programme, to its name, pursues a pacific-liberal agrarian policy. Chen Du-Siu himself declares that it is 'now [?] necessary to confiscate the large estates', but he immediately recalls that we 'must not fall into Left extremism' (Chen Du-Siu's own words) and he adds that we must 'await the further development of the military actions' for the confiscation of the property of the large landowners, that the revolution must first be extended and only later deepened.

But this is simply a blind repetition of the old, well-known and outworn formula of national-liberal deception of the masses: First the victory, then the reform. First we will 'extend' the country—for whom: for the large landowner?—and then, after the victory, we will concern ourselves very tranquilly with the 'deepening'. To this, every intelligent and half-way sensible peasant will answer comrade Chen Du-Siu: 'If the Wuhan government today, when it finds itself encircled by foes and needs our peasant support for life and death—if this government does not dare now to give us the land of the large landowners or does not want to do it, then after it has extricated itself from its encirclement, after it has vanquished the enemy with our help, it will give us just as much land as Chiang Kai-shek gave the workers of Shanghai.' It must be said quite clearly: The agrarian formula of comrade Chen Du-Siu, who is bound hand and foot by the false leadership of the representatives of the Comintern, is objectively nothing else than the formula of the severance of the Chinese Communist Party from the real agrarian movement which is now proceeding in China and which is producing a new wave of the Chinese revolution.

To strengthen this wave and to deepen it we need peasants' Soviets with the unfurled banner of the agrarian revolution, not after the victory but immediately, in order to guarantee the victory.

If we do not want to permit the peasant wave to come to nought and be splattered into froth, the peasants' Soviets must be united through workers' Soviets in the cities and the industrial centres, and to the workers' Soviets must be added the Soviets of the poor population from the urban trade and handwork districts.

If we do not want to permit the bourgeoisie to drive a wedge between the revolutionary masses and the army, then soldiers' Soviets must be fitted into the revolutionary chain.

As quickly as possible, as boldly as possible, as energetically as possible, the revolution must be deepened, not after the victory but immediately, or else there will be no victory.

The deepening of the agrarian revolution, the immediate seizure of the land by the peasants, will weaken Chiang Kai-shek on the spot, bring confusion into the ranks of his soldiers, and set the peasant hinterland in motion. There is no other road to victory and there can be none.

Have we really carried through three revolutions within two decades only to forget the ABC of the first of them? Whoever carries on a *pacific* policy during the agrarian revolution, is lost. Whoever postpones matters, vacillates, temporises, loses time, is lost. The formula of Chen Du-Siu is the surest road to the destruction of the revolution.

Slanderers will be found who will say that our words are dictated by a hatred of the Chinese Communist Party and its leaders. Was it not once said that our position on the Anglo-Russian Committee signified a hostile attitude towards the British Communist Party? The events confirmed the fact that it was we who acted as loyal revolutionists towards the British Communists, and not as bureaucratic sycophants. Events will confirm the fact—they confirm it every day—that our criticism of the Chinese Communists was dictated by a more serious, more Marxist, revolutionary attitude towards the Chinese revolution than was the attitude of the bureaucratic sycophants who approve of everything after the fact, provided that they do not have to foresee for the future.

The fact that the speech of comrade Chen Du-Siu is reprinted in *Pravda* without a single word of commentary, that no article revealing the ruinous course of this speech is devoted to it—this fact by itself must fill every revolutionist with the greatest misgivings, for it is the central organ of Lenin's party that is involved!

Let not the pacifiers and flatterers tell us about 'the unavoidable mistakes of a young Communist party'. It is not a question of isolated mistakes. It is a question of the false basic line, the consummate expression of which is the theses of comrade Stalin.

THE NECESSARY FINAL ACCORD

In the May 9 number of *Sotsialistichesky Vestnik*, it says in the article devoted to the theses of comrade Stalin:

If we strip the envelope of words that is obligatory for the theses of a Communist leader, then very little can be said against the essence of the 'line' traced there. As much as possible to remain in the Kuomintang, and to cling to its Left wing and to the Wuhan government to the last possible moment: 'to avoid a decisive struggle under unfavourable conditions'; not to issue the slogan 'all power to the Soviets' so as not 'to give new weapons into the hands of the enemies of the Chinese people for the struggle against the revolution, for creating new legends that it is not a national revolution that is taking place in China, but an artificial transplanting of Moscow Sovietisation'—what can actually be more sensible for the Bolsheviks now, after the 'united front' has obviously been irremediably destroyed, and so much porcelain has been smashed under the 'most unfavourable conditions'? (*Sotsialistichesky Vestnik*, No. 9 [151] page 1.)

Thus, after *Sotsialistichesky Vestnik*, in its April 23rd number, acknowledged that Martinov analysed the tasks of the Chinese revolution in *Pravda* 'very impressively' and 'entirely in the Menshevik manner', the leading article in the central organ of the Mensheviks declares in its latest number that 'very little can be said against the essence of the "line" traced' in the theses of comrade Stalin. This harmony of political lines hardly requires special elucidation.

But still more: The same article in *Sotsialistichesky Vestnik* speaks further on in a mocking tone—we quote literally!—of '*the line of Radek which, covered with extreme "Left" slogans, (withdrawal from Kuomintang, "propaganda of the Soviet system" etc.), simply desires in reality to give up the game and to step aside. . . .*' (*Sotsialistichesky Vestnik*, No. 9, [151] page 2.) The line of Radek is characterised here with the words of the leading articles and the feuilletons of *Pravda*. After all, it cannot be otherwise: Radek cannot say anything openly in the press about his line, for otherwise the party would learn that Radek's line is being confirmed by the whole course of events. The editors of *Sotsialistichesky Vestnik* not only describe 'the line of Radek' with the words of *Pravda* but also evaluate them in full accord with the articles of *Pravda*: The line of the Opposition, according to Dan, gives the possibility, 'covered with extreme "Left" slogans', in reality 'to give up the game and to step aside'. We have already read in the articles of *Pravda* that 'a mass for the dead must be read' for the Chinese revolution, that the Chinese Communists must 'retire within themselves', that they must renounce 'great deeds and great plans', and that all this is the 'sermon of the liquidation of the Chinese revolution'—if the line of the Oppostion is adopted. This was said literally, for example, in the leading article in *Pravda* of May 16, 1927. As we see, it is word for word the same thing that Dan says, or more correctly, Dan says of the Opposition word for word what *Pravda* has said in a series of its articles. Dan approves the theses of Stalin and derides the 'liquidator' Radek, who covers his liquidation with extremely Left phrases. Everything is clear now: The liquidationism of Radek is the same liquidationism which is evaluated as such by the renowned revolutionist Dan. That is the lesson that the leading articles in *Sotsialistichesky Vestnik* presents to those who are still capable of learning anything.

It is surely portentous that the quoted number of *Sotsialistichesky Vestnik* should arrive in Moscow on the eve of the opening of the session of the Executive Committee of the Communist International, which must consider the problem of the Chinese revolution in its full scope.

May 17, 1927

First Speech on the Chinese Question

DELIVERED AT THE EIGHTH PLENUM OF THE ECCI

COMRADES! In the question under discussion you have been given the theses of comrade Zinoviev which have remained unknown to the Russian party up till now. Zinoviev was not permitted to come here, although he has the full right—politically as well as formally—to do so. I am defending here the theses of comrade Zinoviev as common to us both. The first rule for the political education of a mass party is: It must know not only what is adopted by the Central Committee but also what it rejects, for only in this way does the line of the leadership become clear and comprehensible to the party masses. And that is how things have always been with us until now. The refusal to show the party Comrade Zinoviev's and my own reveals the intellectual weakness, the lack of certainty in their own position, the fear that the theses of the Opposition will appear more correct to the public opinion of the party than the theses of the majority. There can be no other motives for the concealment of our theses.

My attempt to publish a criticism of Stalin's theses in the theoretical organ of the party was unsuccessful. The Central Committee, against whose line in this question my theses are directed, prohibited their publication, as well as the publication of other articles by Zinoviev and me.

Yesterday a decision of the Editorial Committee, signed by comrade Kurella, was distributed here. It relates to information on our proceedings. What is meant by this is not quite clear to me. In any case, the Executive Committee is meeting in a strange atmosphere of silence by the press. Only one article in *Pravda* has been devoted to the Plenum and this article contains a phrase of unheard-of impudence: 'He would be a criminal who would think of shaking the unity of the ranks of the Comintern', etc., etc. Everyone understands what is meant by this. Even before the drafts of the resolutions have been published, *Pravda* brands as a criminal whoever argues against the future resolutions. One can imagine how *Pravda* will inform the party tomorrow about what is taking place here. Meanwhile, here in Moscow every expression of opinion, oral or written, in favour of the Opposition on the basic problems of the Chinese revolution is treated as a crime against the party. The completely false theses of comrade Stalin have been declared *de facto* inviolable. Still more, in the very days of the proceedings of the Executive, those comrades who, in the discussions in their Party cells, protested against the baiting of comrade Zinoviev, are simply expelled from the party or are at least threatened with expulsion. It is in this atmosphere, comrades, that you are acting and deciding. I propose that the Executive decode that every party, the Communist Party of the Soviet Union included, shall publish completely exact and objective reports on our deliberations, supplemented by all the theses and documents distributed here. The problems of the Chinese revolution cannot be stuck into a bottle and sealed up.

Comrades, the greatest of all dangers is the ever-sharpening party regime. Every mistake of the leadership is made 'good', so to speak, through measures against the Opposition. The day the telegram on Chiang Kai-shek's *coup d'état* was made known in Moscow, we said to each other: The Opposition will have to pay dearly for this—especially as demands for payment on their part have not been lacking recently.

The opportunity is always found to frame up a new 'case' of Zinoviev, Kamenev, Trotsky, Piatakov, Smilga, etc., so as to distract the attention of the party from the most burning questions; expulsions of the Opposition, despite the approach of the party congress—or rather just because of it—constantly increase. The same methods in every section of the party: in every factory, in every district, in every city. In this situation there frequently emerge, of necessity, those elements who are always ready to accept in advance everything from above, because nothing is difficult for them. They lull themselves into the hope that after Trotsky or Zinoviev have been overcome, everything will be in order. On the contrary: the regime has its own inner logic. The list has only been opened, not closed. Along this road there are only difficulties and further convulsions.

This regime weighs heavily on the International. Nobody trusts himself to speak a word of criticism openly, on the false pretence of not wanting to harm the Soviet Union. But that is exactly how the greatest harm is done. Our internal policy needs revolutionary international criticism, for the wrong tendencies in foreign policy are only an extension of the incorrect tendencies in our internal policy.

I now turn to the draft resolution of comrade Bukharin. First, a question which directly touches the point on the agenda already acted upon. Listen, comrades:

> The Communist International is of the opinion that parties, and in general all organisations that call themselves workers' parties and workers' organisations, which do not conduct the *most decisive struggle* against intervention in China, which *lull the vigilance of the working class* and propagate a *passive attitude* on this question, objectively (sometimes also subjectively) help the imperialists . . . in the preparation of war against the Soviet Union and in the preparation of new world wars in general.

These ring like honest words. But they become honest

only when they are applied also to the Anglo-Russian Committee. For does it 'conduct the most decisive struggle against intervention in China'? No! Does it not lull the vigilance of the working class? It does. Does it not propagate a passive attitude on this question! Without a doubt. Does it not thereby objectively (in its British half also subjectively) help the imperialists of Britain in their work of preparing the war? Obviously and without a doubt.

Compare this with what was declaimed here yesterday by Kuusinen on the Anglo-Russian Committee, in the language of Kuusinenized Purcellism. Whence this duplicity? The philosophy of customs certificates is far more appropriate in the customs office of a border state than on the tribune of the Comintern. This false and unworthy philosophy must be swept away with a broom.

Let us listen further to Bukharin's resolution:

> The ECCI declares that the development of events [in the Chinese revolution, the estimate of its driving forces made at the last Enlarged Plenum of the CI] has confirmed the prognosis. The ECCI declares especially that the course of events has fully confirmed the prognosis of the Enlarged Plenum on the inevitable departure of the bourgeoisie from the national revolutionary united front and its going over to the side of the counter-revolution.

The workers of Shanghai and Hankow will certainly be surprised when they read that the April events developed in complete harmony with the historical line of march which comrade Bukharin had previously outlined for the Chinese revolution. Could one ever imagine a more malicious caricature and more ridiculous pedantry? The vanguard of the Chinese proletariat was smashed by that same 'national' bourgeoisie which occupied the leading role in the joint party of the Kuomintang, subordinating the Communist party, on all decisive questions, to the organisational discipline of the joint party. After the counter-revolutionary coup, which struck the Chinese workers and the huge majority of the working class of the world like a bolt from the blue, the resolution says: It all took place in accordance with the best rules of the Bukharinist prognosis. This really sounds like a bad joke.

What is to be understood here by a prognosis, what does this so-called prognosis signify under the given conditions? Nothing but an empty phrase on the fact that the bourgeoisie, at a given stage of the bourgeois revolution, must separate itself from the oppressed masses of the people. That this common-place is pathetically called a 'prognosis', is a disgrace to Marxism. This banality does not separate Bolshevism from Menshevism for an instant. Ask Kautsky, Otto Bauer or Dan, and their answer will be: the bloc of the proletariat with the bourgeoisie cannot last for ever. Dan scribbled that in his rag only a short time ago.

But the kernel of the question is the following: To say that the bourgeoisie must separate itself from the national revolution is one thing. But to say that the bourgeoisie must take hold of the leadership of the revolution and the leadership of the proletariat, deceive the working class and then disarm it, smash it, and bleed it to death, is something quite different. The whole philosophy of Bukharin, in his resolution, is founded on the identity of these two prognoses. But this means that one does not want to make any fundamental contrast between the Bolshevik and Menshevik perspectives.

Let us listen to what Lenin said on this question:

The bourgeois politicians have fed and deceived the people with promises in every bourgeois revolution. Our revolution is a bourgeois revolution—therefore the workers must support the bourgeoisie. This is what the good-for-nothing politicians of the liquidator camp say. Our revolution s a bourgeois revolution, is what we Marxists say, and therefore the workers must open the eyes of the people to the deceit of the bourgeois politicians, teach them not to believe them, but to rely on their own forces, on their own solidarity, on their own arms. (March 1917.)

Foreseeing the inevitable departure of the bourgeoisie, Bolshevik policy in the bourgeois revolution is directed towards creating an independent organisation of the proletariat as soon as possible, impregnating it as deeply as possible with mistrust of the bourgeoisie, uniting the masses as soon and as broadly as possible and arming them, aiding the revolutionary uprising of the peasant masses in every way. The Menshevik policy in foreseeing the so-called departure of the bourgeoisie is directed towards postponing this moment as long as possible; while the independence of policy and organisation of the proletariat is sacrificed to this aim, the workers are instilled with confidence in the progressive role of the bourgeoisie, and the necessity of political self-restraint is preached. In order to maintain the alliance with Purcell, the great strike-breaker, he must be appeased by declaiming about cordial relations and political agreement. In order to maintain the so-called bloc with the Chinese bourgeoisie, they must always be whitewashed anew, thereby facilitating the deluding of the masses by the bourgeois politicians.

Yes, the moment of the departure of the bourgeoisie can thereby be postponed. But this postponement is utilized by the bourgeoisie against the proletariat: It seizes hold of the leadership thanks to its great social advantages, It arms its loyal troops, it prevents the arming of the proletariat, political as well as military, and after it has acquired the upper hand it organises a counter-revolutionary massacre at the first serious collision.

It is not the same thing, comrades, whether the bourgeoisie is tossed to one side or it tosses the proletarian vanguard to one side. These are the two roads of the revolution. On what road did the revolution travel up to the coup? The classic road of all previous bourgeois revolutions, of which Lenin said:

The bourgeois politicians have fed and deceived the people with promises in every bourgeois revolution.

Did the false position of the leadership obstruct or facilitate this road of the Chinese bourgeoisie? It facilitated it to a great extent.

To prevent the departure of the bourgeoisie from becoming the destruction of the proletariat, the miserable theory of the bloc of four classes should have been denounced from the very beginning as genuine theoretical and political treason to the Chinese revolution. Was this done? No, just the contrary.

I have not time enough to present a historical description of the development of the revolution and of our differences, which Bukharin had full opportunity to do—extensively and falsely. I am prepared to undertake this retrospective treatment in the theoretical organ of the party or of the International. Unfortunately, Bukharin touches on this question only where we have no opportunity to answer him properly, that is, with facts and quotations.

The following will suffice for today:

1. On March 16, one short month before the coup by Chiang Kai-shek, an editorial in *Pravda* indicted the Opposition for believing that the bourgeoisie stands at the head of the Kuomintang and the national government and is preparing treason. Instead of making this truth clear to the Chinese workers, *Pravda* denied it indignantly. It contended that Chiang Kai-shek submitted to the discipline of the Kuomintang, as if the conflicting classes, especially in the feverish tempo of the revolution, could submit to common political discipline. Incidentally: if the Opposition never had anything to say against the official line, as was said here by Smeral in his ponderous manner, then why are the speeches and articles by Bukharin for the last year filled with accusations against the Opposition on the most burning questions of the Chinese revolution?

If I have time, I will read here a letter by Radek*: it is a repetition of his letter of last July. This letter was written last September and takes up the most burning questions of the Chinese revolution.

2. Only on April 5, that is, only a week before the *coup d'état* by Chiang Kai-shek, Stalin rejected Radek's opinion at a meeting of Moscow functionaries and declared again that Chiang Kai-shek was submitting to discipline, that the admonitions were baseless, that we would use the Chinese bourgeoisie and then toss it away like a squeezed-out lemon. The whole speech of Stalin meant the soothing, the allaying of the uneasiness, the lulling to sleep of our party and the Chinese party. Thousands of comrades listened to this speech. This was on April 5. Truly, the prognosis is not so remarkable as Bukharin may claim. The stenogram of this speech by Stalin was never made public, because a few days later the squeezed-out lemon seized power with his army. As a member of the CC, I had the right to get the stenogram of this speech. But my efforts and attempts were in vain. Attempt it now, comrades, perhaps you will have better luck. I doubt it. This concealed stenogram of Stalin alone, without any other document, suffices to reveal the erroneousness of the official line, and to demonstrate how out of place it is to maintain that the events in Shanghai and Canton 'confirmed' the very line that Stalin defended in Moscow a week before.

3. The CC received a report on March 17 from China, from three comrades who were sent there by the CC. This highly important document gives an actual description of what the line of the CI really looked like. Borodin acted, in the words of the document, sometimes as a Right, at other times as a

---

* The letter was quoted by Vuyovitch in his speech later on. It is printed as an appendix to this volume.—Tr.

Left Kuomintang man, but never as a Communist. The representatives of the CI also acted in the same spirit, by transforming it a little into the Kuomintern; they hindered the independent policy of the proletariat, its independent organisation and especially its armament; to reduce this to a minimum they considered their sacred duty. Heaven forbid, with arms in hand the proletariat would frighten the great spirit of the national revolution, hovering over all the classes. Demand this document! Read it! Study it, so that you will not have to vote blindly.

I could name dozens of other articles, speeches and documents of this type over a period of about one and a half to two years. I am prepared to do it in writing at any moment, with complete accuracy and a statement of date and page. But what has been said is already enough to prove how basically false is the assertion that the events confirmed the 'prognosis' of that time.

Read further in the resolution:

> The ECCI is of the opinion that the tactic of a bloc with the national bourgeoisie in the period of the revolution already passed was fully correct.

Still more. Bukharin contends even today that the renowned formula of Martinov that the national government is the government of the bloc of four classes, suffers from only one trifling defect, that Martinov did not emphasise that the bourgeoisie stands at the head of the bloc. A quite insignificant trifle! Unfortunately, Martinov's masterpiece shows many other defects. For Martinov contends quite openly and clearly in his *Pravda* article that this national Chiang Kai-shek government was no (no!) bourgeois government, but (but!) the four-class-bloc government. Thus is it written for him in the holy scriptures.

What does this mean, anyway—bloc of four classes? Have you encountered this expression in Marxist writing before? If the bourgeoisie leads the oppressed masses of the people under the bourgeois banner, and takes hold of the state power through its leadership, then this is no bloc but the political exploitation of the oppressed masses by the bourgeoisie. But the national revolution is progressive, you reply. To be sure. Capitalist development in backward countries is also progressive. But its progressive character is not conditioned by the economic *co-operation* of the classes, but by the economic *exploitation* of the proletariat and the peasantry by the bourgeoisie. Whoever does not speak of the class struggle but of class co-operation in order to characterise capitalist progress, is not a Marxist but a prophet of peace dreams. Whoever speaks of the bloc of four classes so as to emphasise the progressive character of the political exploitation of the proletariat and peasantry by the bourgeoisie, has nothing to do with Marxism, for herein really lies the political function of the opportunists, of the 'conciliators', of the heralds of peace dreams.

The question of the Kuomintang has the closest connection with this. What Bukharin makes out of it is real political trickery. The Kuomintang is so 'special', something unprecedented, something that can only be characterised by the blue flag and blue smoke—in a word: whoever does not understand this highly complicated 'special thing'—and it cannot be understood for, according to Bukharin, it is just too 'special'—understands nothing about the Chinese revolution. What Bukharin himself understands about it, however, is not to be understood at all from Bukharin's words. The Kuomintang is *a party,* and in time of revolution, it can be understood only as a party. In the recent period, this party has not embodied the 'bloc of four classes', but the leading role of the bourgeoisie over the masses of the people, the proletariat and the Communist party included. The word 'bloc' should not be misused, especially not in the this case where it is done only for the good of the bourgeoisie. Taken politically, a bloc is the expression of an alliance of sides 'with equal rights', who come to an understanding on a certain joint action. Only, this was not the case in China, and still is not to this day. The Communist party was a subordinated part of a party at whose head stood the national-liberal bourgeoisie. Last May, the Communist party bound itself not to criticise even the teachings of Sun Yat Sen, that is, the petty bourgeois doctrine which is aimed not only against imperialism but also against the proletarian class struggle.

This 'special' Kuomintang has assimilated the lesson of the *exclusiveness* of the party which exercises the dictatorship and draws from this the conclusion as regards the Communists: 'Hold your tongue!', for in Russia—they say—there is also only one party at the head of the revolution.

With us the dictatorship of the party (quite falsely disputed theoretically by Stalin) is the expression of the socialist dictatorship of the proletariat. In China we have the bourgeois revolution, and the dictatorship of the Kuomintang is directed not only against the imperialists and the militarists but also against the proletarian class struggle. In that way, the bourgeoisie, supported by the petty bourgeoisie and the radicals, curbs the class struggle of the proletariat and the uprisings of the peasantry, strengthens itself at the cost of the masses of the people and the revolution. We stood for this, we made it easier for them to go on with it, we want to sanction it now also by talking nonsense about the 'special nature' of the Kuomintang without showing the proletariat the vicious class manoeuvres that have been and are concealed behind this 'special nature'.

The dictatorship of a party is a part of the socialist revolution. In the bourgeois revolution, the proletariat must absolutely insure the independence of its own party—at any price, cost what it may. The Communist Party of China has been a shackled party in the past period. It did not have so much as its own newspaper. Imagine what this means in general and especially in a revolution! Why has it not had, and has not yet to this day, its own daily paper? Because the Kuomintang does not want it. Can we tolerate anythink like this? This means disarming the proletariat politically. Then withdrawal from the Kuomintang—cries Bukharin.—Why? Do you want to say thereby that the Communist party cannot exist within the 'revolutionary' Kuomintang as a party? I can accept remaining within a really revolutionary Kuomintang only under conditions of complete political and organisational freedom of action for the Communist party, with a guaranteed common bias for action by the Kuomintang together with the Communist party.

The political conditions for this have been enumerated in the thesis of Zinoviev as well as in my own (No. 39) more precisely in points a, b, c, d, e, f, g, and h. These are the conditions for remaining in the Left Kuomintang. If comrade Bukharin is for remaining unconditionally—under all circumstances and at any price—then we do not go along with him.

(*Remmele*: Where is that in the resolution?)

The maintenance of a bloc or the organisational form of a bloc at any price leads to the necessity of throwing oneself at the feet of one's partner. The Berlin session of the Anglo-Russian Committee teaches us that.

The Communist party must create its own completely independent daily press, at any price. Thereby it will for the first time really begin to live and act as a political party.

Let us read further:

> The ECCI considers radically false the liquidatory [Look, look!] view that the crisis of the Chinese revolution is a long-term defeat.

On this point, we have expressed ourselves in our thesis with complete clarity. That the defeat is great I consider self-evident. To seek to minimise it only means to stand in the way of the education of the Chinese party.

No-one is today in a position to phophesy exactly if the defeat will last, or for how long. At any rate, in our theses we proceed from the possibility of the speedy overcoming of the defeat by the proletariat. But the preliminary condition for this is a correct policy on our part. The policy represented by comrade Chen Du-Siu, the leader of the party, in his speech at the latest convention of the Communist Party of China (published recently in *Pravda*) is basically false on the two most important questions: that of the revolutionary government, and that of the agrarian revolution. If we do not correct with the greatest energy the policy of the Chinese and our own party on these two decisive questions, the defeat will become deeper and weigh heavily on the Chinese working people for a long time. What is most essential concerning this has been said in my thesis, in the postscript to the speech of comrade Chen Du-Siu. I must limit myself greatly, and I point to the theses and other documents. I have promised to read also the letter from Radek to the Central Committee. Unfortunately I cannot here refute wholly frivolous and absurd assertions about the 'surrender' of the Chinese Eastern Railway, etc. Bukharin, like myself, has no documents on this, because the question was considered quite cursorily at one session of the Polburo.

(*Bukharin*: It is shameless to deny this.)

If I am given three minutes for it, I will immediately refute the shamefaced Bukharin, for what he says is a lie. The only thing I proposed at that time—after the words of comrade Rudzutak, who said this railway becomes an instrument of imperialism now and then (for which Bukharin attacked Rudzutak)—was a declaration from our side in which we repeat, in an open and solemn manner, that which we had already said once in the Peking decisions: The moment the Chinese people has created its own democratic unified government, we will freely and gladly hand over the railway to them on the most favourable conditions. The Polburo said: No, at this time such a declaration will be interpreted as a sign of weakness, we will make this declaration a month from now. Although not in agreement with this, I raised no protest against it. It was a fleeting discussion which was only later transformed in a wretched manner, in an untruthful way, then, turned into a rounded-off formula, launched in the party organisation, in the Party cells, with warped insinuations in the press—in a word, dealt with just as has become the custom and practise with us in recent times.

Chairman: Comrade Trotsky, I call your attention to the fact that you have only eight more minutes to speak. The Presidium granted you forty-five minutes and after that I must let the Plenum decide.

Remmele: Besides that, I must request the Plenum to reject certain imputations and expressions; to speak of a shameless Bukharin is the lowest I have yet heard.

Trotsky: If I am reproached for shamelessness and I speak of the shamefaced, protest is made—against me. I speak of the shamefaced Remmele who accuses me of shamelessness. It is you who speak of shamelessness, I always speak only of shamefacedness.

Chairman: I strongly request you to abstain from such expressions. Do not think that you can behave here just as you please.

Trotsky: I bow before the objectivity of the chairman, and withdraw every suspicion of 'shamefacedness'.

I cannot read the whole of Radek's letter; perhaps I will do it when I speak a second time. The letter from Radek, which was sent to the CC in full agreement with myself and Zinoviev, and which raised the most burning questions of the Chinese revolution which we are discussing here today, was not answered by the Polburo of the party. I must therefore now speak only on the general political consequences created by the very heavy defeat of the Chinese revolution.

Comrade Bukharin has already made the attempt to refer to the fact that Chamberlain broke off diplomatic relations.

We were—I have already observed—in a very difficult situation, where we were surrounded by enemies, and Bukharin and other comrades participated then in a great party discussion to find the correct way out of the difficult situation. A revolutionary party can renounce its right to analyse the situation and draw the necessary conclusions for its policy just as little in a difficult situation as in a favourable one. For I repeat again, if a false policy can be harmless in a favourable situation it can become fatal in a difficult situation.

Are the differences of opinion great? Very great, very significant, very important! It cannot be denied that they have become deeper in the course of the last year. No-one would have believed in the possibility of the Berlin decisions of the Anglo-Russian Committee a year ago, no-one in the possibility that the philosophy of the bloc of four classes would be flaunted in *Pravda,* that Stalin would present his squeezed-out lemon on the eve of Chiang Kai-shek's *coup d'état,* just as Kuusinen yesterday presented his customs certificate. Why did this quick development become possible? Because the incorrect line was checked by the two greatest events of the last year, the great strikes in Britain and the Chinese revolution.

Comrades have come forward—and we shall certainly hear such voices again—who said: since the contradictions have become sharpened, the road leads necessarily to two parties. I deny this. We live in a period where contradictions do not ossify, because great events teach us better. There is a great and dangerous push towards the right in the line of the CI. But we have enough confidence in the force of the Bolshevik idea and the power of great events to reject decisively and determinedly every phophecy of split.

The theses of comrade Bukharin are false. And, moreover, in the most dangerous manner. They suppress the most important points of the question. They contain the danger that we shall not only fail to make up for lost time but that we shall lose still more time.

1. Instead of continually sounding alarms about wanting to withdraw from the Kuomintang (which is not proposed at all) the political independence of the Communist party must be put above all other considerations, even that of remaining in the Kuomintang. A separate daily press, relentless criticism also against the Left Kuomintang.

2. The postponement of the agrarian revolution until the territory is secured militarily—the idea of Chen Du-Siu—must be condemned formally, for this programme endangers the life of the revolution.

3. The postponement of the re-organisation of the government until the military victory—a second idea of Chen Du-Siu's—must also be characterised as endangering the life of the revolution. The bloc of Hankow leaders is not yet a revolutionary government. To create and spread any illusions on this score means to condemn the revolution to death. Only the workers', peasants', petty-bourgeois and soldiers' Soviets can serve as the basis for a revolutionary government.

Naturally, the Hankow government will have to adapt itself to the Soviets in some way or other, or else—disappear.

4. The alliance between the Communist party and a really revolutionary Kuomintang must not only be maintained but must be extended and deepened on the basis of mass Soviets.

Whoever speaks of arming the workers without permitting the workers to build Soviets is not serious about arming them. If the revolution develops further—and we are fully confident that it will—the impulse of the workers to build Soviets will grow ever stronger. We must prepare, strengthen and extend this movement, but not hamper and apply brakes to it as the resolution proposes.

The Chinese revolution cannot be advanced if the worst Right deviations are abetted, and smuggled Menshevik goods are allowed to be circulated under the customs seal of Bolshevism—comrade Kuusinen did this for a whole hour yesterday —while on the other hand the really revolutionary warnings of the Left are mechanically smothered.

Bukharin's resolution is false and dangerous. It directs the attack towards the Left. The Communist Party of China, which can and must become a really Bolshevik party in the fire of the revolution, cannot accept this resolution. Our party and the entire Comintern cannot declare this resolution their own. The world historical problem must be openly and honestly discussed by the whole International. The discussion, may it be ever so sharp politically, should not be conducted in the tone of envenomed, personal baiting and slander. All the documents, the speeches, the theses, the articles must be made available to the membership of the International.

The Chinese revolution cannot be stuffed into a bottle and sealed from above with a signet.

Moscow, May 1927.

Second Speech on the Chinese Question

DELIVERED AT THE EIGHTH PLENUM OF THE ECCI

WE ARE ALL OF the opinion that the Chinese revolution lives and will continue to live. That is why the main question is not whether the Opposition issued a warning and when, and where (I assert that it did warn and take it upon myself to prove it); the question is not whether Trotsky or Maslow wanted to surrender the Chinese Eastern Railway; the question is rather what is to be done from now on to pull the revolution out of the morass into which it was led by false policy and to set it on the correct road. I want, in a few words, to go to the heart of the question and show the irreconcilable divergence between our position and Stalin's.

Stalin has again declared himself here against workers' and peasants' Soviets with the argument that the Kuomintang and the Wuhan government are sufficient means and instruments for the agrarian revolution. Thereby Stalin assumes, and wants the International to assume the responsibility for the policy of the Kuomintang and the Wuhan government, as he repeatedly assumed the responsibility for the policy of the former 'national government' of Chiang Kai-shek (particularly in his speech of April 5, the stenogram of which has, of course, been kept hidden from the International).

We have nothing in common with this policy. We do not want to assume even a shadow of responsibility for the policy of the Wuhan government and the leadership of the Kuomintang, and we urgently advise the Comintern to reject this responsibility. We say directly to the Chinese peasants: The leaders of the Left Kuomintang of the type of Wang Chin Wei and Co. will inevitably betray you if you follow the Wuhan heads instead of forming your own independent Soviets. The agrarian revolution is a serious thing. Politicians of the Wang Chin Wei type, under difficult conditions, will unite ten times with Chiang Kai-shek against the workers and peasants. Under such conditions, two Communists in a bourgeois government become impotent hostages, if not a direct mask for the preparation of a new blow against the working masses. We say to the workers of China: The peasants will not carry out the agrarian revolution to the end if they let themselves be led by petty-bourgeois radicals instead of by you, the revolutionary proletarians. Therefore, build up your workers' Soviets, ally them with the peasant Soviets, arm yourselves through the Soviets, draw soldiers' representatives into the Soviets, shoot the generals who do not recognise the Soviets, shoot the bureaucrats and bourgeois liberals who will organise uprisings against the Soviets. Only through peasants' and soldiers' Soviets will you win over the majority of Chiang Kai-shek's soldiers to your side. You, the advanced Chinese proletarians, would be traitors to your class and to your historic mission, were you to believe that an organisation of leaders, petty-bourgeois and compromising in spirit, which has no more than 250,000 members (see the report of Tang Ping Shan), is capable of taking the place of workers', peasants', and soldiers' Soviets embracing millions upon millions. *The Chinese bourgeois-democratic revolution will go forward and be victorious either in the Soviet form or not at all.*

We will say to the Chinese Communists: The programme of comrade Chen Du-Siu, namely, to postpone the 'reorganisation' of the Hankow regime and the confiscation of the large land-owners' land until the war danger is eliminated, is the surest and swiftest road to ruin. The war is a class danger. It can only be ended by crushing the great landowners, by annihilating the agents of imperialism and of Chiang Kai-shek and by the building of Soviets. Precisely in that lies the agrarian revolution, the people's revolution, the workers' and peasants' revolution, i.e., the genuine national revolution (in the Leninist, but not in the Martinovist sense of the term).

Now on the internal questions of the Communist Party of the Soviet Union.

At critical moments like the present, the principal rule of revolutionary policy consists of thinking out a question to the very end and expressing one's opinion completely, with entire clarity, without any hypocrisy, without reservations. It is a question of the Opposition in the CPSU and of what is going to happen in connection with the international difficulties and the prospect of war.

It would be manifestly absurd to believe that the Opposition can simply renounce its views. Such questions are decided by the test of events. An examination of the last half year since the Seventh Plenum has, in our opinion, shown and proved that the line of the Opposition stood the test of the greatest events of the Chinese revolution and made it possible to foresee and foretell correctly every stage in the question of the Anglo-Russian Committee, that is, in essence, the question of Amsterdam, and consequently also of the Second International.

Is common work possible? I have enumerated our diplomats to you, and I named only the most important ones. I could name hundreds and thousands of Opposition party workers in various posts at home. Will anyone dare to say that such Oppositionists, for example, as the People's Commissar for Postal and Telegraphic Communications, Ivan Nikitich Smirnov, or the head of the Workers' and Peasants' Inspection for the Army and

Navy, Muralov, or the People's Commissar for the Interior, Bieloborodov, fulfill their duties worse than others? But the whole trick of the party apparatus consists of removing the Oppositionists from their work, beginning with the skilled workers in the factories. They are persecuted, shifted around, driven out, regardless of the quality of their work, solely and exclusively because of their Opposition viewpoint, which they defend with party methods. As the party Congress approaches, they are trying to send a member of the Central Committee, comrade Smilga, one of the oldest Bolsheviks, one of the heroes of the October revolution and the civil war, one of our outstanding economists, to the Far East, to Khabarovsk, for planning work, that is, simply to isolate him politically. In the same manner, they are trying to get rid of comrade Safarov, who has more than twenty years of uninterrupted party work behind him, by proposing to him to leave as soon as possible, be it for Turkey, or Tierra del Fuego, or the planet Mars, or anywhere else, so long as he disappears. They are trying at all costs to ship one of the oldest party members, Kuklin, a proletarian to the core, a former member of the Central Committee (he was removed from it for supporting the Opposition) to Britain, where he would be practically like a fish out of water. All of them are stainless revolutionists, fighters of the October Revolution and the civil war. The number of examples could be multiplied endlessly. This method is ruinous. It disorganises the party. Common practical work is entirely possible. This has been demonstrated by all our experience. The guarantee for such common work in the interest of our workers' state depends entirely upon the Central Committee which is, it is true, pursuing an exactly contrary course.

I repeat: conscientious common work is possible, despite the deepening of the differences during the last year. On international questions this has appeared clearly, because tremendous events have taken place there. But now developments are entering a new phase in internal questions. Not only war, but also war danger itself puts all questions harshly before us. Every class necessarily examines the fundamental questions of policy when faced with war. The kulak, the functionary, and the Nepman raise their heads and ask: What kind of war will this be, what will we get out of it, with what methods will it be conducted? On the other hand, the town worker, the land worker and the poor peasant will also examine more sharply, in face of the war danger, the achievements of the revolution, the advantages and disadvantages of the Soviet regime, and will ask: In which direction will the relationship of forces be changed by the war? Will it increase the role of the men on top or the masses below? Will it straighten out the proletarian class line of the party or will it accelerate the shift towards the high-ups under the pretext of a 'national war' (in the Stalinist interpretation)?

The bourgeois elements among us have grown very strong; the struggle of the two tendencies has its roots in the classes. Since there is only one party in our country, the struggle goes on inside our party.

With the greatest light-mindedness, or more correctly, with the most criminal light-mindedness, they have spoken here of shattering the Opposition, of splitting off the Opposition, and the speakers were those whose whole past gives them the least right to do so. But I shall not dwell on them. Such people are washed ashore by one wave and washed away by another.

Ustrialov, the shrewdest enemy of Bolshevism, has for some time demanded the expulsion of the Opposition and a split with it. Ustrialov is the representative of the new bourgeoisie which grows out of the Nep, and of the most virile section of the old bourgeoisie which wants to support itself upon the new. Ustrialov does not want to 'skip over any stages'. Ustrialov openly supports the policy of Stalin and only demands of Stalin greater determination in liquidating the Opposition. Ponder over these facts.

On the other hand, when MacDonald appeals against intervention, he demands that the sensible 'practical politicians' should not be prevented from putting an end to 'the propagandists of the Third International'—these are literally MacDonald's words—, that is, that Stalin should not be disturbed in his work of smashing the Opposition. Chamberlain, with his brigand's methods, wants to hasten the same process. The various methods are directed towards one aim: to smash the proletarian line, to destroy the international connections of the Soviet Union, to force the Russian proletariat to renounce its intervention in the affairs of the international proletariat. Can it be doubted that MacDonald will raise no objection to your refusal to permit comrade Zinoviev to attend the sessions of the Comintern? MacDonald will boast of his own farsightedness if you should carry out the policy of destroying and splitting off the opposition. MacDonald will say: The practical politicians are breaking with the propagandists of the Third International.

The attempt to depict the Opposition as a group of leaders is a gross deception. The Opposition is an expression of the class struggle. The organisational weakness of the Opposition by no means corresponds to its specific weight in the party and the working class. The strength of the present party regime lies, among other things, in the fact that it changes the relation of forces in the party by artificial means. The present heavy bureaucratic regime in the party reflects the pressure of other classes upon the proletariat. Yesterday, eighty old party members, tested Bolsheviks, sent a declaration to the Central Committee in which they fully support the standpoint which we are developing here. They are all comrades who have behind them ten, fifteen, twenty and more years of uninterrupted work in the Bolshevik party. To speak of any kind of 'Trotskyism' in the face of all these facts, is to falsify the question in a ridiculous and wretched manner. The revisionists label the revolutionary content of Marxism with the word Blanquism, the more easily to enable them to fight against Marxism. The comrades who are turning away from the Bolshevik line label the revolutionary content of Leninism 'Trotskyism', the more easily to enable them to fight against Leninism. We have had a classic example of this in the speech of comrade Kuusinen, out of whose mouth spoke a provincial German social democrat.

During the most recent period of party development, the blows have been directed only against the Left. The basic reason for this is the defeats of the proletariat in the international field and the strengthening of the Right course flowing from them. The whole history of the working-class movement proves that great defeats result in a temporary triumph of the opportunist line. After the defeat of the great strikes in Britain and of the Chinese Revolution, they want to deliver a new blow to the Opposition, that is, to the Left, revolutionary line in the Communist Party of the Soviet Union and the Communist International. There is no doubt that the most principled, most consummate speech was delivered here by the new leader of the new course, Martinov, the mountebank of the bloc of four classes. What does this signify? A still greater strengthening of the shift to the Right. It means the threat that the tendencies of Ustrialov will triumph. The Ustrialovs do not want to skip over any stages or phases, that is why the Ustrialovs are now openly for Stalin. But they do not, of course, think of remaining with him. For them, he is only a stage. For them, it is a question of destroying the Left barrier in the CPSU, of weakening the proletarian line, of transforming the Soviet system into an instrument of the petty bourgeoisie, so as to proceed from there on the direct road towards the restoration of capitalism, most probably in the Bonapartist form.

The war danger puts all questions harshly. Stalin's line is the line of indecision, of vacillation between Left and Right tendencies with actual support for the Right course. The growth of the war danger will force Stalin to choose. He has made an effort here to show that the choice has already been made. After the massacre of the Chinese workers by the bourgeoisie, after the capitulation of the Political Bureau to Purcell, after the speech of Chen Du-Siu in *Pravda,* Stalin sees the enemy only on the Left and directs his fire against them. Dozens of old and tested Bolshevik party comrades, chiefly from Moscow and Leningrad, warn the party in their collective letter of the threatening internal dangers. We do not doubt that thousands of party fighters will join with them, fighters who do not fear threats or provocations, and who, despite all mechanical barriers, will understand how to penetrate to the public opinion of the party, and to redress the revolutionary line of Bolshevism through the party and by party methods.

Fraternising with Purcell and baiting Zinoviev, eulogising and painting up the bourgeois leaders of the Kuomintang and baiting the Left Opposition in the CPSU and in other parties —one goes closely together with the other. This is a definite course. Against this course we will fight to the end. Stalin said the Opposition stands in one front with Chamberlain, with Mussolini and Chang Tso-lin. To that I answer: Nothing has facilitated the work of Chamberlain so much as the false policy of Stalin, particularly in China. The revolution cannot be made by halves. The London blow is the pay-off for the Martinovist course in China. On this path, only defeats can be accumulated.

Stalin obviously wants to make the attempt to present the Opposition as something like a defence corps for Chamberlain. This is wholly in the spirit of his methods. Yesterday Michael Romanov,* today Chamberlain. But here he

* At the November-December 1927 Plenum of the Executive Committee of the Communist International, during the debate on the Russian question, Stalin sought in every way possible to discredit the stand-

will miscalculate even more than he did with his hopes in Chiang Kai-Shek and Purcell. Chamberlain must be seriously fought against, and the working class in the country and throughout the world must be brought to its feet and united. The masses can be brought to their feet, united and strengthened only through a correct class line. While we fight for a correct revolutionary line against the line of Stalin, we are preparing the best conditions for the struggle against Chamberlain. It is not we who are helping Chamberlain; it is the false policy.

Not a single honest proletarian will believe the insane infamy about the united front between Chamberlain and Trotsky. But the reactionary section of the petty bourgeoisie, the rising kulakdom of the Black Hundreds, can believe this, or pretend to believe this, so as to carry through to the end the suppression of the revolutionary proletarian line and its representatives. If you give the devil of chauvinism a finger, you perish. With his poisoned accusations, Stalin is extending this finger. We say this here and we will say it openly before the international proletariat.

Moscow, May 1927.

---

point of the Opposition by sharp personal attacks upon its leaders. In the concluding remarks on his report, Stalin suddenly 'recalled' that immediately after the March 1917 revolution, Kamenev had joined with a number of rich Siberian merchants in Atchinsk to send a telegram of felicitations to Michael Romanov, to whom the abdicating tsar had turned over the 'right to the throne'. Stalin's 'recollection' of this story created a tremendous disturbance in the hall. Such a story had indeed been circulated by the counter-revolutionists during the early years of the Bolshevik revolution. Not having any foundation in fact, it was formally and publicly denied by Lenin and the party at that time. It was maliciously revived in 1927 out of purely factional considerations.—Tr.

The Sure Road

THE SHANGHAI correspondent of the *Daily Express* reports: 'The peasants of Honan province are occupying the land and executing the big landlords who resist most stubbornly. Everywhere, control is in the hands of the Communists. Workers' Soviets are formed locally which take over administrative authority.' (*Pravda,* May 11, 1927.)

We do not know to what extent the telegram is correct in depicting the situation with such bold strokes. We have no other reports save the telegram. What is the real extent of the movement? Is it not deliberately exaggerated in order to influence the power of imagination of Messrs. MacDonald, Thomas, Purcell and Hicks with the intention of making them more pliant to the policy of Chamberlain? We do not know.

But in this case, it has no decisive significance.

The peasants are seizing the land and exterminating the most counter-revolutionary big landlords. Workers' Soviets are formed locally which take over administrative authority. That is what a correspondent of a reactionary paper communicates. The editorial board of *Pravda* considers this report sufficiently important to incorporate it in the contents table of the most important daily events in the world. We too are of the opinion that this is correct. But it would naturally be premature to contend that the Chinese revolution, after the April *coup d'état* of the bourgeois counter-revolution, has already entered a new and higher stage. After a great defeat, it frequently happens that a part of the attacking masses, which was never submitted to any direct blows, passes over to the next stage of the movement and for a while outstrips the leading detachments which suffered with especial severity in the defeat. Were we to have before us such a phenomenon, the Soviets of Honan would soon disappear, temporarily washed away by the general revolutionary ebb-tide.

But there is not the slightest reason to contend that we have before us only sharp rearguard encounters of a revolution which is ebbing for a long period. In spite of the fact that the April defeat was no separate 'episode', but a very significant stage in the development of the counter-revolution; in spite of the agonising blood drawn from the vanguard detachments of the working class, there is not the least reason to contend that the Chinese revolution has been beaten back for years.

The agrarian movement, since it is more scattered, is less subject to the direct operations of the hangmen of the counter-revolution. There is the possibility that the further growth of the agrarian movement will give the proletariat the opportunity to rise again in the relatively near future and to pass over once more to the attack. Naturally, exact predictions on this point are impossible, especially from afar. The Chinese Communist Party will have to follow attentively the actual course of events and the class groupings in order to catch the moment of a new wave of attack.

The possibility of a new attack, however, will depend not only on the evolution of the agrarian movement but also upon the side towards which the broad, petty-bourgeois masses of the towns develop in the next period. The *coup d'état* of Chiang Kai-shek does not signify only the consolidation of the power of the Chinese bourgeoisie (perhaps less so), but also the re-establishment and the consolidation of the positions of foreign capital in China with all the consequences that flow from them. From this follows the probabality, perhaps even the inevitability —and this in the fairly near future—of a turn of the petty bourgeois masses against Chiang Kai-shek. The petty-bourgeoisie, which is subjected to great sufferings not only by foreign capital but also by the alliance of the national Chinese bourgeoisie with foreign capital, must, after some vacillations, turn against the bourgeois counter-revolution. It is precisely in this that lies one of the most important manifestations of the class mechanics of the national democratic revolution.

Finally, the young Chinese proletariat, by all the conditions of its existence, is so accustomed to privation and sacrifice, has so well 'learned', together with the whole of the oppressed Chinese people, to look death in the eye, that we may expect from the Chinese workers, once they are properly aroused by the revolution, highly exceptional self-abnegation in struggle.

All this gives us the full right to count upon the new wave of the Chinese revolution being separated from the wave which ended with the April defeat of the proletariat, not by long years but by short months. Naturally, nobody can establish the intervals for this either. But we would be incompetent revolutionists if we were not to steer our course upon a new rise, if we were not to work out any programme of action for it, any political road or any organisational forms.

The April defeat was no 'episode', it was a heavy class defeat; we will not take up here an analysis of the reasons for it. We want to speak in this article of tomorrow and not of yesterday. The heaviness of the April defeat lies not only in the fact that the proletarian centres were struck a sanguinary blow. The heaviness of the defeat lies in the fact that the workers were crushed by those who until then had stood at their head. Such a violent turn must produce not only physical disorganisation but also political confusion in the ranks of the proletariat. This confusion, which is more dangerous to the revolution than the defeat itself, can be overcome only by a clear, precise, revolutionary line for tomorrow.

In this sense, the telegram of the Shanghai correspondent of the reactionary British newspaper has especial significance. In it is shown what road the revolution in China can tread should it succeed in the next period in reaching a higher level.

We have said above that the peasants' liquidation of the big landlords of Honan, like the creation of workers' Soviets, may be the sharp conclusion of the last wave or the commencement of a new one, since the matter is considered from afar. This contrast of two waves can lose its significance if the interval between them is long, namely, a few weeks or even a few months. However the matter may be (and here only advice can be given, especially from a distance), the symptomatic significance of the Honan events is thoroughly clear and incontestable, regardless of their extent and sweep. The peasants and the workers of Honan are showing the road which their movement can tread, now that the heavy chains of their bloc with the bourgeoisie and the big landlords have been smashed. It would be contemptible and philistine to believe that the agrarian problem and the workers' problem in this revolution, gigantic in its tasks and in the masses it has drawn in its train, can be solved by decree from above and by arbitration committees. The worker himself wants to break the backbone of the reactionary bourgeoisie and to teach the manufacturers to respect the proletarian, his person and his rights. The peasant himself wants to sever the ties of his dependence upon the big landlords who exhaust him with their usurious practices and enslave him. Imperialism, which violently hampers the economic development of China by its customs, its financial and its military policy, condemns the worker to beggary and the peasant to the cruellest enslavement. The struggle against the big landlords, the struggle against the usurer, the struggle against the capitalists for better working conditions, is thus raised by itself to the struggle for the national independence of China, for the liberation of its productive forces from the bonds and chains of foreign imperialism. There is the principal and the mightiest foe. It is mighty not only because of its warships, but also directly by its inseparable connections with the heads of the banks, the usurers, the bureaucrats and the militarists, with the Chinese bourgeoisie, and by the more indirect but no less intimate ties with the big commercial and industrial bourgeoisie.

All these facts demonstrate that the pressure of imperialism is in no sense an external, mechanical pressure which welds all the classes together. No, it is a very deep-lying factor of internal action which accentuates the class struggle. The Chinese commercial and industrial bourgeoisie carries behind it the supplementary force of foreign capital and foreign bayonets in every one of its serious collisions with the proletariat. The masters of this capital and these bayonets play the role of more experienced and more adroit operators, who included the blood of the Chinese workers in their accounts just as they do with raw rubber and opium. If one wants to drive out foreign imperialism, if one wants to conquer the enemy, then his 'peaceful', 'normal' hangman's and robber's work in China must be rendered impossible. This cannot be attained, naturally, on the road of compromise of the bourgeoisie with foreign imperialism. Such a compromise may increase the share of the Chinese bourgeoisie in the product of the labour of the Chinese workers and peasants by a few per cent. But it will signify the deeper penetration of foreign imperialism into the economic and political life of China, the deeper enslavement of the Chinese worker and peasant. Victory over foriegn imperialism can only be won by means of the toilers of town and country driving it out of China. For this, the masses must really rise, millions strong. They cannot rise under the bare slogan of national liberation, but only in direct struggle against the big landlords, the military satraps, the usurers, the capitalist brigands. In this struggle, the masses are already rising, steeling themselves, arming themselves. There is no other road of revolutionary training. The big bourgeois leadership of the Kuomintang (the gang of Chiang Kai-shek) has opposed this road with all means. At first, only from within, by means of decrees and prohibitions, but when the 'discipline' of the Kuomintang did not suffice, with the aid of machine guns. The petty bourgeois leadership of the Kuomintang hesitates out of fear of a too stormy development of the mass movement. By their whole past, the petty-bourgeois radicals are more accustomed to looking to the top, to seeking combinations of all sorts of 'national' groups, than to looking down below, to the real struggle of millions of workers. But if vacillations and irresolution are dangerous in all things, then in the revolution they are disastrous. The workers and peasants of Honan are showing the way out of the vacillations, and by that, the road to save the revolution.

It is not necessary to explain that only this road, that is, the deeper mass sweep, the greater social radicalism of the programme, the unfurled banner of workers' and peasants' Soviets, can seriously preserve the revolution from military defeats from without. We know this from our own experience. Only a revolution on whose banner the toilers and the exploited plainly inscribe their won demands is capable of winning the living sympathy of the soldiers of capitalism. We experienced and tested this out in the waters of Archangel, Odessa and other places. The leadership of compromise and treason did not preserve Nanking from destruction, and gave the enemy ships access to the Yangtse. A revolutionary leadership, given a mighty social sweep of the movement, can succeed in making the waters of the Yangtse too hot for the ships of Lloyd George, Chamberlain and MacDonald. In any case, it is only along this road that the revolution can seek and find its defence.

We have repeatedly said above that the agrarian movement and the formation of Soviets can signify the conclusion of yesterday and the beginning of tomorrow. But this does not depend upon objective conditions alone. Under present conditions, the subjective factor has an enormous, perhaps a decisive significance: a correct formulation of the tasks, a firm and clear leadership. If a movement like the one that has begun in Honan is left to its own resources, it will inevitably be crushed. The confidence of the insurrectionary masses will be increased tenfold as soon as it feels a firm leadership and greater cohesion with it. A clear-headed leadership, generalising matters in the political field and connecting them up organisationally, is alone capable of preserving the movement to a greater or lesser degree from incautious or premature side-leaps and from so-called 'excesses', without which, however, as the experience of history teaches, no really revolutionary movement of the millions can reach its goal.

The task consists of giving the agrarian movement and the workers' Soviets a clear programme of practical action, an internal cohesion and a broad political goal. Only on this basis can a really revolutionary collaboration of the proletariat and the petty-bourgeoisie be constituted and developed, a genuine alliance of struggle of the Communist party with the Left Kuomintang. The cadres of the latter can in general only constitute and steel themselves if they do it in most intimate contact with the revolutionary struggles of the peasants and the poor population of the city. The agrarian movement, led by peasants' and workers' Soviets, will confront the Left Kuomintang people with the necessity of finally choosing between the Chiang Kai-shek camp of the bourgeoisie and the camp of the workers and peasants. To put the fundamental class questions openly, that is the only way under present conditions to put an end to the vacillation of the petty-bourgeois radicals and to compel them to tread the only road which leads to victory. This can be done by our Chinese party with the support of the whole Communist International.

Moscow, May 27, 1927.

Hankow and Moscow

WHAT IS happening in Hankow now? We can only judge from the telegraphic fragments which TASS does not give to the press.

The Left Kuomintang continues to chew the cud of the theory of the solidarity of the workers, peasants and the bourgeoisie in the 'national revolution' and recommends to the workers and peasants to observe discipline—towards the bourgeoisie.

The Central Committee of the Communist party (or the Executive Committee of the Kuomintang?) calls upon the trade unions to mind 'their own affairs' and to leave to the authorities of the Kuomintang the struggle against the counter-revolution.

The leader of the Communist party, Chen Du-Siu, adjures the peasants to wait for land until the external foe is conquered.

From Moscow comes the warning not to create Soviets 'prematurely'.

In the meantime, imperialism exerts pressure upon Chiang Kai-shek, and Chiang Kai-shek, through the bourgeoisie of Hankow, upon the Left Kuomintang.

The Left Kuomintang demands discipline and patience from the workers and the peasants.

This is the general picture. Its meaning is completely clear.

What is the Moscow leadership doing these days? We know nothing about it. But we need not doubt that under the influence of the recent extremely disquieting telegrams from Hankow, Moscow is sending advice there with approoixmately the following content: 'As much of the agrarian revolution as possible'; 'as many of the masses as possible in the Kuomintang', and so forth. The Communist ministers transmit these counsels to the government and to the Central Executive Committee of the Kuomintang.

In this manner, the work of the Communist party is divided into two parts: aloud, it implores the workers and peasants *to wait;* but in an undertone it whisperingly adjures the bourgeois government *to make haste.* But the revolution is a revolution precisely because the masses do not want to wait. The bourgeois 'radicals' are afraid to make haste precisely because they are bourgeois radicals. And the Communist party, instead of bringing the masses to their feet, instead of occupying the land, and building Soviets, loses time with sterile counsels to both sides, in accordance with the sacrosanct prescription of Martinov on the bloc of four classes and on the replacement of the revolution by an arbitration committee.

The collapse of this policy is absolutely inevitable. Unless we correct it sharply, instantly and resolutely, the collapse will take place in the immediate future. Then a lot of papers, with Moscow's advice on them, will be brandished before our eyes: 'As much of the agrarian revolution as possible, as many of the masses as possible in the Kuomintang.' But then we will repeat just what we say today: Such counsels are humbug. The whole revolution cannot be made dependent upon whether or not the pusillanimous bourgeois leadership of the Kuomintang accepts our well-meaning advice. It cannot accept it. The agrarian revolution cannot be accomplished with the consent of Wang Chin Wei, but in spite of Wang Chin Wei and in struggle against him.

That is why the first task is to free our hands, to withdraw the Communist ministers from the national government, to call upon the masses to occupy the land immediately and to build up Soviets.

But for this we need a really independent Communist party, which does not implore the leaders, but resolutely leads the masses. There is no other road and there can be none.

Moscow, May 28, 1927.

Is It Not Time to Understand?

TODAY'S *Bulletin of TASS* [Soviet Telegraphic Agency], Number 118, not for the press, contains a few telegrams of exclusively political importance. These telegrams are not kept concealed from public opinion because they may cause harm to the Soviet state or the Chinese revolution, but because they prove the faultiness of the official course and the correctness of the line of the Opposition. We cite only the two especially striking telegrams:

'*Shanghai, May 24. Tass.—The central political council in Nanking has decided to make Feng Yu-hsiang a member of the council.*'

That Chiang Kai-shek has made Feng Yu-hsiang a member of the council (for the time being, perhaps, without the consent of the 'cautious' Feng Yu-hsiang) is now known to the whole world. But it must remain a secret from the Soviet workers. Why? Because Feng Yu-hsiang has until recently been presented to us at home as a genuine 'worker' or 'peasant', as a reliable revolutionist, and so forth, that is, all the mistakes that were previously made with Chiang Kai-shek, were again made with Feng Yu-hsiang. Now, for the last few week, all telegrams concerning the more than dubious conduct of Feng Yu-hsiang have been concealed. Why? To what end? Obviously, because some are waiting with the secret hope: perhaps he will not betray us after all! And if he does betray us, they will say: this completely verifies our prediction on the abandonment of the national revolution by the bourgeoisie. But now? Instead of warning the Chinese workers and the party, instead of stirring the masses of workers, peasants and soldiers to adopt really revolutionary measures against the treason of the generals, we keep quiet, we conceal the telegrams in our pockets. That will not help. The class logic of the revolutionary struggle cannot be concealed in one's pocket.

The second telegram:

THE SITUATION IN HANKOW

'Hankow, May 23. Tass.—The Central Committee of the Communist party has proposed to the "Hupeh League for Strengthening the Revolutionary Front" to set in order the relations between the workers and the petty-bourgeoisie. The Central Committee emphasised the necessity of increasing discipline among the workers and of obedience to the decrees of the National Government and declared that the trade unions have not the right to arrest anyone, and must always apply to the authorities when they consider the arrest of this or that person necessary.'

This telegram is even more important than the first. For every serious revolutionist, it illuminates the whole situation and shows the absolute faultiness of the official line, the down-right disastrousness of this line, and the absolute correctness of the line of the Opposition.

Just think: the trade unions in the territory of the Hankow government are arresting the enemies of the revolution. This means that the trade unions, by the whole logic of the situation, are forced to assume the tasks of revolutionary Soviets. Now what does the Central Committee of the Communist party do? It recommends to the trade unions to refrain from non-legal actions, to submit to the 'decrees' of the Wuhan authorities, and in case of emergency, when a counter-revolutionist, a traitor,

or conspirator has to be arrested or shot, to apply respectfully
to the authorities who, in all probability, are related or allied
to the conspirator. Is this not a mockery of the revolution, of
its needs and of its most elementary tasks? Instead of arousing
the masses to settle with the enemy right on the spot, the
Wuhan government forbids it. Still more, it forbids it not in
its own name, but through the medium of the Communist
party. The Central Committee of the Communist party, in this
case, plays the role of a political clerk to cowardly bourgeois
radicals and pseudo-radicals, who tremble before the revolutionary masses and believe together with Martinov that the
revolution can be carried out through arbitration commissions
but not through the liquidation of the enemy by the masses.
Isn't this monstrous? Isn't this a mockery of the revolution?

It is noteworthy, besides, that the 'Hupeh League for the
Strengthening of the Revolutionary Front' is given a special
commission, namely, to set in order 'the relations between the
workers and the petty-bourgeoisie'. These relations cannot be
set in order by a special League and not by special instructions,
but only by a correct policy. The Soviets of workers and of
semi-proletarian city poor must be the broad organs of such
a daily revolutionary policy. If the trade unions are forced to
assume the functions of Soviets, they will in certain cases almost
inevitably leave out of consideration or injure the legitimate
interests of the city petty-bourgeois. Thus, the absence of Soviets
also hits the petty-bourgeoisie and undermines its alliance with
the proletariat.

Such is the situation in reality. The trade unions, driven
forward by the masses, seek to correct the errors of the
Chinese and Moscow leadership, and are proceeding to the
immediate liquidation of the enemy. The Central Committee
of the Communist party, however, which ought to be the
inspirer and leader of this summary liquidation, holds back
the workers, and calls upon them to increase their 'discipline'

(towards the bourgeoisie), and to bow mutely before the connivance of the Hankow Kerenskys and Tseretellis with the agents of imperialism, of the bourgeoisie and of Chiang Kai-shek.

There is the Martinovist policy for you, not in words but in deeds!

A whole series of telegrams, especially from Tokyo, speaks of the 'crumbling' of the Hankow government, of its impending downfall, and so forth. Of course such telegrams must be taken with the greatest caution. These are telegrams from an enemy, who awaits the downfall of the revolution, hopes for it, is on the watch for it, and thinks up all kinds of things and lies. But the two above-mentioned telegrams, like many others of a similar kind which arrive almost every day, compel us to recognise the fact that *the position of the Hankow government can become hopeless*. If it prevents the workers and peasants from putting an end to the counter-revolutionists, it will collapse. By its false policy, the Central Committee of the Communist party is accelerating its collapse. Should the Hankow government crash under the assault of the workers', peasants' and soldiers' Soviets, we will surely not regret it. And it will collapse because it opposes the creation of Soviets. If the Hankow government is supported in this ruinous policy, if the Chinese workers and peasants are restrained from immediately eliminating the enemy, and from building Soviets, then *the Chinese Communist Party is helping the Hankow government to collapse in the shortest time,* and to die an inglorious death, not at the hands of the worker and peasant masses, but at the hands of bourgeois reaction. What is more, with such a policy the Hankow government, before it 'collapses', will most probably unite with Chiang Kai-shek—against the workers and peasants.

Is it not really time to understand this?

Moscow, May 28, 1927.

The Canton Insurrection

1. STAGES OF THE CHINESE REVOLUTION

THE FIRST STAGE of the Kuomintang was the period of domination by the national bourgeoisie, under the apologetic banner of the 'bloc of four classes'. The second period, after the Chiang Kai-shek *coup d'état,* was an experiment in parallel and 'independent' domination by Chinese Kerenskyism. While the Russian Populists, together with the Mensheviks, openly gave their short-lived 'dictatorship' the form of dual power, the Chinese 'revolutionary democracy' did not reach even that stage. And inasmuch as history in general does not work to order, there is nothing left for us but to understand *that there is not and that there will not be* any other 'democratic' *dictatorship* than the one exercised by the Kuomintang since 1925. This remains true regardless of whether the semi-unification of China accomplished by the Kuomintang is maintained in the coming period or whether the country is again dismembered. But precisely when the class dialectics of the revolution, having spent all its other resources, put on the order of the day the *dictatorship of the proletariat,* with the numberless millions of oppressed and downtrodden of town and country on its side, the ECCI advanced the slogan of the *democratic* dictatorship (that is, bourgeois democracy) of the workers and peasants. The reply to this formula was the Canton insurrection which, lifted the curtain over a new stage, or, more correctly, over with all its prematurity, with all the adventurism of its leaders, the coming, the *third* Chinese revolution. This must be emphasised.

Trying to insure themselves against the sins of the past, the leaders criminally forced the trend of events at the end of last year and brought about the Canton miscarriage. However, even a miscarriage can teach us a good deal concerning the organism of the mother and the process of birth. The tremendous theoretical and even decisive significance of the Canton events for the fundamental problems of the Chinese revolution is due precisely to the fact that we have here what happens so rarely in history and in politics: *a laboratory experiment on a gigantic scale.* We paid for it dearly, but that makes it all the more imperative for us to digest the lessons.

One of the fighting slogans of the Canton insurrection, as *Pravda* (No. 31) relates, was the watchword: 'Down with the Kuomintang!' The Kuomintang banners and signs were torn and trampled upon. But it was already after the 'betrayal' of Chiang Kai-shek and that of Wang Chin Wei (not a betrayal of his class, but of our . . . illusions) that the ECCI pompously declared: 'We will not give up the Kuomintang banner.' The workers of Canton prohibited the Kuomintang, *proclaiming all its tendencies illegal.* This means that to solve the basic national tasks, not only the big bourgeoisie but also the small bourgeoisie failed to advance a political power, a party, a faction, in conjunction with which the proletarian party might be able to solve the tasks of the bourgeois democratic revolution. The key to the position lies in the fact that the *problem of winning the movement of the poor peasants already fell entirely on the shoulders of the proletariat,* and the Communist party directly; the approach to a real solution of the bourgeois-democratic tasks of the revolution necessitated the concentration of all the power in the hands of the proletariat.

As to the short-lived Canton Soviet government, *Pravda* reports:

> In the interests of the workers, the decrees of the Canton Soviet proclaimed . . . workers' control of production through factory committees, the nationalisation of big industry, transportation and the banks.

Then, measures are mentioned such as the 'confiscation of all dwellings of the big bourgeoisie for the benefit of the labourers. . . .'

Thus, it was the Canton workers who were in power and what is more, the government was actually in the hands of the Communist party. The programme of the new government included not only the confiscation of the feudal lands, in so far as such exist in Kwangtung at all, and workers' control of production, but also the nationalisation of big industry, the banks and transportation and even the confiscation of the dwellings of the bourgeoisie and all their property for the benefit of the workers. The question arises: If these are the methods of a bourgeois revolution what will the proletarian revolution in China look like?

Notwithstanding the fact that the instructions of the ECCI said nothing about the proletarian dictatorship and socialist measures; notwithstanding the fact that Canton, when compared with Shanghai, Hankow and other industrial centres of the country, has more of a petty-bourgeois character, the revolutionary upheaval effected *against the Kuomintang* led automatically to the proletarian dictatorship which, at its very first steps, found itself compelled by the entire situation to take more radical measures than those with which the October revolution began. And this fact, in spite of its paradoxical appearance, is quite a normal outcome of the social relations of China as well as of the whole development of the revolution.

Large and middle-scale landownership (as it exists in China) is most closely intertwined with urban, including foreign capitalism. There is no landowning caste in China in opposition to the bourgeoisie. The most wide-spread, generally-hated exploiter in the village is the usurious wealthy peasant, the agent of urban banking capital. The agrarian revolution has therefore just as much of an anti-bourgeois as it has of an anti-feudal character in China. The first stage of our October revolution, in which the wealthy peasant marched hand in hand with the middle and poor peasant, and frequently at their head, against the landlord, will not, or will hardly at all, take place in China. The agrarian revolution there will be from the very beginning, and also later on, an uprising not only against the few landlords and bureaucrats, but also against the wealthy peasants and usurers. Whereas in Russia the poor peasant committees acted only in the second stage of the October revolution, towards the middle of 1918, in China they will appear on the scene, in one form or another, as soon as the agrarian movement revives. The breaking-up of the rich peasants will be the first and not the second step in the Chinese October.

The agrarian revolution, however, does not constitute the only basis of the present historical struggle in China. The most radical agrarian revolution, the general division of land (the Communist party will naturally support it to the very end), will not by itself be a way out of the economic blind alley. It is now essential for China to have national unity and economic sovereignty, that is, customs autonomy, or more correctly, a monopoly of foreign trade; this means: *emancipation from world imperialism,* for which China remains the most important source not only of enrichment but also of existence, constituting a safety valve against internal explosions of capitalism, today in Europe and tomorrow in America.

This is what determines in advance the gigantic scope and monstrous sharpness of the struggle through which the masses of China must pass, the more so now, when the depth of the stream of the struggle has already been measured and felt by all of its participants.

The enormous role of foreign capitalism in Chinese industry, its habit of relying directly on its own 'national' bayonets in order to defend its rapacity, makes the programme of workers' control in China even less realisable than it was in Russia. The direct expropriation of the foreign capitalist enterprises, and later also the Chinese capitalist enterprises, will most likely be made imperative by the struggle, on the very morrow of the victorious insurrection.

The same objective social and historical causes which determined the 'October' outcome of the Russian revolution rise before us in China in a still more accentuated form. The bourgeois and the proletarian poles of the Chinese nation are opposed to each other even more intransigently, if this is possible, than they were in Russia, inasmuch as, on the one hand, the Chinese bourgeoisie is directly bound up with foreign imperialism and its military machine and, on the other hand, the Chinese proletariat has from the very beginning established relations with the Comintern and the Soviet Union. Numerically, the Chinese peasantry constitutes an even more overwhelming mass than the Russian peasants; but, crushed in the vice of world contradictions upon the solution of which in one way or another its fate depends, the Chinese peasantry is even less capable than the Russian of playing a *leading* role. This is now no longer a theoretical forecast; it is a fact tested through and through and from all sides.

These fundamental and incontrovertible social and political pre-requisites of the third Chinese revolution show not only that the formula of a democratic dictatorship has *hopelessly outlived its usefulness,* but also that the third Chinese revolution, in spite of the extreme backwardness of China or more correctly, because of this great backwardness, as compared with Russia, will not have a 'democratic' period, be it even for six months, as was the case in the October revolution (November 1917 to July 1918); it will be compelled from the very beginning to effect the most decisive shake-up and abolition of bourgeois property in town and country.

True, this prospect does not harmonise with the pedantic and schematic conception concerning the relationships between economics and politics. But the responsibility for this harmony which disturbs the newly adopted prejudices to which the October revolution already dealt a serious blow, does not devolve upon 'Trotskyism' but upon *the law of uneven development*. In the given case, it is exactly in place.

It would be pedantry to contend that the Chinese Communist Party, had it pursued a Bolshevik policy in the revolution of 1925-1927, would *certainly* have come to power. But it is pitiful philistinism to contend that this possibility was entirely out of the question. The mass movement of workers and peasants was absolutely sufficient for it, as was also the collapse of the ruling classes. The national bourgeoisie sent its Chiang Kai-sheks and Wang Chin Weis to Moscow; through its Hu Han Mins it knocked on the door of the Comintern, precisely because it felt itself hopelessly weak in the face of the revolutionary masses; it realised its weakness and sought to insure itself in advance. Neither the workers nor the peasants would have followed the national bourgeoisie if we ourselves had not drawn them behind it with a lasso. Had the Comintern pursued a more or less correct policy, the outcome of the struggle of the Communist party for the masses would have been determined in advance: the Chinese proletariat would have supported the Communists, while the peasants' war would have supported the revolutionary proletariat.

If, at the beginning of the northern campaign, we had begun to organise Soviets in the 'liberated' districts (and the masses were instinctively fighting for that) we would have rallied to our side the agrarian uprisings, we would have built *our own* army; we would have undermined the opposing armies and— notwithstanding the youthfulness of the Communist Party of

China—it would have been able, with a judicious Comintern guidance, to mature in these years of stress and to come to power, if not in the whole of China at once, then at least in a considerable part of it. And above all, we would have had a *party*.

But precisely in the sphere of leadership something absolutely monstrous occurred, a veritable historical catastrophe: the authority of the Soviet Union, of the Bolshevik party and of the Comintern went entirely to the support, first of Chiang Kai-shek, against an independent policy of the Communist party, and then to the support of Wang Chin Wei, as the leader of the agrarian revolution. After having trampled underfoot the very basis of Lenin's policy and paralysed the young Chinese Communist Party, the ECCI determined in advance the victory of Chinese Kerenskyism over Bolshevism, of the Chinese Miliukovs over the Kerenskys, and of Japanese and British imperialism over the Chinese Miliukovs.

In this and in this alone lies the meaning of what happened in China in the course of 1925-1927.

DEMOCRATIC DICTATORSHIP OR DICTATORSHIP OF THE PROLETARIAT?

How did the last Plenum of the ECCI evaluate the experiences acquired in the Chinese revolution, including the experiences of the Canton insurrection? What prospect did it outline for the future? The resolution of the February (1928) Plenum, the key to the corresponding parts of the draft programme of the Sixth Congress, says concerning the Chinese revolution:

> It is wrong to characterise it as a 'permanent' revolution [the position of the representative of ECCI]. The tendency to skip [?] over the bourgeois-democratic phase of the revolution with a simultaneous [?] appraisal of the revolution as a 'permanent revolution' is a mistake similar to that which Trotsky made in 1905 [?].

The ideological life of the Comintern since Lenin's departure from its leadership, that is, since 1923, has consisted primarily of a struggle against so-called 'Trotskyism' and particularly against the 'permanent revolution'. How then could it happen that on the fundamental question of the Chinese revolution, not only the Central Committee of the Communist Party of China, but even the official representative of the Comintern, that is, the leader who was especially instructed for the job, should have fallen into the same 'error' for which hundreds of people are now exiled to Siberia and put in prison? The struggle around the Chinese problem has raged for about two and a half years. When the Opposition declared that the old Central Committee of the Chinese Communist Party (Chen Du-Siu), under the influence of wrong instructions from the Comintern, conducted an opportunist policy, this was declared to be a 'slander'. The leadership of the Communist Party or China was declared flawless. The well-known Tang Ping Shan clamoured, with the general approval of the Seventh Plenum of the ECCI, that

> . . . as soon as the first manifestations of Trotskyism made their appearance, the Communist Party of China and the Young Communist League immediately adopted a unanimous resolution against Trotskyism. (Stenographic report, page 205.)

However, notwithstanding all these 'achievements', when events unfolded their tragic logic, which led to the first, and later on to the second, even more terrific debacle of the revolution, the leaders of the Communist Party of China, from having been a model, were re-christened in twenty-four hours as Mensheviks, and turned out. At the same time, it was declared that the new leaders fully represented the line of the Comintern. But as soon as another serious phase came, the new Central Committee of the Communist Party of China was accused of having passed over (as we have always seen, not in words, but in deeds), to the position of the so-called 'permanent revolution'.

This was the path chosen also by the representative of the Comintern. This striking and unbelievable fact can be explained only by the glaring 'scissors' between the instructions of the ECCI and the real dynamics of the revolution.

We will not dwell here upon the myth of the 'permanent revolution' of 1905 which was put forward in 1924 in order to sow confusion and bewilderment. We will confine ourselves to an analysis of how this myth broke down on the question of the Chinese revolution.

The first paragraph of the February resolution, from which we have taken the above passage, motivates its negative attitude towards the so-called 'permanent revolution' as follows:

> The present period of the Chinese revolution is a period of the bourgeois-democratic revolution which has not been completed either from the economic viewpoint (the agrarian revolution and the abolition of feudal relations) or from the viewpoint of the national struggle against imperialism (the unification of China and the establishment of national independence), or from the viewpoint of the class nature of the government (the dictatorship of the proletariat and the peasantry).

This motivation is an unbroken chain of blunders and contradictions.

The ECCI taught that the Chinese revolution must guarantee China an opportunity to develop along the path of socialism. This object could be attained only if the revolution did not stop merely at the solution of the bourgeois-democratic tasks, but by growing over from one stage into another, that is, by constantly (or *permanently*) developing, led China towards socialist development. This is precisely what Marx understood by the term 'permanent revolution'. How then can one speak of a non-capitalist path of development of China on the one hand, and on the other, deny the permanent character of the revolution in general?

But—objects the resolution of the ECCI—the revolution has not been completed, either from the viewpoint of the agrarian revolution or from the viewpoint of the national struggle against

imperialism. Hence the conclusion about the bourgeois-democratic nature of the 'present period of the Chinese revolution'.
In reality, the 'present period' is a period of counter-revolution.
The ECCI apparently wants to say that the new rise of the
Chinese revolution, or more correctly, *the third Chinese revolution,* will have a bourgeois-democratic character, in view of
the fact that the second Chinese revolution of 1925-1927 solved
neither the agrarian problem nor the national problem. However,
even with this correction, the argumentation rests upon a
complete failure to understand the experiences and lessons of the
Chinese as well as of the Russian revolution.

The revolution of February 1917 in Russia left unsolved all
the internal and international problems which led to the revolution—feudalism in the villages, the old bureaucracy, the war
and the economic ruin. Based upon this, not only the SRs and
the Mensheviks, but also a considerable section of the leaders
of our own party, tried to show Lenin that the 'present period
of the revolution is a period of the bourgeois-democratic
revolution'. On this essential point, the resolution of the ECCI
merely copies the objections made to Lenin in 1917 by the opportunists, against the struggle for the proletarian dictatorship.

Furthermore, the bourgeois-democratic revolution proves to
be uncompleted not only from the economic and national stand-
points, but also from the 'viewpoint of the class nature of the
government (the dictatorship of the proletariat and the
peasantry)'. This can only mean one thing: the Chinese proletariat has been forbidden to fight for power so long as there
is no 'real' democratic government at the helm in China. Unfortunately, it is not pointed out where this is to come from.

The confusion is further increased by the fact that the
slogan of Soviets was rejected for China in the course of two
years on the sole ground that Soviets can be organised only
during the transition towards the proletarian revolution (Stalin's
'theory'). But when the Soviet revolution broke out in Canton

and its participants arrived at the conclusion that this is the transition to the proletarian revolution, they were accused of 'Trotskyism'. Can a party be trained in such a way and can it be helped in this manner to solve the greatest tasks?

To save a hopeless situation, the resolution of the ECCI (breaking with the entire trend of its thought), hastily advances its last argument—from imperialism. We find that the tendency to skip over the bourgeois-democratic phase

> . . . is all [!] the more harmful because such a formulation of the question excludes [?] the greatest national peculiarity of the Chinese revolution, which is a semi-colonial revolution.

The only meaning that these senseless words can have is that the imperialist yoke will be overthrown by some sort of dictatorship other than the proletarian. But this means that the 'greatest national peculiarity' has been dragged in at the last moment only in order to present in bright colours the Chinese national-bourgeois or the Chinese petty-bourgeois 'democracy'. They can have no other meaning. But we have sufficiently examined this only 'meaning' in our chapter concerning the 'nature of the colonial bourgeoisie'. There is no need to return to this subject.

China is still confronted with an enormous, terrific, bloody and prolonged struggle for such elementary aims as the liquidation of the most 'Asiatic' forms of slavery, the national emancipation and unification of the country. But it is precisely from here, as the march of events has shown, that further petty-bourgeois leadership or even half leadership in the revolution is impossible. The unification and emancipation of China is now an international task. It is no less international than the existence of the USSR. This task can be solved only by means of a desperate struggle of the suppressed, hungry and downtrodden masses under the direct leadership of the proletarian vanguard, a struggle not only against world imperialism, but also against its economic and political agency in China—

the bourgeoisie, including also the 'national' and democratic bourgeois flunkeys. And that is the road, leading towards the proletarian dictatorship.

Beginning with April 1917, Lenin explained to his opponents who accused him of having adopted the position of the 'permanent revolution', that the dictatorship of the proletariat and the peasantry was partly realised in the epoch of dual government. He explained later that it was further realised during the first period of Soviet power, from November 1917 until July 1918, when the peasants, together with the workers, effected the agrarian revolution, while the working class had not yet proceeded with the confiscation of the factories and plants, but experimented with workers' control. As to the 'class nature of the government', the SR-Menshevik 'dictatorship' gave all that it could give—the dual-government miscarriage. As to the agrarian revolution, it gave birth to a healthy and strong child; only, the proletarian dictatorship acted as the midwife. In other words, that which the theoretical formula of 'the dictatorship of the proletariat and the peasantry' sought to unite was disunited i the course of the actual class struggle.

The empty shell of the half government was provisionally entrusted to Kerensky and Tseretelli; the real kernel of the agrarian-democratic revolution fell to the lot of the victorious working class. This is the dialectical dissociation of the democratic dictatorship which the leaders of the ECCI failed to understand. They have landed in a political blind alley, mechanically condemning any 'skipping over the bourgeois-democratic stage' and endeavouring to guide the historical process by means of circular letters. *If we are to understand by the bourgeois-democratic stage the completion of the agrarian revolution by means of a 'democratic distatorship', then it was none other than the October revolution which boldly 'skipped over' the bourgeois-democratic stage.* Should it not be condemned for having done so?

Why is it that what was historically inevitable and the highest expression of Bolshevism in Russia, proves to be 'Trotskyism' in China? Apparently in accordance with the same logic which proclaims that the theory of the Martinovs, branded for twenty years by Bolshevism in Russia, was suitable for China.

But can such a comparison be made with Russia at all? The slogan of a democratic dictatorship of the proletariat and the peasantry—we reply—was built up by the leaders of the ECCI exclusively and entirely by the method of analogy, but of a formal and literal analogy and not a material and historical analogy. An analogy between China and Russia is absolutely admissible if one finds the proper key to it; this analogy was used excellently by Lenin, and not after the fact but beforehand, as if he had foreseen the future blunders of the epigones. Lenin had hundreds of times to defend the October proletarian revolution which dared to capture power, *notwithstanding the fact* that the bourgeois-democratic problems had not yet been solved. *Precisely because of that, precisely for that purpose,* replied Lenin.

On January 16, 1923, Lenin wrote in answer to the pedants who, in their arguments against the capture of power, referred to the economic immaturity of Russia for socialism which was 'incontestable' for Lenin (Volume 18, Part 2, page 119):

> For instance, it does not even occur to them that Russia— standing as she does on the borderline between the civilised countries and the countries which this war had for the first time definitely brought into the orbit of civilisation, that is, all the Oriental, non-European countries—might therefore and was indeed bound to reveal certain peculiar features which, while of ocurse in keeping with the general line of world development, distinguish her revolution from all previous revolutions in West-European countries, and which introduce certain partial innovations in passing to the Oriental countries. (*Ibid.,* page 118.)

The 'peculiar feature' which brings Russia *closer* to the Eastern countries was seen by Lenin in the fact that the young proletariat, at the very dawn of the movement, had to take hold of the broom so as to sweep from its road to socialism all feudal barbarism and every other kind of rubbish.

Consequently, if we are to proceed from Lenin's analogy between China and Russia, we must say: from the standpoint of the *'political nature of the power'*, all that could have been obtained through the democratic dictatorship was tried out in China: first in Sun Yat Sen's Canton, then on the road from Canton to Shanghai which was crowned by the Shanghai *coup d'état,* and finally in Wuhan, where the Left Kuomintang appeared in its chemically pure aspect, that is, according to the instructions of the ECCI, as an organiser of the agrarian revolution, but in reality as its hangman. The social content of the bourgeois-democratic revolution will have to be completed by the first period of the coming dictatorship of the Chinese proletariat and the rural poor. To advance at present the slogan of the democratic dictatorship of the proletariat and the peasantry, when the role not only of the Chinese bourgeoisie but also of 'democracy' has already been tested through and through, when it has become absolutely certain that 'democracy' will, in the coming struggles, play its role of hangman even more than in the past, simply means to create the means of covering up the new forms of Kuomintangism and to set a trap for the proletariat.

For the sake of completeness, let us recall here what Lenin said briefly about those Bolsheviks who continued to counterpose to the Social Revolutionary-Menshevik experience, the slogan of a 'genuine' democratic dictatorship:

'Whoever speaks only of a "revolutionary democratic dictatorship of the proletariat and the peasantry" is behind the times, and has passed over to the side of the petty-bourgeoisie against the proletarian class struggle. He should be relegated to the archives of pre-revolutionary "Bolshevik" relics (we might call them the archives of the "old" Bolsheviks).' (Volume XIV, Part 1, page 29.)

These words have a timely ring even today.

Of course, it is by no means a question of calling the Communist Party of China immediately to revolt to capture power. The tempo depends entirely upon the circumstances. The consequences of a defeat cannot be eliminated simply by revising one's tactics. The revolution is now subsiding. The verbiage, half concealed by the resolution of the ECCI, about an imminent revolutionary resurgence, *because* numberless people are being executed in China and a terrific commercial and industrial crisis is raging in the country, is criminal light-mindedness and nothing else. After three overwhelming defeats, an economic crisis does not rouse, but on the contrary depresses the proletariat, which, as it is, has already been bled white; the executions only destroy the politically weakened party. We are in a period of ebb-tide in China and consequently in a period of theoretical deepening, of the critical self-education of the party, of the creation and strengthening of firm points of support in all the spheres of the labour movement, of the organisation of rural nuclei of the leadership and unification of partial, at first defensive and later offensive, battles of the workers and rural poor.

How will a new mass movement begin? What circumstances will give the proletarian vanguard, at the head of the multitudinous millions, the necessary revolutionary impulse? This cannot be foretold. Whether internal processes alone will be sufficient or whether an impulse from without will come to the fore the future will show.

There are enough reasons to assume that the crushing of the Chinese revolution, conditioned directly by the false leadership, will permit the Chinese and foreign bourgeoisie to overcome, in some measure, the terrific economic crisis which exists in the country at the present time; naturally, this will be accomplished upon the backs of the workers and peasants. This phase of 'stabilisation' will again group together the workers, give them cohesion, imbue them with a class confidence in themselves so as later on to set them up against the enemy more sharply, but upon a higher historical plane. It is only with a new rising wave of the proletarian movement that one will be able to speak seriously about the prospect of an agrarian revolution.

It is not excluded that the first period of the coming third revolution may repeat, in a greatly abridged and modified form, the stages which have already been gone through, for example, by presenting some new parody of the 'common national front'. But this first period will probably suffice to permit the Communist party to put before the popular masses its 'April theses', that is, its programme and tactics for the capture of power. But what does the draft of the programme of the Comintern say on this subject?

> The transition to the proletarian dictatorship is possible here [in China] only after a series of preparatory stages [?], only as a result of a whole period of the growing over [?] of the bourgeois-democratic revolution into the socialist revolution.

In other words, all the 'stages' that have already been gone through are not taken into account. What has been left behind, the draft programme still sees ahead. This is exactly what is meant by dragging behind the tail. It leaves gates wide open for new experiments in the spirit of the Kuomintang course. Thus, the concealment of the old blunders inevitably prepares the road for new errors.

If we enter the new rise, which will develop at an incomparably more rapid rate than the last one, with the outlived plan of 'democratic dictatorship', there can be no doubt that the third revolution will be lost just as the second one was.

ADVENTURISM AS A PRODUCT OF OPPORTUNISM

The second paragraph of the same resolution of the February Plenum of the ECCI says:

> The first wave of the broad revolutionary movement of the workers and peasants which, in the main, proceeded under the slogans and to a considerable extent *under the leadership of the Communist party, is over.* It ended in a number of centres of the revolutionary movement with *heavy defeats* for the workers and peasants, with the physical extermination of the Communists and of the revolutionary cadres of the labour and peasant movement in general. [Our emphasis.]

When the 'wave' was surging high, the ECCI said that the movement was entirely under the blue banner and leadership of the Kuomintang which even took the place of Soviets. It is precisely on that ground that the Communist party was subordinated to the Kuomintang. But that is exactly why the revolutionary movement ended with 'heavy defeats'. Now, when these defeats have been recognised, an attempt is being made to delete the Kuomintang from the past as if it had never existed, as if the ECCI had not proclaimed the blue banner its own.

Formerly we were told that there were no defeats either in Shanghai or in Wuhan, there were merely transitions of the revolution 'into a higher phase'. That is what we were taught. Now the sum total of these transitions is suddenly declared to be 'heavy defeats for the workers and peasants'. However, in order to mask to some extent this unprecedented political bankruptcy of perspective and judgment, the concluding paragraph of the resolution says:

> The ECCI makes it the duty of all sections of the Comintern to fight against the social-democratic and Trotskyist slander to the effect that the Chinese revolution has been liquidated [?].

In the first paragraph of the resolution we were told that 'Trotskyism' consisted of estimating the Chinese revolution as *permanent,* that is, a revolution which is now growing over from the bourgeois to the socialist phase. From the last paragraph, we learn that according to the 'Trotskyists', 'the Chinese revolution has been liquidated'. How can a *liquidated* revolution be a *permanent* revolution? This is Bukharin all the way through. Only complete and reckless irresponsibility permits of such contradictions which undermine all revolutionary thought at its roots.

If we are to understand by the 'liquidation' of the revolution the fact that the offensive of the workers and the peasants has been set back and drowned in blood, that the masses are in a state of retreat, that before another onslaught there must be, apart from many other things, a molecular process at work among the masses which requires a certain period of time the duration of which cannot be determined beforehand; if 'liquidation' is to be understood in this way, it does not in any way differ from the 'heavy defeats' which the ECCI has at last been compelled to recognise.

Or are we to understand the term liquidation literally, as the actual elimination of the Chinese revolution, that is, of the very possibility and inevitability of its revival at a new stage? One can speak of such a perspective seriously only in two cases: if China were doomed to dismemberment and complete ruin—an assumption for which there is not the slightest reason; or else, if the Chinese bourgeoisie were to prove capable of solving the basic problems of Chinese life in its own non-revolutionary way. Is it not this last variant which the theoreticians of the 'bloc of four classes', who forced the Communist party under the yoke of the bourgeoisie, seek to ascribe to us now?

History repeats itself. The blind who could not grasp the extent of the defeat of 1923, accused us for a year and a half of looking at the German revolution as 'liquidators'. Yet even this lesson, which cost the International so dearly, did them no good. At the present time, picking up their old formulae, they simply apply them no longer to Germany, but to China.

It is true that the need of finding 'liquidators' is far more acute than it was four years ago; for at the present time, it is too obvious that if anybody did 'liquidate' the second Chinese revolution, it was the authors of the course towards the Kuomintang.

The strength of Marxism lies in its ability to foretell. In this sense, the Opposition can point to a complete confirmation of its prognoses by experience: first, concerning the Kuomintang as a whole, then concerning the 'Left' Kuomintang and the Wuhan government, and finally, concerning the 'deposit' made on the third revolution, that is, on the Canton insurrection. What other confirmation could there be of a correct theoretical standpoint?

The very same opportunist line which, by the policy of capitulation to the bourgeoisie, already brought the revolution, at its first two phases, the heaviest defeats, 'grew over' in the third phase, into a policy of adventurous attacks upon the bourgeoisie, and made the defeat final.

If the leadership had not been in such a hurry yesterday to skip over the defeats which it had brought about, it would have begun by explaining to the Communist Party of China that victory is not gained at one blow, that on the road to insurrection there is still a period of intense, constant and fierce struggles for political influence on the workers and peasants.

On September 17, 1927, we said to the Presidium of the ECCI:

> Today's papers report that the revolutionary army has taken Swatow. The armies of Ho Lung and Yeh-Ting have now been marching for a few weeks. *Pravda* calls these armies revolutionary armies. But the question I ask is: what prospects does the movement of the revolutionary army which captured Swatow open up before the Chinese revolution? What are the slogans of the movement? What is its programme? What should be its organisational forms? What has become of the slogan of Soviets, which *Pravda* suddenly put forward (for a day) in July?

Without first organising the Communist party against the Kuomintang in its entirety, without agitation among the masses for Soviets and a Soviet government, without an independent mobilization of the masses under the slogan of the agrarian revolution and national emancipation, without the creation, extension and strengthening of the local Soviets of workers', soldiers' and peasants' deputies, the uprising of Ho Lung and Yeh-Ting, even leaving aside their opportunist policy, could not fail to be an isolated adventure, a pseudo-Communist Makhno feat; it could not but clash against its own isolation, and it has clashed.

The Canton insurrection was a broader and deeper rehearsal of Ho Lung's and Yeh-Ting's adventure, only with infinitely more tragic consequences.

The February resolution of the ECCI combats certain putschistic tendencies in the Communist Party of China, that is, the tendencies towards armed skirmishes. It does not say, however, that these tendencies are a reaction to the entire opportunist policy of 1925-1927, and an unavoidable consequence of the purely military orders, handed down from above, to 'change step' without appraising all that had been done, without an open revaluation of the basis of the tactics, without a clear prospect. Ho Lung's march and the Canton insurrection were (and under such circumstances, had to be) outbursts of putschism.

A real antidote to putschism, as well as to opportunism, cannot be had without a clear understanding of the truth that, from now on, it devolves entirely upon the Communist Party of China to guide the armed insurrection of the workers and the poor peasants, to capture power and to institute a revolutionary dictatorship. If it thoroughly assimilates an understanding of this, it will be little inclined to improvise military attacks on towns, or armed insurrections in traps, or to chase humbly after the enemy's banner.

The resolution of the ECCI condemns itself to sterility by the fact alone that while arguing most abstractly concerning the inadmissability of skipping over stages and the harmfulness of putschism, it ignores entirely the class content of the Canton insurrection and the short-lived Soviet regime which it brought into existence. We Oppositionists hold that this insurrection was an adventure of the leadership in an effort to 'save its prestige'. But it is clear to us that even an adventure develops according to certain definite laws which are determined by the structure of the social environment. That is why we seek to discover in the Canton insurrection the features of the coming stage of the Chinese revolution. These features correspond fully with our theoretical analysis of the Canton uprising. But how much more imperative is it for the ECCI, which holds that the Canton rising was a correct and proper link in the chain of struggle, to give a clear class characterisation of the Canton insurrection. Yet, there is not a word about this in the resolution of the ECCI, although the Plenum met immediately after the Canton events. Is this not the most convincing proof that the present leadership of the Comintern, stubbornly pursuing a false policy, is compelled to play on alleged errors of 1905 and other years, without daring to approach the Canton insurrection of 1927, the significance of which completely upsets the schema of the revolution in the East which is outlined in the draft programme?

Soviets and Revolution

In the February resolution of the ECCI, the representative of the Comintern, 'comrade N. and others', are made responsible for the 'absence of an *elected* Soviet in Canton as an organ of insurrection' (emphasis in the original). In this charge we have, in reality, an astounding admission.

The report in *Pravda,* written on the basis of first-hand

documents (No. 31), stated that there was a Soviet government established in Canton. But it said nothing about the fact that the Canton Soviet was *not* an elected organ, that is, that it was not a *Soviet*—for how can there be a Soviet which has not been elected? We learn this for the first time from the resolution. Let us reflect for a moment on the significance of this fact. The ECCI tells us now that a Soviet is necessary for an armed insurrection, but not before. But when the insurrection is decided upon, it appears that there is no Soviet! To set up an elected Soviet is not at all an easy matter: it is necessary that the masses should know from experience what a Soviet is, that they should understand its form, that they should have accustomed themselves in the past to the election of Soviets. Of this, there was not a sign in China, as the slogan of Soviets was declared to be a Trotskyist slogan precisely in the period when it should have become the nerve centre of the entire movement. When, however, a date was fixed in all haste for an insurrection so as to skip over their own defeats, they simultaneously had to *appoint* a Soviet. If we were not to expose the roots of this error to the very bottom, the slogan of Soviets itself might be turned into a noose for strangling the revolution.

Lenin explained to the Mensheviks in his time that the basic historical task of the Soviets is to organise, or to help to organise, the capture of power, so that on the morrow after the victory, it may become the machinery of that power. The epigones—not disciples, but epigones—draw from this the conclusion that Soviets may be organised only when the twelfth hour of the insurrection has struck. On the basis of Lenin's broad generalisation they write, *post factum,* a short prescription which does not serve the interests of the revolution but acts to their detriment.

Before the Bolshevik Soviets captured power in October 1917, the SR and Menshevik Soviets had existed for nine months. Twelve years prior to that, the first revolutionary Soviets existed in Petersburg and in Moscow and in many other towns. Before the Soviet of 1905 embraced the factories and plants of the capital, there was a printers' Soviet in Moscow during the strike, and a few months prior to that, in 1905, a mass strike in Ivanovo-Voznesensk set up a leading committee which already presented all the principal features of a Soviet of workers' deputies. Between the first attempt at setting up a Soviet of deputies and the gigantic experiment of setting up a Soviet government, more than twelve years rolled by. Of course, such a period is not absolutely essential for all countries, China included. But to think that the Chinese workers are capable of organising Soviets on the basis of a short prescription which is substituted for Lenin's broad generalisation, means the replacement of the dialectics of revolutionary action by a pedant's impotent and importunate decree. Soviets must be set up not on the eve of uprisings, with the slogan of the immediate capture of power— for if the matter has reached the point of the capture of power, if the masses are prepared for an armed insurrection *without Soviets,* it means that there have been other organisational forms and methods which made possible the performance of the preparatory work to ensure the success of the uprising: the question of Soviets then becomes of secondary importance and is reduced to a question of organisational technique, or still lower, to a question of name. The task of the Soviets is not merely to issue the call for the insurrection or to carry out that insurrection, but *to lead the masses toward the insurrection through the necessary stages.* At first, the Soviet does not rally the masses to the slogan of an armed insurrection, but to partial slogans; it is only later, step by step, that they are brought towards the insurrection without scattering them on the road and without allowing the vanguard to become isolated from the class as a whole. The Soviet appears most frequently and primarily in connection with strikes which have before them the prospect of revolutionary development, but are, at the given moment, limited to economic demands. The masses must feel and understand, while in action, that the Soviet is *their* organisation, that it marshals their forces for the struggle, for resistance, for self-defence, and for the offensive. They can feel and understand this not through a one-day action and in general not through one act, but through the experience of several weeks, months and perhaps years, with intermissions or without. That is why only a bureaucratic leadership of epigones can restrain the rising and mutinous masses from the creation of Soviets, under conditions when the country is passing through a period of revolutionary upheavals, and when the working class and the poor peasants see before them the prospect of capturing power, even if only in one of the later phases, and even if that prospect can be envisaged in the given phase only by a small minority. That was always our conception of the Soviets. We valued the Soviet as that broad and elastic organisational form which is grasped by the masses who have just awakened, in the very first phase of their revolutionary action, and which is capable of uniting the working class in its entirety, regardless of how large a section of it has, in the given phase, already matured to the point of understanding the task of capturing power.

Is any further documentary evidence necessary? Here, for instance, is what Lenin wrote about the Soviets in the epoch of the first revolution:

> The Russian Social-Democratic Labour Party [that was then the name of the party] has never refused, *at moments of greater or lesser revolutionary unrest,* to utilise certain non-party organisations, such as Soviets of workers' deputies, in order to strengthen the influence of the social-democrats over the working class and to consolidate the social-democratic labour movement. (Volume 13, page 215. Our emphasis.)

One could cite such historical quotations without number. But the question appears to be clear enough without that.

In contradiction to this, the epigones have converted the

Soviets into a parade uniform which the party puts on the proletariat on the eve of the capture of power. But that is just when we find that Soviets cannot be improvised in twenty-four hours, by order, with the direct object of an armed insurrection. Such experiments must inevitably assume a fictitious character and the absence of the conditions necessary for the capture of power be marked by the external ceremonial of the Soviet system. That is what happened in Canton, where the Soviet was simply appointed to pay respects to the ritual. That is where the epigones' formulation of the question leads to.

In the polemics on the Chinese events, the Opposition was accused of the following alleged crying contradiction: whereas at the beginning of 1926 the Opposition came forward with the slogan of Soviets for China, its representatives spoke against the slogan of Soviets for Germany in the autumn of 1923. On no other point, perhaps, has the scholastic spirit in political thought been expressed so strikingly as on this. Yes, we demanded for China, *at the right time,* the creation of Soviets as *independent* organisations of workers and peasants, *when the wave ran high.* The chief significance of the Soviets was to be that of *setting up the workers and peasants against the bourgeoisie of the Kuomintang* and its Left wing agency. The slogan of Soviets in China meant, in the first place, the break-up of the suicidal, shameful 'bloc of the four classes' and the withdrawal of the Communist party from the Kuomintang. The centre of gravity consequently lay not in a sterile organisational form, but in a class political line.

In the autumn of 1923 in Germany, on the contrary, it was a question of organisational form only. As a result of the extreme passivity, the backwardness, and the tardiness of the leadership of the Comintern and of the Communist Party of Germany, the favourable moment for a call for the organisation of Soviets was missed; under pressure from below, the factory committees occupied in the labour movement of Germany, by the autumn of 1923, the place which, provided the Communist party had followed a correct and daring policy, would no doubt have been occupied much more successfully by Soviets.

The acuteness of the situation had in the meantime reached its highest degree. To lose further time would mean definitely to miss a revolutionary situation. The uprising was finally put on the agenda with very little time left. To advance the slogan of Soviets under such conditions would have been the greatest doctrinaire stupidity conceivable. The Soviet is not a talisman which has within itself the power of saving everything. In a situation such as had then developed, the creation of Soviets in a hurry would only have duplicated the factory committees. It would have become necessary to deprive the latter of their revolutionary functions and to pass these over to the newly created Soviets which enjoyed no authority as yet. And at what time? Under conditions when each day counted. This would have meant to substitute for revolutionary action a most injurious game of playing with trifles in the field of organisation.

That the Soviet organisational form can be of gigantic importance is irrefutable, provided, however, that it reflects a correct political line at the proper time. It can, on the other hand, be of no less negative importance if it is converted into a fiction, a talisman, an empty shell. German Soviets, created at the very last moment in the autumn of 1923, would have added nothing politically, they would only have caused organisational confusion. What happened in Canton was even worse. The Soviet which was created in a hurry, only so as to observe the ritual, was merely a camouflage for an adventurist putsch. That is why we found out, after it was all over, that the Canton Soviet was just one of those old Chinese dragons—it was simply drawn on paper. The policy of marionettes and paper dragons is not our policy. We were against improvising Soviets by telegraph in Germany in September 1923. We were for the creation of Soviets in China in 1926. We were against carnival Soviets in Canton in December 1927. There are no contradictions there. On the contrary, we see in it a deep integral understanding of the dynamics of the revolutionary movement and of its organisational forms.

The question of the role and the significance of the Soviets, which has been distorted, confused and obscured by the theory and practice of recent years, has not been illuminated in the least in the draft programme.

Alma-Ata, July 1928.

The Chinese Question after the Sixth Congress

THE LESSONS and the problems in the strategy and tactics of the Chinese revolution constitute at the present time the greatest teaching for the international proletariat. The experience gained in 1917 has been altered, disfigured and falsified to the point of unrecognisability by the epigones brought to power on the waves of defeats of the world's working class. Henceforth, one is compelled to extract the 1917 revolution from beneath mountains of impurities under which it has been buried. The revolution has verified the policy of Bolshevism by resorting to the method of *reductio ad absurdum*. The strategy of the Communist International in China was a gigantic game of 'losers win' The young generation of revolutionists must be taught the alphabet of Bolshevism by using the Chinese antithesis contrasted to the experience gained in October. China itself has a world importance. But what happens in this country decides not only its own fate, but the destiny of the Communist International in the full sense of the world. Not only has the Sixth Congress not drawn up the correct balance or introduced clarity, but on the contrary, it has consecrated the errors committed and has supplemented them by a new confusion which can create for the Chinese Communist Party a hopeless situation for a whole series of years. The bureaucratic thunderbolts of excommunication will manifestly fail to reduce us to silence when the fate of the international revolution is at stake. It is just those who excommunicate us who are the ones directly responsible for the defeats suffered; that is why they dread the shedding of light.

*   *   *

In the past five years, no party has suffered so cruelly from the opportunist leadership of the Communist International as the Chinese CP. We have had in China a perfect example (and that is just the reason why it led to a catastrophe) of the application of the Menshevik policy to a revolutionary epoch. What is more, Menshevism had a monopoly at its disposal, for it was protected against Bolshevik criticism by the authority of the Communist International and by the material apparatus of the Soviet power. This combination of circumstances is unique in its kind. As a result, one of the greatest revolutions, according to its possibilities, was completely confiscated by the Chinese bourgeoisie; it served to strengthen the latter, something which, from all the data in our possession, the bourgeoisie had no reason to count on. The mistakes of opportunism have not yet been repaired. The whole course of the Congress discussion, the reports of Bukharin and Kuusinen, the speeches of the Chinese Communists—all these indicate that the line of conduct followed by the leadership in Chinese politics not only was false but remains false to this day. Passing over from the opportunism openly practised in the form of collaboration (1924-1927), it made an abrupt zig-zag at the end of 1927 by resorting to adventures. After the Canton insurrection, it rejected putschism and passed into the third phase, the most sterile one, seeking to combine the old opportunistic premises with a purely formal, ineffectual radicalism, which at a certain period bore in Russia, the names of 'ultimatism' and 'otsovism', and which constitutes the worst variety of ultra-Leftism.

No Chinese Communist can any longer take a single step forward now without first having estimated at its right value the opportunist leadership which led to destruction in the three stages (Shanghai, Wuhan, Canton) and without having completely understood the immense break produced by these defeats in the social and political, the internal and international position of China.

The Congress discussion showed what gross and perilous illusions still subsist in the conceptions of Chinese Communist leaders. While defending the Canton insurrection, one of the Chinese delegates referred triumphantly to the fact that after the defeat suffered in this city, the membership of the party did not decrease but grew. Even here, thousands of miles from the theatre of the revolutionary events, it seems incredible that such monstrous information could have been presented to a world Congress without immediately encountering an indignant refutation. However, thanks to observations made on another point by a speaker, we learn, that while the CPC has gained (for how long?) tens of thousands of new members among the peasants, it has on the other hand lost the majority of its workers. It is this menacing process, characterising without the possibility of error a certain phase of *decline* of the party, that the Chinese Communists describe at the Congress as a sign of growth and progress. While the revolution is beaten in the cities and in the most important centres of the workers' and the peasants' movement, there will always be, especially in a country as vast as China, fresh regions, fresh just because they are backward, containing not yet exhausted revolutionary forces. On the distant periphery, the beginnings of the revolutionary wave will yet swell for a long time. Without having direct data on the situation in the Chinese-Moslem regions of the South-west, it is difficult to speak with precision of the probability of a revolutionary ferment being produced there in the approaching period. But the whole past of China renders such an eventuality possible. It is quite evident that this movement would only be a belated echo of the battles of Shanghai, Hankow and Canton. After the decisive defeat suffered by the revolution in the cities, the party, for a certain time, can still draw tens of thousands of new members from the awakening peasantry. This fact is important as a precursory sign of the great possibilities in the future. But in the period under consideration it is only one form of the dissolution and the liquidation of the CPC, for, by losing its proletarian nucleus, it ceases to be in conformity with its historical destiny.

An epoch of revolutionary decline is by its very essence pregnant with dangers for a revolutionary party. In 1852, Engels said that such a party, having let a revolutionary situation escape it, or having suffered a decisive defeat in it, inevitably disappears from the scene for a certain period of history. The counter-revolutionary epoch strikes a revolutionary party all the more cruelly if the crushing of the revolution is caused, not by an unfavourable relationship of forces, but by the patent and indisputable blunders of the leadership, as was exactly the case in China. Add to all this the brief existence of the Chinese party, the absence in it of firmly tempered cadres and solid traditions; add to it, finally, the alterations made so light-heartedly in the leadership which, there as everywhere else, was converted into the responsible manager expiating the mistakes of the Communist International. Taken together, all this creates veritably fatal conditions for the CPC during the counter-revolutionary epoch, the duration of which cannot be determined in advance.

It is only by clearly and courageously posing the fundamental questions of today and yesterday that one can avert for the CPC the fate which Engels spoke of, in other words, liquidation, from the political point of view, for a certain period.

We have examined the class dynamics of the Chinese revolution in a special chapter of the criticism to which we submitted the fundamental theses of the draft programme of the Communist International. Today, we see no need of adding anything to this chapter, or, for that matter, of introducing any modifications into it. We arrived there at the conclusion that the subsequent development of the Chinese revolution can only take place in the form of the struggle of the Chinese proletariat, drawing hundreds of millions of poor peasants to the conquest of power. The solution of fundamental bourgeois-democratic problems in China depends entirely on the dictatorship of the proletariat. To oppose to this the democratic dictatorship of the proletariat and peasantry is to devote oneself to a reactionary attempt which seeks to drag the revolution back to stages already traversed by the coalition in the Kuomintang. This general political diagnosis, containing the strategical line of conduct for the coming period of the Chinese revolution, or more exactly, of the third Chinese revolution of the future, in no way annuls the question of the tactical problems of today and tomorrow.

1. THE PERMANENT REVOLUTION AND THE CANTON INSURRECTION

In November 1927, the plenum of the Central Committee of the Chinese party decided that

> The objective circumstances existing at the present time in China are such that the duration of a directly revolutionary situation will be measured not by weeks or by months, but by long years. The Chinese revolution has a lasting character, but on the other hand, it has no stops. By its character, it constitutes what Marx called a permanent revolution.

Is this right? Intelligently understood, it is right. But it must be understood according to Marx and not according to Lominadze. Bukharin, who showed up the latter precisely for having employed this formula, was no closer to Marx than the author of it. In capitalist society, every real revolution, above all if it takes place in a large country, and more particularly now, in the imperialist epoch, tends to transform itself into a permanent revolution; in other words, not to come to a halt at any of the stages it reaches, not to confine itself up to the complete transformation of society, up to the final abolition of class distinctions, consequently, up to the complete and final suppression of the very possibility of new revolutions. That is just what the Marxian conception of the proletarian revolution consists of, being distinguished by that from the bourgeois revolution, limited by its national scope as much as by its specific objectives. The Chinese revolution contains within itself tendencies to become permanent in so far as it contains the possibility of the conquest of power by the proletariat. To speak of the permanent revolution without this and outside of it, is like trying to fill the cask of the Danaides. Only the proletariat, after having seized the state power and having transformed it into an instrument of struggle against all the forms of oppression and exploitation, in the interior of the country as well as beyond its frontiers, gains therewith the possibility of assuring a continuous character to the revolution, in other words, of leading it to the construction of a complete socialist society. A necessary condition for this is to carry out consistently a policy which prepares the proletariat in good time for the conquest of power. Now, Lominadze has made of the possibility of a permanent development of the revolution (on the condition that the Communist policy be correct) a scholastic formula guaranteeing at one blow and for all time a revolutionary situation 'for many years'. The permanent character of the revolution thus becomes a law placing itself above history, independent of the policy of the leadership and of the material development of revolutionary events. As always in such cases, Lominadze and company resolved to announce their metaphysical formula regarding the permanent character of the revolution only after the political leadership of Stalin, Bukharin, Chen Du-Siu and Tang Ping Shan had thoroughly sabotaged the revolutionary struggle.

After having assured the continuity of the revolution for many years, the plenum of the Central Committee of the Chinese Communist Party, freed from any further doubts, deduces from this formula conditions favourable to the insurrection.

> . . . Not only is the strength of the revolutionary movement of the toiling masses of China not yet exhausted, but it is precisely only now that it is beginning to manifest itself in a new advance of the revolutionary struggle. All this obliges the plenum of the Central Committee of the Chinese Communist Party to recognise that a directly revolutionary situation exists today (November 1927) throughout China.

The Canton insurrection was deduced from a similar evaluation of the situation with perfect inevitability. Had a revolutionary situation really existed, the mere fact of the defeat of Canton would have been a special episode, and in any case, would not have transformed the uprising of this city into an adventure. Even in face of unfavourable conditions for the insurrection of Canton itself or its environs, the leadership would have had as its duty to do all that was necessary to realise the revolt most rapidly in order thus to disperse and weaken the forces of the enemy and to facilitate the triumph of the uprising in the other parts of the country.

However, not after 'many years' but after a few months, it had to be acknowledged that the political situation had declined abruptly, and that before the Canton insurrection. The campaign of Ho Lung and Yeh-Ting were already developing in an atmosphere of revolutionary decline, the workers were separating themselves from the revolution, the centrifugal tendencies were gaining in strength. This is in no way contradictory to the existence of peasant movements in various provinces. That is how it always is.

Let the Chinese Communist ask themselves now: Would they have dared to decide upon fixing the Canton insurrection for December had they understood that for the given period the fundamental forces of the revolution were exhausted and that the great decline had commenced? It is clear that if they had understood in good time this radical break in the situation, they would in no case have put on the order of the day the appeal for the armed uprising in Canton. The only way of explaining the policy of the leadership, in fixing and carrying out this revolt, is that it *did not understand the meaning* and the consequences of the defeats in Shanghai and Hupeh. There can be no other interpretation of it. But the lack of understanding can all the less excuse the leadership of the Communist International since the Opposition had warned in good time against the new situation and the new dangers. It found itself accused for this, by idiots and calumniators, of having the spirit of liquidators.

The resolution of the Sixth Congress confirms the fact that an inadequate resistance to 'putschistic moods' produced the fruitless uprisings in Hunan, in Hupeh, etc. What is to be understood by 'putschistic moods'? The Chinese Communists, in conformity with the directions of Stalin and Bukharin, judged that the situation in China was directly revolutionary and that the partial revolts had every chance of being extended successfully to the point of becoming a general insurrection. In this way, the launching of these surprise attacks resulted from an erroneous estimation of the circumstances in which China found itself towards the second half of 1927, as a result of the defeats suffered.

In Moscow, they could prattle about the 'directly revolutionary situation', accuse the Oppositionists of being liquidators, while providing for themselves beforehand against the future (especially after Canton) by making reservations on the subject of 'putschism'. But on the theatre of events, in China itself, every honest revolutionist was duty bound to do everything he could in his corner to hasten the uprising, since the Communist International had declared that the general situation was propitious for an insurrection on a national scale. It is on this question that the regime of duplicity reveals its deliberately criminal character.

At the same time the resolution of the Congress says:

> The Congress deems it entirely inexact to attempt to consider the Canton insurrection as a putsch. It was a heroic rearguard [?] battle of the Chinese proletariat, fought in the course of the period which has just passed in the Chinese revolution; in spite of the crude mistakes committed by the leadership, this uprising will remain the standard of the new Soviet phase of the revolution.

Here confusion reaches its zenith. The heroism of the Cantonese proletariat is brought in evidence as a screen to cover up the faulty leadership, not of Canton (which the resolution casts off completely) but of Moscow, which only yesterday spoke not of a 'rearguard battle' but of the overthrow of the government of the Kuomintang.

Why is the appeal to insurrection denounced as putschism *after* the experience of Canton? Because, thanks to this experience, the inopportuneness of the uprising was confirmed. The leadership of the Communist International had need of a new object lesson in order to discover what already appeared quite clear without it. But are not these supplementary lessons for backward people, gven in life, too costly to the proletariat?

Lominadze, one of the infant prodigies of revolutionary strategy, swore at the Fifteenth Congress of the Communist Party of the Soviet Union that the Canton insurrection was necessary, right and salutary, precisely because it inaugurated an era of the direct struggle of the workers and peasants for the conquest of power. He met with agreement. At the Sixth Congress, Lominadze recognised that the insurrection did not inaugurate an era of triumph but concluded one of defeat.

Nevertheless, just as before, the uprising is considered necessary, right and salutary. Its name has simply been changed: from a clash between the vanguard of the forces at hand, they made a 'rearguard battle'. Everything else remains as in the past. The attempt to escape the criticism of the Opposition by hiding behind the heroism of the Cantonese workers has as much weight as, let us say for example, the attempt of General Rennenkampf to take shelter behind the heroism of the Russian soldiers whom he drowned by his strategy in the Masurian swamps. The proletarians of Canton are guilty, without having committed mistakes, simply of an excess of confidence in their leadership. Their leadership was guilty of having had a blind confidence in the leadership of the Communist International which combined political blindness with the spirit of adventurism.

It is radically false to compare the Canton insurrection of 1927 with that of Moscow in 1905. During the whole of 1905, the Russian proletariat rose from one plane to the other, wresting concessions from the enemy, sowing disintegration in its ranks, concentrating around its vanguard ever greater popular masses. The October 1905 strike was an immense victory, having a world historical importance. The Russian proletariat had its own party, which was not subordinated to any bourgeois or petty bourgeois discipline. The self-esteem, the intransigence, the spirit of offensive of the party, rose from stage to stage. The Russian proletariat had created Soviets in dozens of cities, not on the eve of the revolt but during the process of a strike struggle of the masses. Through these Soviets, the party established contact with the vast masses; it registered their revolutionary spirit; it mobilised them. The Tsarist government, seeing that each day brought a change in the relationship of forces favourable to the revolution, passed over to the counter-offensive and thus prevented the revolutionary leadership from being able to gain the time needed for continuing to mobilise its forces. Under these conditions, the leadership could and should have staked everything so as to be able to test by deeds the state of mind of the last decisive factor: the army. This was the meaning of the insurrection of December 1905.

In China, events developed in a directly opposite way. The Stalinist policy of the Chinese Communist Party consisted of a series of capitulations before the bourgeoisie, accustoming the workers to support patiently the yoke of the Kuomintang. In March 1926 the party capitulated before Chiang Kai-shek; it consolidated his position while weakening its own; it discredited the banner of Marxism; it converted itself into an auxiliary instrument of the bourgeois leadership. The party extinguished the agrarian movement and the workers' strikes by putting into practice the directions of the Executive Committee of the Communist International on the bloc of four classes. It renounced the organisation of Soviets so as not to disturb the situation at the rear of the Chinese generals. It thus delivered to Chiang Kai-shek the workers of Shanghai, bound hand to foot. After the crushing of Shanghai, the party, in conformity with the directions of the Executive Committee of the Communist International, placed all its hopes in the Left Kuomintang, the so-called 'centre of the agrarian revolution'. The Communists entered the Wuhan government, which repressed the strike struggle and the peasants' uprisings. They thus prepared a new and still crueller devastation of the revolutionary masses. After all this, an instruction entirely permeated with the spirit of adventurism was issued, ordering an immediate orientation towards the insurrection. It is from this that was first born the adventure of Ho Lung and Yeh-Ting, and the even more painful one of the Canton *coup d'état*.

No, all this does not resemble the insurrection of December 1905 at all.

If an opportunist calls the events of Canton an adventure it is because it was an *insurrection*. If a Bolshevik employs the same designation for these facts, it is because it was an *inopportune insurrection*. It is not for nothing that a German proverb says that when two men say the same thing it does not mean the same thing. The officials *à la* Thälmann can continue, on the subject of the Chinese revolt, to recount to the German Communists the 'apostasy' of the Opposition. We will know how to teach the German Communists to turn their backs on the Thälmanns. In actuality, the question of evaluating the Canton insurrection is the question of the teachings drawn from the Third Congress, in other words, of a lesson where the life of the German proletariat was at stake.

In March 1921 the Communist Party of Germany sought to engage in an insurrection by basing itself upon an active minority of the proletariat in the face of the passive spirit of the majority, which was tired, distrustful, expectant, as a result of all the preceding defeats. Those who directed this attempt at the time also sought to take shelter behind the heroism of which the workers gave proof in the March battles. However, the Third Congress did not congratulate them for this attempt when it condemned the spirit of adventurism of the leadership. What was our judgment in those days of the March events? 'Their essence,' we wrote, 'is summed up in the fact that the young Communist party, alarmed by a manifest decline in the workers' movement, made a desperate attempt to profit by the intervention of one of the most active detachments of the proletariat in order to "electrify" the working class and, if possible, to bring matters to a decisive battle.' (L. Trotsky, *Five Years of the Communist International,* page 333.) Thälmann has not understood a thing of all this.

From July 1923 on, we demanded, to the great astonishment of Klara Zetkin, Warski and other old, very venerable but incorrigible social-democrats, that the date of the insurrection in Germany be fixed. Then, at the beginning of 1924, when Zetkin declared that at that moment she envisaged the eventuality of an uprising with much 'more optimism' than during the preceding year, we could only shrug our shoulders.

> An elementary truth of Marxism says that the tactics of the socialist proletariat cannot be the same in face of a revolutionary situation as when this situation does not exist. (Lenin, *Works*, Volume XV, page 499.)

Today, everybody acknowledges this A B C verbally, but how far they still are from applying it in reality!

It is not a question of knowing what the Communists must do when the masses are rebelling *of their own accord*. That is a special question. When the masses arise, the Communists must be with them, organising and instructing them. But the question is posed differently: What did the leadership do and what should it have done during the weeks and months that immediately preceded the Canton insurrection? The leadership was duty bound to explain to the revolutionary workers that as a consequence of defeats, due to an erroneous policy, the relationship of forces had veered entirely in favour of the bourgeoisie. The great masses of workers who had fought tremendous battles, dispersed by the encounters, abandoned the field of battle. It is absurd to believe that one can march towards a peasant insurrection when the proletarian masses are departing. They must be grouped together again, fight defensive battles, avoiding a general battle, which obviously does not hold out any hope. If *in spite of* such a work of clarification and education, *contrary* to it, the masses of Canton had rebelled (which is very unlikely) the Communists would have had to put themselves at their head. But it is just the reverse that happened. The uprising had been commanded in advance, deliberately and with premeditation, based upon a false appreciation of the whole atmosphere. One of the detachments of the proletariat was drawn into a struggle which obviously held out no hope, and made easier for the enemy the annihilation of the vanguard of the working class. Not to say this openly, is to deceive the Chinese workers and to prepare new defeats. The Sixth Congress did not say it.

Does all this signify that the Canton insurrection *was only an adventure,* allowing of but one conclusion, that is, that the leadership was entirely incompetent? No, that is not the sense of our criticism. The Canton insurrection showed that even after enormous defeats, with the manifest decline of the revolution, even in non-industrialised Canton, with its petty-bourgeois traditions of Sun-Yat-Senism, the proletariat was able to rise in revolt, to fight valiantly and to conquer power. We have here a fact of enormous importance. It shows anew how considerable is the weight of the proletariat in its own right, how great is the political role which it can eventually play, even if the working class is relatively weak in numbers, in a historically backward country, where the majority of the population is composed of peasants and scattered petty-bourgeois. This fact, once more after 1905 and 1917, completely demolishes the philistines *à la* Kuusinen, Martinov and consorts, who teach us that one cannot dream of speaking of the dictatorship of the proletariat in 'agrarian' China. Yet the Martinovs and the Kuusinens are at the present time the daily inspirers of the Communist International.

The Canton insurrection showed at the same time that at the decisive moment the proletariat was unable to find, even in the petty bourgeois capital of Sun-Yat-Senism, a single *political ally* having a distinct form, not even among the debris of the Kuomintang, of the Left or the ultra-Left. This means that the vital task of establishing the alliance between the workers and the poor peasants in China devolves exclusively and directly upon the Communist party. The accomplishment of this task is one of the conditions for the triumph of the coming third Chinese revolution. And the victory of the latter will restore the power to the vanguard of the proletariat, supported by the union of the workers and the poor peasants.

If 'apostasy' must be spoken of, the traitors to the heroes and the victims of the Canton insurrection are those who seek to rid themselves of the teachings of this uprising in order to conceal the crimes of the leadership. The lesson to draw is the following:

1. The Canton insurrection showed that only the proletarian vanguard in China is capable of carrying out the uprising and of capturing power. The revolt showed, after the experience of collaboration between the Communist party and the Kuomintang, the complete lack of vitality and the reactionary character of the slogan of the democratic dictatorship of the proletariat and the peasantry, opposed to the slogan of the dictatorship of the proletariat drawing the poor peasants behind it.

2. The Canton insurrection, conceived and executed contrary to the course of development of the revolution, accelerates and deepens the decline of the latter, facilitating the annihilation of the proletarian forces by the bourgeois counter-revolution. This stamps the inter-revolutionary period with a painful, chronic and lasting character. The greatest problem now is the renascence of the Communist party as the organisation of the vanguard of the proletariat.

These two conclusions are equally important. It is only by considering them simultaneously that the situation can be judged and the perspectives fixed. The Sixth Congress did neither the one nor the other. By taking as its point of departure the resolutions of the Ninth Plenum of the Executive Committee of the Communist International (February 1928) which assured us that the Chinese revolution 'is continuing', the Congress slipped up in its flight to the point of declaring that this revolution has now entered into a preparatory phase. But this flight will not help anything. We must speak clearly and sincerely, recognise firmly, openly, brutally the breach that has taken place, adapt the tactics to it and at the same time follow a line of conduct which leads the vanguard of of the proletariat through the insurrection to its preponderant role in the Soviet China of the future.

2. The Inter-Revolutionary Period and the Tasks That Present Themselves in the Course of It

Bolshevik policy is characterised not only by its revolutionary scope, but also by its political realism. These two aspects of Bolshevism are inseparable. The greatest task is to know how to recognise in time a revolutionary situation and to exploit it to the end. But it is no less important to understand when this situation is exhausted and is converted, from the political point of view, into its antithesis. Nothing is more fruitless and worthless than to show one's fist after the battle. That, however, is just where Bukharin's speciality lies. First, he proved that the Kuomintang and the Soviets are the same thing, and that the Communists can conquer power through the Kuomintang, avoiding the fray. And when this same Kuomintang, with the aid of Bukharin, crushed the workers, he began to show his fist. In so far as he did nothing but amend or 'complete' Lenin, his caricatured aspect did not exceed certain modest limits. In so far as he pretends to give leadership himself, profiting by the total lack of knowledge in international questions on the part of Stalin, Rykov and Molotov, little Bukharin swells up until he becomes a gigantic caricature of Bolshevism. His strategy reduces itself to finishing off and mutilating, in the epoch of decline, that which escaped alive in the abortive and besmirched revolutionary period.

It must be distinctly understood that there is not, at the present time, a revolutionary situation in China. It is rather a counter-revolutionary situation that has been substituted there, transforming itself into an inter-revolutionary period of indefinite duration. Turn with contempt from those who would tell you that this is pessimism and lack of faith. To shut one's eyes to facts is the most infamous form of lack of faith.

There remains in China a revolutionary situation in all its profundity, in so far as all the internal and international contradictions of the country can find their solution only on the road of the revolution. But from this point of view, there is not a single country in the world where there does not exist a revolutionary situation which must inevitably manifest itself openly with the exception of the USSR, where, in spite of five years of opportunist back-sliding, the Soviet form of the proletarian dictatorship still opens up the possibility of a renascence of the October revolution by means of reformist methods.

In certain countries, the eventuality of the transformation of the potential revolution into an active revolution is closer; in others it is further off. It is all the more difficult to divine in advance what will be the rotation followed, since it is determined not only by the acuteness of the international contradictions, but also by the intersection of world factors. One may very reasonably assume that the revolution will be accomplished in Europe before taking place in North America. But the predictions which announce that the revolution will break out in Asia first and then in Europe already have a more conditional character. It is possible, even probable, but it is not at all inevitable. New difficulties and complications, like the occupation of the Ruhr in 1923, or else the accentuation of the commercial and industrial crisis, under the pressure of the United States, can in the nearest future confront the European states with a directly revolutionary situation, as was the case in Germany in 1923, in England in 1926 and in Austria in 1927.

The fact that only yesterday China was passing through a

stirring revolutionary phase does not bring closer the revolution for today and tomorrow, but on the contrary, makes it more distant. In the course of the period which followed the revolution of 1905, it produced great revolutionary disturbances and *coups d'état* in the countries of the East (Persia, Turkey, China). But in Russia itself, the revolution revived only twelve years later, in connection with the imperialist war. Naturally, these intervals are not obligatory for China. The general speed of the evolution of world contradictions has now been accelerated. That is all that can be said. But one must take into account and bear in mind that in China itself the revolution is at the present time laid over into an indefinite future. And moreover: the consequences of the defeat of the revolution have not yet been completely exhausted. In Russia the wave of fall and decline went through the years 1907-1908, 1909 and partly 1910, when, thanks in large measure to the revival of industry, the working class began to come to life. A no less abrupt descent confronts the Chinese Communist Party. The latter must know how to cling to every ledge, to hold tenaciously to every point of support so as not to tumble down and be smashed.

The Chinese proletariat, beginning with its vanguard, must assimilate the enormous experiences of the defeats and, by acting with new methods, recognise the new environment; it must redress its shattered ranks; it must renew its mass organisations; it must establish with greater clarity and distinctness than before what its attitude must be towards the problems which are arising before the country: national unity and liberation, revolutionary agrarian transformation.

On the other hand, the Chinese bourgeoisie must squander the capital accumulated by its victories. The contradictions which exist within itself, as well as between it and the outside world, must once more lay themselves bare and become sharpened. A new regrouping of forces must have its repercussions in the peasantry, reviving its activity. It is precisely all this that will signify that there is a renascence of the revolutionary situation on a higher historical basis.

> . . . Those who have had to live, said Lenin on February 23, 1918, through the long years of revolutionary battles at the time of the ascension of the revolution and at the time when it sank into the abyss, when the revolutionary appeals to the masses found no echo among them, know that in spite of everything the revolution always rose anew. . . . (Lenin, *Works,* Volume XX, part 2, page 217.)

The pace that the Chinese revolution will follow in 'rising anew', will depend not only upon objective conditions but also upon the policy of the Communist International.

The resolution of the Congress wheels diplomatically around these essential questions, planting reservations to the Right and the Left which will permit it to save itself, that is, like the lawyers, it creates motives in advance which will permit it to squash the case or appeal it.

It is true that this resolution recognises that 'the slogan of mass uprising becomes a propaganda slogan and it is only to the extent . . . that a new rise of the revolution matures that it will again become immediately applicable in practice'. Let us point out in passing that as late as February of this year such an attitude was called Trotskyism. No doubt it must be understood that this term signifies the ability to take into account facts and their consequences more rapidly than is done by the leadership of the Communist International.

But the resolution of the Congress does not go beyond this transformation of the armed insurrection into a propaganda slogan. The reports say nothing more on this point. What is to be expected in the very next period? What must be prepared for? What line must be followed in the work to be effected? No perspective is established. To understand how much needs to be learned over again from the very bottom in this question, let us again cast a glance upon yesterday, upon the very same resolution of the Chinese Central Committee, which furnishes the most striking manifestation of 'revolutionary' lightmindedness doubled by opportunism.*

The Plenum of the Central Committee of the Chinese Communist Party, directed by the infant prodigies of Left Centrism, decided in November 1927, on the eve of the insurrection at Canton:

> In evaluating the general political situation created in China after the counter-revolutionary *coup d'état* in Hunan, the Central Committee of the Chinese Communist Party, already in its theses of August, formulated the affirmation that stabilisation of the bourgeois military reaction in China was *entirely impossible* on the basis of the present social, economic and political relationships.

In this remarkable thesis, dealing with *stabilisation,* the same operation was carried through as was done with the *revolutionary situation.* These two conceptions have been transformed into certain substances, irremediably opposed to each other. If the revolutionary situation is assured for 'many years' in the face of no matter what circumstances, it is clear that stabilisation, no matter what happens, is 'absolutely impossible'. The one supplements the other in a system of metaphysical principles. Bukharin and his friendly-enemy, Lominadze, do not understand in such a case that the *revolutionary situation,* as well as its opposite, *stabilisation,* are not only the premises of the class struggle but also constitute its living content. Outside of this struggle, neither the one nor the other exists. We once wrote that stabilisation is an 'object' of the class struggle and not an arena established for it in advance. The proletariat wants to develop and utilise a situation of crisis, the bourgeois wants to put an end to it

---

* It goes without saying that *Pravda* has not published this resolution to which we have already referred above. It can only be found in the 'Material on the Chinese Question' (No. 10, 1928. Issued by the Chinese Sun Yat Sen University), and is very hard to procure. It is this same resolution which is officially charged with 'Trotskyism', although it is, in reality, nothing but Stalino-Bukharinist opportunism upside-down.

and to overcome it by its stabilisation. Stabilisation is the 'object' of the struggle of these fundamental class forces. Bukharin first sneered at this definition; then he introduced it textually, as contraband, into his printed report to one of the plenums of the Executive Committee of the Communist International. But in acknowledging our formula, directed especially against his scholasticism, Bukharin failed absolutely to understand the meaning of our definition. As to the capricious leaps that Lominadze executes towards the Left, their radius is very restricted, for the valiant infant prodigy does not dare break Bukharin's thread. Naturally, absolute stabilisation is absolutely opposed to an absolute revolutionary situation. The conversion of these absolutes into each other is 'absolutely impossible'. But if one descends from these ridiculous theoretical summits, it turns out that before the complete and final triumph of socialism, the relatively revolutionary situation will very likely be converted more than once into relative stabilisation (and *vice versa*). All other conditions remaining equal, the danger of the conversion of a revolutionary situation into bourgeois stabilisation is all the greater the less capable is the proletarian leadership of exploiting the situation. The leadership of the Chiang Kai-shek clique was superior to that of Chen Du-Siu and of Tang Ping Shan. But it is not this leadership that decided: foreign imperialism guided Chiang Kai-shek by threats, by promises, by its direct assistance. The Communist International directed Chen Du-Siu. Two leaderships of world dimensions crossed swords here. That of the Communist International, through all the stages of the struggle, appeared as absolutely forthless, and it thus facilitated to the highest degree the task of the imperialist leadership. In such conditions, the transformation of the revolutionary situation into bourgeois stabilisation is not only not 'impossible', but is absolutely inevitable. Even more: it is accomplished, and within certain limits it is completed.

Bukharin has announced a new period of 'organic' stabilisation for Europe. He gave assurances that one need not expect, in the course of the coming years in Europe, any renewal of the Vienna events or in general any revolutionary conclusions. Why? One does not know. The struggle for the conquest of power is entirely thrust aside by the struggle to be conducted against war. On the other hand, stabilisation in China is denied, just as the Fifth Congress denied it in Germany after the defeat of the revolution of 1923. Everything passes and everything changes, except the mistakes of the leadership of the Communist International.

The defeat of the workers and the peasants in China corresponds inevitably to a political consolidation of the Chinese ruling classes; and that is precisely the point of departure for economic stabilisation. A certain establishment of order in domestic circulation and in foreign commercial relations, following upon the pacification or the abatement of the civil war regions, automatically brings with it a restoration of economic activity. The vital needs of the completely devastated and exhausted country must make a path for themselves to some degree or other. Commerce and industry must begin to re-establish themselves. The number of employed workers must increase.

It would be blindness to close one's eyes to the existence of certain political premises for the subsequent development of the productive forces of the country which, of course, take on the forms of capitalist servitude. The political premises alone do not suffice. There is still needed an economic impulsion without which the disorganisation could be overcome only with relative slowness. This external shock may be furnished by the influx of foreign capital. America has already cut across the field, outstripping Japan and Europe, by consenting, for the sake of form, to conclude an 'equal treaty'. The domestic depression, in the face of the available resources, makes more than likely an extensive economic intervention in China by the United States, before which the Kuomintang will evidently hold the door wide 'open'. One cannot doubt the fact that the European countries, especially Germany, fighting against the rapidly aggravated crisis, will seek to debouch upon the Chinese market.

Given the vast area of China and its multitudinous population, even feeble success in the field of road construction, even a simple growth in transportation security, accompanied by a certain regulation of the exchange, must automatically produce a considerable increase of commercial circulation and by the same sign an enlivening of industry. At the present time, the most important capitalist countries, among them and far from occupying last place, the United States, preoccupied with an outlet for their automobiles, are interested in the establishment of all kinds of roads.

In order to stabilise the Chinese exchange and to mark out the roads, a large loan from abroad is required. The possibility of concluding it is discussed and recognised as quite real in the influential Anglo-Saxon financial press. They speak of an international banking consortium to amortise the old debts of China and to grant it new credits. The well-informed press is already calling the future affair 'the most important in world history'.

It is impossible to predict to what extent these grandiose projects will be put into effect without being better acquainted with all the documents, which relate in part to operations that take place behind the scenes. But there can be no doubt about the fact that for the near future the course of events will follow this direction. Right now, the press is bringing dozens of news items indicating that the extremely relative pacification of China and its still more relative unification have already given an impetus in the most diversified fields of economic life.

A good harvest in almost the whole of China is acting in the same sense. The diagrams of domestic circulation, of imports and exports, show patent signs of progress.

Manifestly, one should not repeat the mistake committed yesterday, only the other way around. One should not attribute to semi-colonial capitalist stabilisation I do not know what rigid, unchangeable—in a word, metaphysical—traits. It will be a very lame stabilisation, exposed to all the winds of world politics as well as to the still uneliminated internal dangers. Nevertheless, this very relative bourgeois stabilisation is radically distinguished from a revolutionary situation. To be sure, the fundamental material relations of the classes have remained the same. But the political relationships of their forces for the period in view have been rudely altered. This is expressed also by the fact that the Communist party has been almost completely driven back to its starting point. It will have to regain its political influence by proceeding almost from the beginning. What has been gained is experience. But this gain will be positive instead of negative on the single condition that the experience is judiciously assimilated. In the meantime, the bourgeoisie is acting with greater assurance, with greater cohesion. It has gone over to the offensive. It is setting itself great tasks for the morrow The proletariat is falling back; it is far from always offering resistance to blows. The peasantry, deprived of any kind of centralised leadership, boils over here and there without having any real chances of success. Now, world capital is coming to the aid of the Chinese bourgeoisie with the clear intention of bowing down still lower to the ground, through the intermediary of the latter, the Chinese toiling masses. There is the mechanism of the process of stabilisation. The day after tomorrow, when Bukharin runs his head into the facts, he will proclaim that heretofore the stabilisation might have been considered as 'incidental', but it is now clear that it is 'organic'.

The process of economic recovery will, in turn, correspond to the mobilisation of new tens and hundreds of thousands of Chinese workers, to the tightening up of their ranks, to the increase of their specific gravity in the social life of the country and by that an increase in their revolutionary self-confidence. It is superflous to explain that the re-animation of Chinese commerce and industry will soon give point to the problem of imperialism. However, were the Communist Party of China, influenced by the scholasticism of Bukharin and Lominadze, to turn its back to the process really taking place in the country, it would lose an economic point of support for the recovery of the workers' movement. At the beginning, the augmentation of the specific gravity and the class self-confidence of the proletariat will make itself felt in a rebirth of the strike struggle, in the consolidation of the trade unions. It is needless to say that serious possibilities are thus opened up before the Chinese Communist Party. Nobody knows how long it will have to remain in a clandestine existence. In any case, it is necessary to reinforce and to perfect the illegal organisations in the course of the coming period. But this task cannot be accomplished outside of the life and the struggle of the masses. The illegal apparatus will have all the greater possibilities to develop itself if the legal and semi-legal organisations of the working class surround it closely and the more profoundly it will penetrate into them. The Chinese Communist Party must not have doctrinaire blinkers over its eyes, and it must keep its hands on the pulse of the economic life of the country. It must put itself at the head of strikes at the proper time, charge itself with the resurrection of the trade unions and the struggle for the eight-hour day. It is only under these conditions that its participation in the political life of the country can obtain a serious foundation.

*   *   *

'There cannot even be any question,' said one of the Chinese delegates at the Congress, 'of a consolidation of the power of the Kuomintang.' (*Pravda*, August 28, 1928.) This is false. There most assuredly can be a 'question' of a certain consolidation, even fairly considerable, of the power of the Kuomintang for a certain period of time, even for a fairly important period.

The Chinese bourgeoisie, with an ease which it never expected, has won decisive victories, for the period in view, against the workers and the peasants. The re-awakening of its class consciousness which followed made itself clearly felt at the economic conference which met at the end of June in Shanghai and which represented, so to speak, the economic pre-parliament of the Chinese bourgeoisie. It showed that it wanted to reap the fruits of its triumph. Across this road stand the militarists and the imperialists with whose aid it vanquished the masses. The bourgeoisie wants customs autonomy, that stumbling block to economic independence, to the completest possible unification of China; the abolition of internal customs which disorganise the market; suppression of the arbitrariness of the military authorities who confiscate the rolling stock of the railroads and encroach upon private property; finally, the reduction of armaments, which today constitute a too heavy burden upon the economy of the country. It is to this, also, that belongs the creation of a unified currency and the establishment of order in administration. The bourgeoisie has formulated all its demands in its economic pre-parliament. From the formal point of view, the Kuomintang has taken note of it, but being entirely divided among the regional military cliques, it constitutes at the present time an obstacle to the realisation of these measures.

The foreign imperialists represent an even stronger one. The bourgeoisie considers, and not without cause, that it will exploit the contradictions between the imperialists with all the greater success, and that it will obtain an all the more favourable compromise with them, should it be successful in compelling the military cliques of the Kuomintang to submit to the centralised apparatus of the bourgeois state. It is in this sense that the aspirations of the most 'progressive' elements of the bourgeoisie and of the democratic petty-bourgeoisie are now being directed. It is out of this that is born the idea of the National Assembly to crown the victories won, a means of bridling the militarists, the authorised state representative of the Chinese bourgeoisie for doing business with foreign capital. The economic animation which is already visible cannot but give courage to the bourgeoisie, obliging it to regard with particular hositility anything that impairs the regularity of the circulation of merchandise and disorganises the national market. The first stage of economic stabilisation will certainly increase the chances of success of Chinese parliamentarism and will consequently require that the Chinese Communist Party give evidence, in this question too, of timely political initiative.

For the Chinese bourgeoisie, having vanquished the workers and the peasants, it can only be a question of an arch-censored assembly, perhaps by simply giving formal representation to the commercial and industrial associations on the basis of which the economic conference of Shanghai was convoked. The petty-bourgeois democracy, which will inevitably begin to stir, seeing that the revolution declines, will formulate more 'democratic' slogans. In this manner, it will seek to establish contact with the higher strata of the popular masses of town and country.

The 'constitutional' development of China, at least in its next stage, is intimately bound up with the internal evolution of the Kuomintang, in whose hands the state power is at present concentrated in every respect. The last plenum of the Kuomintang, in August, decided, so far as can be understood, to convene for the first of January 1929 the party congress which was adjourned for so long a time owing to the centre's fear of losing power (as we see, the peculiarity of 'China' is not very peculiar). The agenda of the congress includes the problem of the Chinese constitution. It is true that certain internal or external events may cause the collapse not only of the January congress of the Kuomintang but also of the whole constitutional era of stabilisation of the Chinese bourgeoisie. This eventuality always remains a possibility. But unless new factors intervene, the question of the state regime in China, the constitutional problems, will occupy the centre of public attention in the next period.

What attitude will the Communist party take? What will it set up against the Kuomintang's draft of a constitution? Can the Communist party say that since it is preparing, as soon as a new rise takes place, to create Soviets in the future, it makes no difference to it *up to then* whether there exists or does not exist in China a National Assembly, that it matters little if it is censored or embraces the whole people? Such an attitude would be superficial, empty and passive.

The Communist party can and should formulate the slogan of a Constituent Assembly with full powers, elected by universal, equal, direct and secret suffrage. In the process of agitation for this slogan, it will obviously be necessary to explain to the masses that it is doubtful if such an assembly will be convened, and even if it were, it would be powerless so long as the material power remains in the hands of the Kuomintang generals. From this flows the possibility of broaching in a new manner the slogan of the arming of the workers and the peasants. The revival of political activity, connected with that of economy, will once more bring the agrarian problem to the foreground. But for a certain period it may find itself posed on the parliamentary field, that is, on the field of the attempts by the bourgeoisie and primarily by the petty-bourgeois democracy to 'solve' it by legislative means.

Obviously, the Communist party cannot adapt itself to bourgeois legality, that is, capitulate before bourgeois property. It can and should have its own finished and rounded-out project for the solution of the agrarian problem on the basis of the confiscation of landed property exceeding a certain area, varying in accordance with the different provinces. The Communist project of the agrarian law must be in essence the formula of the future agrarian revolution. But the Communist party can and should introduce its own formula into the struggle for the National Assembly and into the Assembly itself, should this ever be convened.

The slogan of the National (or Constituent) Assembly is thus intimately linked up with those of the eight-hour day, the confiscation of the land and the complete national independence of China. It is precisely in these slogans that the democratic stage of the development of the Chinese revolution will express itself. In the field of international policy, the Communist party will demand an alliance with the USSR. By judiciously combining these slogans, by advancing each of them at the proper time, the Communist party will be able to tear itself out of its clandestine existence, make a bloc with the masses, win their confidence, and thus speed the coming of the period of the creation of Soviets and of the direct struggle for power.

Well-defined historical tasks are deduced from the democratic stage of the revolution. But by itself the democratic character of these tasks does not at all determine as yet what classes, and in which combination, will solve these problems. At bottom, all the great bourgeois revolutions solved problems of the same type, but they did it through a different class mechanism. By fighting for democratic tasks in China in the inter-revolutionary period, the Communist party will re-assemble its forces, will check up on itself, upon its slogans and its methods of action. If it should succeed, in this connection, in passing over a period of parliamentarism (which is possible, even probable, but far from inevitable), this will permit the proletarian vanguard to scrutinise its enemies and adversaries by examining them through the prism of parliament. In the course of the pre-parliamentary and parliamentary period, this vanguard will have to conduct an intransigent struggle to win influence over the peasants, to guide the peasantry directly from the political point of view. Even if the National Assembly should be realised in an arch-democratic manner, the fundamental problems would nevertheless have to be solved by force. Through the parliamentary period, the Chinese Communist Party would arrive at a direct and immediate struggle for power, but by possessing a maturer historical basis, that is, surer premises for victory.

We have said that the existence of the parliamentary stage was probable, but not inevitable. A new disintegration of the country, as well as external causes, may prevent its realisation; at all events, in the first case, a movement in favour of parliaments for various regions might come forward. But all this does not remove the importance of the struggle for a democratically convoked National Assembly which would by itself be an entering wedge between the groupings of the possessing classes and would broaden the framework of the proletariat's spirit of activity.

We know in advance that all the 'leaders' who preached the bloc of the four classes, the arbitration commissions instead of strikes, who gave telegraphic orders that the agrarian movement should not be extended, who counselled that the bourgeoisie should not be terrorised, who prohibited the creation of Soviets, who subordinated the Communist party to the Kuomintang, who acclaimed Wang Chin Wei as the leader of the agrarian revolution—that all these opportunists, guilty of the defeat of the revolution, will now attempt to outbid the Left wing and to charge our way of putting the question with containing 'constitutional illusions' and a 'social-democratic deviation'. We deem it necessary to warn the Communists and the advanced Chinese workers in time against the hollow, false radicalism of yesterday's favourites of Chiang Kai-shek. One cannot rid oneself of a historical process by faked quotations, by confusion, by mile-long resolutions, in general, by every sort of apparatus and literary trick, which seeks to escape facts and classes. Events will come and furnish the test. Those for whom the tests of the past are not enough have only to wait for the future. Only, let them not forget that this verification nevertheless is effected on the bones of the proletarian vanguard.

3. THE SOVIETS AND THE CONSTITUENT ASSEMBLY

We hope that it is not necessary to raise here the general question of formal, that is, of bourgeois democracy. Our attitude towards it has nothing in common with the sterile anarchist negation. The slogan and the norms of democracy, from the formal point of view, are deduced in a different way for the various countries of a well-defined stage in the evolution of bourgeois society. The democratic slogans contain for a certain period not only illusions, not only deception, but also an animating historical force. 'So long as the struggle of the working class for full power is not on the order of the day, it is our duty to utilise every form of bourgeois democracy.' (Lenin *Works,* January 20, 1919, Volume XX, Part 2, page 298.)

From the *political* point of view, the question of formal democracy is for us not only that of the attitude to be observed towards the petty-bourgeois masses, but also towards the worker masses, to the extent that the latter have not yet acquired a revolutionary class consciousness. Under the conditions of progress of the revolution, during the offensive of the proletariat, the eruption of the lower strata of the petty-bourgeoisie in political life was manifested in China by agrarian revolts, by conflicts with the governmental troops, by strikes of all kinds, by the extermination of lower administrators. At the present moment, all the movements of this type are obviously diminishing. The triumphant soldiery of the Kuomintang dominates society. Every day of stabilisation will lead more and more to collisions between this militarism and the bureaucracy on the one hand, and on the other, not only the advanced workers but also the petty-bourgeois masses who predominate in the population of the country and towns, and even, within certain limits, the big bourgeoisie. Before these collisions develop to the point of becoming an open revolutionary struggle, they will pass, from all the available facts, through a 'constitutional' stage. The conflicts between the bourgeoisie and its own military cliques will inevitably draw in the upper layer of the petty bourgeois masses, through the medium of a 'third party' or by other means. From the standpoint of economics and of culture, the former are extraordinarily feeble. Their political strength lies in their numbers. Therefore, the slogans of formal democracy win over, or are capable of winning over, not only the petty bourgeois masses but also the broad working masses, precisely because they reveal to them the possibility, which is essentially illusory, of opposing their will to that of the generals, the country squires and the capitalists. The proletarian vanguard educates the masses by using this experience, and leads them forward.

The experience of Russia shows that during the progress of the revolution, the proletariat organised in Soviets can, by a correct policy, directed towards the conquest of power, draw behind it the peasantry, fling it against the front of formal democracy embodied in the Constituent Assembly, and switch it on the rails of Soviet democracy. In any case, these results were not attained by simply opposing the Soviets to the Constituent Assembly, but by drawing the masses towards the Soviets while maintaining the slogans of formal democracy up to the very moment of the conquest of power and even after it.

> That in the Russia of September-November 1917, the working class of the cities, the soldiers and the peasants, as a result of a number of special conditions, found themselves admirably prepared for the adoption of the Soviet regime and the dissolution of the most democratic of the bourgeois parliaments—that is an undeniable and perfectly established historical fact. Yet the Bolsheviks did not boycott the Constituent Assembly; far from it, they participated in the elections not only before but even after the conquest of political power by the proletariat. . . .
>
> Even a few weeks before the victory of the Soviet republic, even *after* this victory, the participation in a parliament of bourgeois democracy, far from injuring the revolutionary proletariat, helps it *to prove* to the backward masses that these parliaments deserve to be dissolved, *facilitates* the success of their dissolution, brings nearer the moment when it could be said that bourgeois parliamentarism had 'had its day politically'. (Lenin, *Works,* Volume XVII, 1920. *The Infantile Sickness of Communism,* page 149.)

When we adopted direct practical measures to disperse the Constitutent Assembly, I recall that Lenin insisted particularly on having sent to Petrograd one or two regiments of Lettish light infantry, composed largely of agricultural workers. 'The Petrograd garrison is almost entirely peasants; may it not hesitate in face of the Constituent?' That is how Lenin formulated his preoccupations. It was not at all a question of political 'traditions'; indeed, the Russian peasantry could have no serious traditions of parliamentary democracy. The essence of the question lies in the fact that the peasant mass, aroused to historical life, is not at all inclined to place confidence in advance in a leadership coming from the cities, even if it is proletarian, especially during a non-revolutionary period; this mass seeks a simple political formula which would express *directly* its own political strength, that is, the predominance of numbers. The political expression of the domination of the majority is formal democracy.

Naturally, to affirm that the popular masses can and should never and under no conditions 'leap' over the 'constitutional' step, would be to manifest a ridiculous pedantry in the spirit of Stalin. In certain countries, the epoch of parliamentarism lasts long decades and even centuries. In Russia, it was only prolonged for the few years of the pseudo-constitutional regime and the one day of existence of the Constituent. From the historical point of view, one can perfectly well conceive of situations where even these few years and this one day would not exist. Also, if the revolutionary policy had been correct, if the Communist party had been completely independent of the Kuomintang, if the Soviets had been established in 1925-1927, the revolutionary development could already have led China today to the dictatorship of the proletariat by passing beyond the democratic phase. But even in that case, it is not impossible that the formula of the Constituent Assembly, not tried by the peasantry at the most critical moment, not tested, and consequently still containing illusions, could, at the first serious difference between the peasantry and the proletariat, on the very morrow of the victory, become the slogan of the peasants and the petty-bourgeoisie of the cities against the proletariat. Important conflicts between the proletariat and the peasantry, even in face of favourable conditions for the alliance, are quite inevitable, as is witnessed by the experience of the October revolution. Our greatest advantage lay in the fact that the majority of the Constituent Assembly, which had grown in the struggle of the dominant parties for the continuation of the war and against the confiscation of the land by the peasants, had profoundly compromised itself, even in the eyes of the peasantry, already at the moment of the convocation of the Constituent Assembly.

*   *   *

How does the resolution of the Congress, adopted after a reading of Bukharin's report, characterise the present period of the development of China and the tasks to be deduced from this period? Paragraph 54 of this resolution says:

> At the present time, the principal task of the party, in the period between two waves of revolutionary progress, is to fight to win the masses, that is, mass work among the workers and the peasants, the re-establishment of their organisations, the utilisation of all discontentment against the landed proprietors, the bourgeoisie, the generals, the foreign imperialists. . . .

There is really a classic example of double meaning in the manner of the most renowned oracles of antiquity. The present period is characterised as being 'between two waves of revolutionary progress'. We know this formula. The Fifth Congress applied it to Germany. A revolutionary situation does not develop uniformly, but by successive waves of ebb and flow. This formula has been chosen with premeditation, so as to be able to interpret it as recognising the existence of a revolutionary situation, in which there takes place simply a 'calm' before the tempest. At all events, they will also be able to explain it by pretending to acknowledge a whole period between two revolutions. In both cases, they will be able to begin the new resolution with the words: 'as we foresaw' or 'as we predicted'.

Every historical prognosis inevitably contains a conditional element. The shorter the period over which this prognosis extends, the greater is this element. In general, it is impossible to establish a prognosis with which the leaders of the proletariat would, in the future, no longer have need of analysing the situatioon. A prognosis has not the significance of command but rather of an orientation. One can and one must make reservations on the point up to which it is conditional. In certain situations, one can furnish a number of variants of the future, delimiting them with reflection. One can, finally, in a turbulent atmosphere, completely abandon prognosis for the time being and confine oneself to giving the advice: Wait and see! But all this must be done clearly, openly, honestly. However, in the course of the last five years, the prognoses of the Communist International have constituted not directives but rather traps for the leaderships of the parties of the various countries. The principal aim of the 'prognoses' is: to inspire veneration towards the wisdom of the leadership, and in case of defeat, to save its 'prestige', that supreme fetish of weak people. It is a method of oracular announcement and not of Marxian investigation. It presupposes the existence on the scene of action of 'scapegoats'. It is a demoralising system. The ultra-Leftist mistake committed by the German leadership in 1925 flowed precisely from this same perfidious, double-meaning manner of formulating the question on the subject of the 'two waves of revolutionary progress'. The resolution of the Sixth Congress can cause just as many misfortunes.

We have known the wave of the period before Shanghai, and then that of Wuhan. There have been many more partial and localised waves. They all rose in the general revolutionary progress of 1925-1927. But this historical ascension is exhausted. This must be understood and said clearly. Important strategic consequences are to be deduced from it.

The resolution speaks of the necessity of utilizing 'all discontentment against the landed proprietors, the bourgeoisie, the generals, the foreign imperialists'. This is incontestable, but it is too indefinite. Utilise it how? If we find ourselves between two waves of continuous revolutionary progress, then every manifestation of discontentment, no matter how small its importance, can be considered as the famous (according to Zinoviev-Bukharin) 'beginning of the second wave'. Then the propaganda slogan of the armed insurrection will have to be transformed immediately into a slogan of action. From this can grow a 'second wave' of putschism. The party will utilise quite differently the discontentment of the masses, if it considers it by reckoning with a correct historical perspective. But the Sixth Congress does not possess this 'bagatelle', a correct historical perspective, on any question. The Fifth Congress was a failure because of this deficiency. It is on this score that the whole Communist International can also break its neck.

After having once more condemned the putschistic tendencies for which it itself prepares the ground, the resolution of the Congress continues:

> On the other hand, certain comrades have fallen into an opportunist error: they put forward the slogan of the National Assembly.

The resolution does not explain what the opportunism of this slogan consists of. The scalded cat fears even cold water.

Only the Chinese delegate, Strakhov, in his closing speech on the lessons of the Chinese revolution, tried to furnish an explanation. Here is what he says:

> From the experience of the Chinese revolution, we see that when the revolution in the colonies [?] draws close to the decisive moment, the question is clearly posed: Either the dictatorship of the landed proprietors and the bourgeoisie, or that of the proletariat and the peasantry.

Naturally, when the revolution (and certainly not only in the colonies) 'draws close to the decisive moment', then every mode of action in the Kuomintang style, that is to say, all collaborationism, is a crime involving fatal consequences: one can then conceive only of a dictatorship of the possessors or a dictatorship of the workers. But as we have already seen, even in such moments, in order to triumph over parliamentarism as revolutionists, one must have nothing in common with the sterile negation of it. Strakhov, however, goes even further:

> There [in the colonies], bourgeois democracy cannot exist; only the bourgeois dictatorship, operating openly, is possible. . . . It cannot have there . . . any constitutional path.

This is a doubly inexact extension of a correct thought. If, during 'decisive moments' of the revolution, bourgeois democracy is inevitably torpedoed (and that not only in the colonies), this in no wise signifies that it is impossible during inter-revolutionary periods. But it is Strakhov and the whole Congress who do not want to recognise that the 'decisive moment', during which it was precisely the Communists who occupied themselves with the worst democratic fictions within the Kuomintang, has already passed. Now, before a new 'decisive moment', a long period must be passed through, during which the *old* questions will have to be approached in a *new* manner. To assert that in the colonies there can be no constitutional or parliamentary periods of evolution, is to renounce the utilisation of methods of struggle which are essential to the highest degree, and is, above all, to make hard for oneself a correct political orientation, by driving the party into a blind alley.

To say that for China, as, moreover, for all the other states of the world, there is no way out towards a free, in other words, a socialist development, by following the parliamentary path, is one thing, is right. But to claim that in the evolution of China, or of the colonies, there can be no constitutional period or stage, that is another thing, that is wrong. There was a parliament in Egypt, which is at the present time dissolved. It may come to life again. There is a parliament in Ireland, in spite of the semi-colonial situation of that country. The same holds true for all the states of South America, not to speak of the dominions of Great Britain. There exist semblances of 'parliaments' in India. They can also develop later on: in such matters, the British bourgeoisie is pretty flexible. What reason is there for asserting that after the crushing of the revolution which has just taken place, China will not pass through a parliamentary or pseudo-parliamentary phase, or that it will not go through a serious political struggle to gain this stage of evolution? Such an assertion has no foundation at all.

The same Strakhov says that it is precisely the Chinese opportunists who aspire to substitute the slogan of the National Assembly for that of Soviets. This is possible, probable, even inevitable. It was proved by all the experience of the world labour movment, of the Russian movement in particular, that the opportunists are the first to cling to parliamentary methods, in general to everything which resembles parliamentarism, or even approaches it. The Mensheviks clung to activity in the Duma *as against* revolutionary activity. The utilisation of parliamentary methods inevitably brings up all the dangers connected with parliamentarism: constitutional illusions, legalism, a penchant for compromises, etc. These dangers and maladies can only be combated by a revolutionary course in policies. But the fact that the opportunists put forward the slogan of the struggle for the National Assembly in no way constitutes an argument in favour of a formal, negative attitude on our part towards parliamentarism. After the *coup d'état* of June 3, 1907 in Russia, the majority of the leading elements of the Bolshevik party favoured boycotting the mutilated and tricked Duma. This did not prevent Lenin from coming forward resolutely in favour of the utilisation of even the 'parliamentarism' of June 3, at the party conference which at that time still united the two factions. Lenin was the only Bolshevik who voted with the Mensheviks in favour of participation in the elections. Obviously, Lenin's 'participation' had nothing in common with that of the Mensheviks, as was shown by the whole subsequent march of events; it was not opposed to the revolutionary tasks, but served them for the epoch included between two revolutions. While utilising the counter-revolutionary pseudo-parliament of June 3, our party, in spite of its great experience of the Soviets of 1905, continued to conduct the struggle for the Constituent Assembly, that is, for the most democratic form of parliamentary representation. The right to renounce parliamentarism must be won by uniting the masses around the party and by leading them to struggle openly for the conquest of power. It is naive to think that one can simply substitute for this work the mere renunciation of the revolutionary utilisation of the contradictory and oppressive methods and forms of parliamentarism. This is the crudest error of the resolution of the Congress, which makes here a flippant ultra-Leftist leap.

Just see how everything is turned topsy-turvy. According to the logic of the present leadership, and in conformity with the sense of the resolutions of the Sixth Congress of the Communist International, China is not approaching its 1917, but rather its 1905. *That is why* the leaders conclude mentally: Down with the slogan of formal democracy! There really does not remain a single joint which the epigones have not taken care to dislocate. How can the slogan of democracy, and especially the most radical one, the democratic representation of the people, be rejected in the condition of a non-revolutionary period, if the revolution has not accomplished its most immediate tasks from the point of view of the unity of China and its purging of all its feudal and military-bureaucratic rubbish?

So far as I know, the Chinese party has not had a programme of its own. The Bolshevik party arrived at the October revolution and accomplished it while armed with its old programme, in the political part of which the slogans of democracy occupied an important place. In his time, Bukharin attempted to suppress this minimum programme, just as he came forward later on against transitional demands in the programme of the Communist International. But this attitude of Bukharin's remained recorded in the history of the party only as an anecdote. As is known, it was the dictatorship of the proletariat which accomplished the democratic revolution in Russia. The present leadership of the Communist International absolutely does not want to understand this either. But our party led the proletariat to the dictatorship only because it defended with the greatest energy, doggedness and devotion all the slogans and demands of democracy, including popular representation based upon universal suffrage, responsibility of the government to the representatives of the people, etc. Only such an agitation permits the party to preserve the proletariat

from the influence of petty-bourgeois democracy, to undermine
its influence among the peasantry, to prepare the alliance of the
workers and the peasants, and to draw into its ranks the most
resolute revolutionary elements. Was all this nothing but opportunism? *Spoitie, svietik, nie stydities!**

*   *   *

Strakhov says that we have the slogan of Soviets and that
only opportunists can substitute for it the slogan of the
National Assembly. This argument unmasks in most exemplary
manner the erroneous character of the Congress resolution. In
the discussion, nobody confuted Strakhov. On the contrary, his
position was approved; it was ratified in the principal tactical
resolution. It is only now that one sees clearly how numerous
are those in the present leadership who went through the experience of one, two, or even three revolutions, letting themselves be drawn in by the course of events and the leadership
of Lenin, but without themselves reflecting upon the meaning
of what was happening and without assimilating the greatest
lessons of history. One is therefore obliged to repeat again
certain elementary truths.

In my criticism of the programme of the Communist International, I have shown how the epigones have monstrously
disfigured and mutilated the thought of Lenin, which affirms
that the Soviets are organs of insurrection and organs of power.
From it was drawn the conclusion that Soviets can be created
only on the 'eve' of the insurrection. This grotesque idea found
its most consummate expression in the same resolution, recently
revealed by us, of the November Plenum of the Chinese Central
Committee held last year. It says there:

Soviets can and should be created as organs of revolutionary power
only when we are in the midst of an important, incontestable pro-

* 'Sing, my dove, be not abashed!' From a popular Russian song.—Tr.

gress of the revolutionary movement of the masses and when the *solid* victory of the uprising is *assured*.

The first condition: 'important progress', is incontestable. The second condition: 'guarantee of victory', and what is more, of a 'solid' one, is simply pedantic stupidity. In the rest of the text of the resolution this stupidity, however, is developed at length:

> The creation of Soviets obviously cannot be approached when victory is not yet absolutely guaranteed, for it might then happen that all attention is concentrated solely upon elections to the Soviets and not upon the military struggle, as a consequence of which petty-bourgeois democratism might instal itself, which would weaken the revolutionary dictatorship and would create a danger for the leadership of the party.

The spirit of Stalin, refracted through the prism of the infant prodigy, Lominadze, hovers over these immortal lines. However, all this is simply absurd. During the Hongkong strike, during the Shanghai strikes, during all the subsequent violent progress of the workers and the peasants, Soviets should and could have created as organs of an open revolution mass struggle which, *sooner or later* and not at all at one blow, would lead to the insurrection and the conquest of power. If, in the phase under consideration, the struggle did not rise to the point of insurrection, obviously the Soviets too would be reduced to nothing. They cannot become 'normal' institutions of the bourgeois state. But in that case, too, that is, if the Soviets are liquidated before the insurrection, the working masses make an enormous acquisition, familiarising themselves with the the Soviets in practice, identifying themselves with their mechanism. During the following stage of the revolution, the more successful and more extensive creation of Soviets will thus be guaranteed: although, even in the phase that follows it may be that they do not lead directly, not only to victory, but even not to the insurrection.

Let us recall this very distinctly: the slogan of Soviets can and must be put forward from the first stages of the revolutionary progress of the masses. But it must be a real progress. The working masses must flock to the revolution, rally under its standard. The Soviets furnish an expression, from the organisational point of view, to the centripetal force of revolutionary progress. But in this way, it holds true at the same time that during the period of revolutionary ebb-tide and of the development of centrifugal tendencies in the masses, the slogan of Soviets will be doctrinaire, lifeless, or what is just as bad, it will be the slogan of adventurists. The Canton experience showed this better than anything else, in a striking and tragic manner.

At the present time, the slogan of Soviets in China has an importance only from the point of view of perspective, and in this sense it has a propaganda value. One would not be conforming to anything at all by opposing the Soviets, the slogan of the third Chinese revolution, to the National Assembly, that is, to the slogan that flows from the debacle of the second Chinese revolution. Abstentionism, in an inter-revolutionary period, especially after a cruel defeat, would be a suicidal policy.

One might say (for there are many sophists in the world) that the resolution of the Sixth Congress does not at all mean abstentionism: there is no National Assembly, nobody is as yet convoking it or promising to convoke it, consequently there is nothing to boycott. Such reasoning, however, would be too pitiable, purely formal, infantile, Bukharinistic. If the Kuomintang were compelled to proclaim the convocation of a National Assembly, would we boycott it in the given situation? No. We would pitilessly unmask the lie and duplicity of the Kuomintang's parliamentarism, the constitutional illusions of the petty bourgeoisie: we would demand the complete extension of electoral rights; at the same time we would throw ourselves into the political arena to oppose, in the struggle for the parliament, in the course of the elections and in the parliament itself, the workers and the poor peasants to the possessing class and their parties. Nobody would presume to foretell how great would be the results thus obtained for the present party, debilitated and reduced to a clandestine existence. If the policy were correct, the advantages could be very considerable. But in this case, is it not clear that the party can and must not only participate in the elections if the Kuomintang promulgates them, but also demand that they be held by mobilising the masses around this slogan?

From the political point of view the question is already posed, every new day will confirm it. In our criticism of the programme, we spoke of the probability of a certain economic stabilisation in China. The newspapers have since then brought dozens of indications of the economic revival that is beginning (see the *Bulletin of the Chinese University*). Now it is no longer a supposition, but a fact, even though it is only in its very first phase. But it is just in the course of the first phase that the tendencies must be perceived, otherwise it will not be a revolutionary policy that is pursued, but a dragging at the tail of events. The same holds true for the political struggle around the questions of the constitution. This is now no longer a theoretical forecast, that is, a simple possibility, but something more concrete. It is not for nothing that the Chinese delegate frequently recurs to the theme of the National Assembly; it is not by chance that the Congress thought it necessary to adopt a special (and a particularly false) resolution on the subject of this question. It is not the Opposition which has posed this question, but rather the evolution of Chinese political life. Here too one must know how to perceive a tendency at the very outset. The more audaciously and resolutely the Communist party comes forward with the slogan of the democratic Constituent Assembly, the less place it will leave all sorts of intermediary parties, the more solid will be its own success.

If the Chinese proletariat is obliged to live a few more years (even if it were only another year) under the regime of the Kuomintang, could the Chinese Communist Party abandon the struggle for the extension of legal possibilities of all sorts, for the freedom of press, of assembly, of organisation, of strike, etc.? Were it to abandon this struggle, it would transform itself into a lifeless sect. But that is a struggle on the democratic plane. Soviet power signifies the monopoly of the press, of assembly, etc., in the hands of the proletariat. Perhaps the Chinese Communist Party will put forward these slogans precisely at this time? In the situation under consideration, it would be a mixture of childishness and madness. The Communist party is fighting at present not for power, but to maintain, to consolidate and to develop its contact with the masses for the sake of the struggle for power in the future. The struggle to win the masses is inevitably bound up with the struggle conducted against the violence which the Kuomintang bureaucracy practices towards the mass organisations, their meetings, their press, etc. During the period that is to follow immediately, will the Communist party fight for freedom of the press or will it leave this to be done by a 'third party'? Will the Communist party confine itself to presenting democratic, isolated, partial demands (freedom of the press, of assembly, etc.), which would amount to liberal reformism, or will it put forward the most consistent slogans of democracy? In the political sphere, this signifies popular representation based upon universal suffrage.

*   *   *

One might ask if the Democratic Constituent Assembly is 'realisable' after a defeated revolution in a semi-colonial China encircled by the imperialists. This question can only be answered by conjectures. But the simple criterion of the possibility of realising some demand, in the face of conditions existing in bourgeois society or in a given state of this society, is not decisive for us. It is very probable, for example, that the monarchical power and the House of Lords will not be swept away before the establishment of the revolutionary dictatorship of the proletariat. Nevertheless, the British Communist Party must formulate among its partial demands this one as well. It is not by devoting oneself to empirical conjectures as to the possibility of realising some transitional demand or not, that the question relating to it is settled. It is its social and historical character that decides: is it progressive from the point of view of the subsequent development of society? Does it correspond to the historical interests of the proletariat? Does it strengthen the consciousness of the latter? Does it bring it closer to its dictatorship? Thus for example, the demand for the prohibition of trusts is petty-bourgeois and reactionary and, as the experiences of America have shown, it is completely Utopian. Under certain conditions, on the contrary, it is entirely progressive and correct to demand workers' control over the trusts, even though it is more than doubtful that this will ever be realised within the framework of the bourgeois state. The fact that this demand is not satisfied so long as the bourgeoisie rules must push the workers to the revolutionary overthrow of the latter. Thus, the impossibility of realising a slogan from the political point of view can be no less fruitful than the relative possibility of putting it into practice.

Will China come for a certain period to democratic parliamentarism? What will be the degree of its democratism? What strength and what duration will it have? All this is a matter of conjecture. But it would be radically wrong to base oneself on the supposition that parliamentarism is unrealisable in China in order to conclude that we cannot hale the cliques of the Kuomintang before the tribunal of the Chinese people.

The idea of the representation of the entire people, as has been shown by the experience of all the bourgeois revolutions and especially those which liberated nationalities, is the most elementary, the most simple and the one most apt to embrace really vast popular strata. The more the ruling bourgeoisie resists this demand of the 'entire people', and the more the proletarian vanguard rallies around our banner, the riper the political conditions will become to win the real victory against the bourgeois state, little matter whether it be the military state of the Kuomintang or the parliamentary.

It may be said: a real Constituent Assembly will not be convoked except through the Soviets, that is through the insurrection. Would it not be simpler to begin with Soviets and to confine oneself to them? No, it would not be simpler. It would be just like putting the cart before the horse. It is very likely that it will not be possible to convoke the Constitutent Assembly except through the Soviets and that in this way the Assembly might become superfluous even before its birth. This may happen, just as it may not happen. If the Soviets, through whose medium a 'real' Constitutent Assembly might be called together, were already here, we would see if it was still necessary to proceed with its convocation. But there are no Soviets at the present time. One cannot start to establish them except at the beginning of a new advance of the masses, which may take place in two or three years, in five years, or more. There are no Soviet traditions at all in China. The Communist International conducted an agitation in that country against Soviets and not in favour of them. In the meantime, however, constitutional questions are beginning to emerge from every cranny.

Can the Chinese revolution, in the course of its new stage, leap over formal democracy? It follows from what has been said above that, from the historical point of view, such a possibility is not excluded. But it is entirely inadmissible to approach the question guided by this possibility, which is the most distant and the least likely. It is to manifest lightmindedness in the political domain. The Congress adopts its decisions for more than one month, and even, as we know, for more than a year. How then can the Chinese Communists be left bound hand and foot, by designating as opportunism the form of political struggle which, from the next stage onwards, may acquire the greatest importance?

*   *   *

It is incontestable that by entering the path of struggle for the Constituent Assembly, the Menshevik tendencies in the Chinese Communist Party may be revived and strengthened. It is no less important to fight against opportunism when the policy is directed towards parliamentarism or towards the struggle for it, than when one is confronted with a direct revolutionary offensive. But, as has already been said, it does not follow from this that the democratic slogans should be called opportunistic, but that guarantees and Bolshevik methods of struggle for these slogans must be worked out. In broad outline, these methods and guarantees are the following:

1. The party must have in mind and must explain that in comparison with its principal aim, the conquest of power with arms in hand, the democratic slogans have only an auxiliary, a provisional, an episodic character. Their fundamental importance consists of the fact that they permit us to debouch on the revolutionary road.

2. In the process of the struggle for these slogans of democracy, the party must shatter the constitutional and democratic illusions of the petty bourgeoisie and of the reformists who express their opinions, by explaining that power in the state is not obtained by the democratic forms of the vote, but by property and by the monopoly of information and armaments.

3. While making full use of the differences of views existing within the petty and the big bourgeoisie on the subject of constitutional questions; while opening up every possible road towards an openly exercised field of activity; while fighting for the legal existence of the trade unions, the workers' clubs, the labour press; while creating, whenever and wherever possible, legal political organisations of the proletariat under the direct influence of the party; while trying as soon as possible to legalise more or less the various fields of activity of the party; the latter must above all assure the existence of its illegal, centralized, well-built apparatus, directing all the branches of the party's activity, legal as well as illegal.

4. The party must develop systematic revolutionary work among the troops of the bourgeoisie.

5. The leadership of the party must implacably unmask all the opportunist hesitations seeking a reformist solution of the problems confronting the proletariat of China and must cut off all the elements who consciously pull towards the subordination of the party to bourgeois legalism.

It is only by taking these conditions into account that the party will preserve the necessary proportions in the various branches of its activity, will not let pass a new turn in the situation which leads towards a revolutionary advance, so that its first steps proceed along the road of the creation of Soviets, of mobilising the masses around them and of opposing them to the bourgeois state, with all its parliamentary and democratic camouflage, should this happen to be realised.

4. Once More on the Slogan of the Democratic Dictatorship

The slogan of the Constituent Assembly is just as little opposed to the formula of the democratic dictatorship as it is to that of the dictatorship of the proletariat. Theoretical analysis and the history of our three revolutions indicate that.

In Russia, the formula of the democratic dictatorship of the proletariat and the peasantry was the algebraic expression, in other words, the most general, the broadest expression of the collaboration of the proletariat and the lower strata of the peasantry in the democratic revolution. The logic of this formula was conditioned by the fact that its fundamental magnitude had not been checked up in action. In particular, it was not possible to predict quite categorically if, in the conditions of the new epoch, the peasantry would be capable of becoming a more or less *independent* political power, to what extent it would be such, and what would the reciprocal political relations of the allies in the dictatorship which would result from it. The year 1905 did not bring the question to the point of a decisive verification. The year 1917 showed that when the peasantry bears on its back a party (the Socialist-Revolutionaries) independent of the vanguard of the proletariat, this party proves to be in complete dependence upon the imperialist bourgeoisie. In the course of the period from 1905 to 1917, the growing imperialist transformation of the petty-bourgeois democracy as well as of international social democracy, made gigantic progress. It was because of this that in 1917 the slogan of the democratic dictatorship of the proletariat and the peasantry was really realised in the dictatorship of the proletariat, drawing with it the peasant masses. By this very token, the 'transformation by growth' of the revolution, passing from the democratic phase to the socialist stage, took place with the dictatorship of the proletariat already established.

In China, the slogan of the democratic dictatorship of the proletariat and the peasantry might still have had a certain political logic, much more limited and episodic than in Russia, if it had been formulated at the right time in 1925-1926, in order to test out the animating forces of the revolution, so as to be replaced, also at the right time, by the dictatorship of the proletariat, drawing behind it the poor peasants. All that is necessary has been said about this in *The Criticism of the Draft Programme*. Here, it still remains to ask: Does not the present inter-revolutionary period, bound up with a new regrouping of class forces, allow one to discern possibilities of the rebirth of the slogan of the democratic dictatorship? To this we reply: No, it makes this possibility disappear completely. The period of inter-revolutionary stabilisation corresponds to the development of the productive forces, to the growth of the national bourgeoisie, to the growth and the increase of the cohesion of the proletariat, to the accentuation of the differentiation in the villages and to the continuation of the capitalist degeneration of democracy *à la* Wang Chin Wei or any other petty-bourgeois democrat, with their 'third party', etc. In other words, China will pass through processes analogous in their broad outlines to those through which Russia passed under the regime of June 3. We were certain in our time that this regime would not be eternal, nor of long duration, and that it would terminate by a revolution. That is what happened (somewhat aided by the war). But the Russia which came out of the regime of Stolypin was no longer what it had been when it entered it. The social changes which the inter-revolutionary regime will introduce in China depend especially upon the duration of this regime. But the general tendency of these modifications is henceforth indisputable: it is the sharpening of the class contradictions and the complete elimination of the petty-bourgeois democracy as an independent political power. But this signifies precisely that in the third Chinese revolution, a 'democratic' coalition of the political parties would acquire a still more reactionary and more anti-proletarian content than that of the Kuomintang in 1925-1927. There is therefore nothing left to do but to make a coalition of classes under the direct leadership of the proletarian vanguard. That is the road of October. It involves many difficulties, but there exists no other.

5.   APPENDIX

A Remarkable Document on the Policy and the Regime of
the Communist International

We referred above several times to the remarkable resolution of the Plenum of the Central Committee of the Chinese Communist Party (November 1927), precisely the one which the Ninth Plenum of the Executive Committee of the Communist International charged with 'Trotskyism', and about which Lominadze justified himself in such a variegated manner while Stalin very monotonously slunk off in silence. In reality, this resolution is a combination of opportunism and adventurism, reflecting with perfect precision the policy of the Executive Committee of the Communist International before and after July 1927. In condemning this resolution *after the defeat of the Canton insurrection,* the leaders of the Communist International not only did not publish it but did not even quote from it. It was too embarrassing for them to show themselves in the Chinese mirror. This resolution was published in a special *Documentation,* accessible to very few, printed by the Chinese Sun Yat Sen University (No. 10).

No. 14 of the same publication, which reached our hands when our work (*The Chinese Question After the Sixth Congress*) was already completed, contains a no less remarkable document, even though of a different, that is, of a critical character: it is a resolution adopted by the Kiangsu District Committee of the Chinese Communist Party on May 7, 1928, in connection with the decisions of the Ninth Plenum of the Executive Committee of the Comintern. Remember that Shanghai and Canton are part of the province of Kiangsu.

This resolution, as has already been said, constitutes a truly remarkable document, in spite of the errors in principle and the political misunderstandings it contains. The essence of the resolution amounts to a deadly condemnation not only of the decisions of the Ninth Plenum of the Executive Committee of the Communist International, but in general, of the whole leadership of the Comintern in the questions of the Chinese revolution. Naturally, in conformity with the whole regime existing in the Comintern, the criticism directed against the Executive Committee of the CI bears a camouflaged and conventionally diplomatic character. The immediate point of the resolution is directed against the Central Committee itself as against a responsible ministry under an irresponsible monarch who, as is known, 'can do no wrong'. There are even polite eulogies for certain parts of the resolution of the ECCI. This whole way of approaching the question by 'manoeuvring' is in itself a harsh criticism of the regime of the Communist International; hypocrisy is inseparable from bureaucratism. But what the resolution says in essence about the political leadership and its methods has a much more damning character.

'After the August 7 (1927) conference,' the Kiangsu Committee relates, 'the Central Committee formulated a judgment on the situation which was tantamount to saying that even though the revolution had suffered a triple defeat, it is nevertheless going through a rising phase.' This appreciation is entirely in conformity with the caricature which Bukharin makes of the theory of the permanent revolution, a caricature which he applied first to Russia, then to Europe and finally to Asia. The actual events of the struggle, that is, the three defeats, are one thing and the permanent 'rise' is another.

The Central Committee of the Chinese party draws the following conclusion from the resolution adopted by the Eighth Plenum of the Executive Committee of the Communist International (in May):

Wherever this is objectively possible, we must *immediately* prepare and organise armed insurrections.

What are the political premises for this? The Kiangsu Committee declares that in August 1927

the political report of the Central Committee pointed out that the *workers* of Hunan, after the cruel *defeat, are abandoning the leadership of the party*, that we are not confronted with an objectively revolutionary situation . . . but in spite of this . . . the Central Committee says plainly that the general situation, from the economic, political and social [precisely!—L.T.] point of view is favourable to the insurrection. Since *it is already no longer possible to launch revolts in the cities,* the armed struggle must be transferred to the villages. That is where the centres of the uprising must be, while the town must be an auxiliary force. (Page 4.)

Let us recall that immediately after the May Plenum of the Executive Committee of the Communist International, which entrusted the leadership of the agrarian revolution to the Left Kuomintang, the latter began to exterminate the workers and peasants. The position of the ECCI became completely untenable. At all costs, there had to be, and that without delay, 'Left' actions in China to refute the 'calumny' of the Opposition, that is, its irreproachable prognosis. That is why the Chinese Central Committee, which found itself between the hammer and the anvil, was obliged, in August 1927, to turn the proletarian policy topsy-turvy all over again. Even though there was no revolutionary situation and the working masses were abandoning the party, this Committee declared that the economic and social situation was, in its opinion, 'favourable to the insurrection'. In any case, a triumphant uprising would have been very 'favourable' to the prestige of the Executive Committee of the Comintern. Given the fact that the workers were abandoning the revolution, it was therefore necessary to turn one's back to the towns and endeavour to launch isolated uprisings in the villages.

Already at the May Plenum (1927) of the ECCI, we pointed out that the adventurist uprisings of Ho Lung and Yeh-Ting were inevitably doomed to defeat because of insufficient political preparation and because they were bound up with no movement of the masses. That is just what happened. The resolution of the Kiangsu Committee says on this subject:

> In spite of the defeat of the armies of Ho Lung and Yeh-Ting in Kwangtung, even after the November Plenum the Central Committee persists in clinging to the tactic of immediate uprisings and takes as its point of departure an estimation leading to the direct ascent of the revolution.

For understandable reasons, the Kiangsu Committee passes in silence over the fact that this appreciation was also that of the Executive Committee of the Comintern itself, which treated as 'liquidators' those who correctly estimated the situation, and the fact that the Chinese Central Committee was forced, in November 1927, on pain of being immediately overthrown and expelled from the party, to present the decline of the revolution as its rise.

The Canton insurrection sprang up by basing itself upon this tip-tilted manner of approaching the question; manifestly, this uprising was not regarded as a rear-guard battle (only raging madmen could have urged passing over to the insurrection and to the conquest of power through a 'rear-guard battle'); no, this uprising was conceived as part of a general *coup d'état*. The Kiangsu resolution says on this point:

> During the Canton insurrection of December, the Central Committee decided once more to launch an immediate uprising in Hunan, Hupeh and Kiangsu in order to defend Kwangtung, in order to extend the framework of the movement all over China (this can be verified from the information letters of the Central Committee, Nos. 16 and 22). These measures flowed from a subjective estimation of the situation and did not correspond to the objective circumstances. Obviously, under such conditions defeats will be inevitable. (Page 5.)

The Canton experience frightened the leaders not only of China but also of Moscow. A warning was issued against putschism, but in essence the political line did not change. The orientation remained the same: towards insurrection. The

Central Committee of the Chinese Communist Party transmitted this ambiguous instruction to the lower bodies; it also warned against the tactic of skirmishes, while setting down in its circulars academic definitions of adventurism.

'But being given the fact that the Central Committee based itself in its estimation of the revolutionary movement, upon an uninterrupted advance,' as the Kiangsu resolution says correctly and pointedly, 'no modifications were brought into this question at the bottom. The forces of the enemy are far too greatly under-rated and at the same time, no attention is paid to the fact that our organisations have lost contact with the masses. . . . Therefore, in spite of the fact that the Central Committee had sent its information letter No. 28 (on putschism) everywhere, it did not at the same time correct its mistakes.' (Page 5.)

Once more, it is not a question of the Central Committee of the Chinese party. The February Plenum of the Executive Committee of the Communist International introduced no modifications into its policy either. While warning against the tactics of skirmishes in general (in order to insure itself against all eventualities), the resolution of this Plenum pounced furiously upon the Opposition which spoke of the necessity of a resolute change in the whole orientation. In February 1928, the course continued as before to lead towards insurrection. The Central Committee of the Chinese Communist Party only served as a mechanism to transmit this instruction. The Kiangsu Committee says:

The Central Committee circular No. 38, of March 6 [take careful note: March 6, 1928!—L.T.] shows very clearly that the Central Committee still finds itself under the influence of illusions about a favourable situation for general insurrection in Hunan, Hupeh and Kiangsu, and the possibility of conquering power throughout the province of Kwangtung. The radical quarrel over the choice of Changsha or Hankow as the centre of insurrection still continued between the Political Bureau of the Central Committee and the instructor of the Central Committee in Hunan and Hupeh. (Page 5.)

Such was the disastrous significance of the resolution of the February Plenum, not only false in principle, but deliberately ambiguous from the practical point of view. The thought concealed behind this resolution was always the same: if, contrary to expectations, the uprising extends itself, we shall refer to that part which speaks against the liquidators; if the insurrection goes no further than partisan affrays, we will point a finger at that part of the resolution which warns against putschism.

Even though the Kiangsu resolution nowhere dares to criticise the Executive Committee of the Communist International (everybody knows what this costs), nevertheless, in none of its documents has the Opposition dealt such deadly blows to the leadership of the Comintern as does the Kiangsu Committee in its arraignment, aimed formally at the Central Committee of the Chinese Communist Party. After listing chronologically the policies of adventurism month after month, the resolution turns to the general causes for the disastrous course.

'How is one to explain,' asks the resolution, 'this erroneous estimation of the situation established by the Central Committee which influenced the practical struggle and contained serious errors? It is to be explained as follows:

'1. The revolutionary movement was estimated as an uninterrupted ascent [the "permanent revolution" à la Bukharin-Lominadze!—L.T.].

'2. No attention was paid to the loss of contact between our party and the masses, nor to the decomposition of the mass organisations at the turning point of the revolution.

'3. No account was taken of the new regrouping of class forces inside the enemy camp during this turn.

'4. No consideration was given to leading the movement in the cities.

'5. No attention was paid to the importance of the anti-imperialist movement in a semi-colonial country.

'6. During the insurrection, no account was taken of the objective conditions, nor of the necessity of applying different methods of struggle in conformity with them.

'7. A peasant deviation made itself felt.

'8. The Central Committee, in its estimation of the situation, was guided by a subjective point of view.'

It is doubtful if the Kiangsu Committee has read what the Opposition wrote and said on all these questions. One can even say with certainty that it did not read it. As a matter of fact, if it had, it would have feared to formulate with such precision its considerations, coinciding entirely in this part with ours. The Kiangsu Committee repeated our words without suspecting it.

The eight points enumerated above, characterising the false line of the Central Committee (that is, the Executive Committee of the Communist International) are equally important. If we wish to say a few words on the fifth point, it is simply because we have here a particularly striking confirmation 'by facts' of the justice of our criticism in its most essential features. The Kiangsu resolution charges the policy of the Central Committee with neglecting the problems of the anti-imperialist movement in a semi-colonial country. How could this happen? By the force of the dialectic of the false political line; mistakes have their dialectic like everything else in the world. The point of departure of official opportunism was that the Chinese revolution is essentially an anti-imperialist revolution, and that the yoke of imperialism welds together all the classes or at the very least 'all the living forces of the country'. We objected that a successful struggle against imperialism is only possible by means of an audacious extension of the class struggle,

and consequently, of the agrarian revolution. We rose up intransigently against the attempt to subordinate the class struggle
to the abstract criterion of the struggle against imperialism
(substitution of arbitration commissions for the strike movement,
telegraphic advice not to stir up the agrarian revolution, prohibit-
ing the formation of Soviets, etc.). This was the first stage of
the question. After Chiang Kai-shek's *coup d'état,* and especially
after the 'treason' of the 'friend' Wang Chin Wei, there was
a turn about face of 180 degrees. Now, it turns out to be that
the question of customs independence, that is, of the economic
'(and consequently, the political)' sovereignty of China is a
secondary 'bureaucratic' problem (Stalin). The essence of the
Chinese revolution was supposed to consist of the agrarian
upheaval. The concentration of power in the hands of the
bourgeoisie, the abandonment of the revolution by the workers,
the schism between the party and the masses, were appraised
as secondary phenomena in comparison with the peasant revolts.
Instead of a genuine hegemony of the proletariat, in the anti-
imperialist as well as in the agrarian struggle, that is, in the
democratic revolution as a whole, there took place a wretched
capitulation before the primitive peasant forces, with 'secondary'
adventures in the cities. However, such a capitulation is the
fundamental premise of putschism. The whole history of the
revolutionary movement in Russia, as well as in other countries,
is witness to that. The events in China of the past year have
confirmed it.

In its estimation and its warnings, the Opposition took as
its point of departure general theoretical considerations, basing
itself upon official information, very incomplete and sometimes
deliberately distorted. The Kiangsu Committee has as its point
of departure facts which it observed directly at the centre of
the revolutionary movement; from the theoretical point of
view this Committee still writhes in the toils of Bukharinist
scholasticism. The fact that its empirical conclusions coincide

completely with our own has, in politics, the same significance as, for example, the discovery in laboratories of a new element whose existence was predicted in advance on the basis of theoretical deductions has in chemistry. Unfortunately, the triumph from the theoretical point of view of our Marxian analysis, in the case before us, has as its political foundation mortal defeats for the revolution.

*   *   *

The abrupt and essentially adventurist turn in the policy of the Executive Committee of the Communist International in the middle of 1927 could not but provoke painful shocks in the Chinese Communist Party, which was taken off its guard by it. Here we pass from the political line of the Executive Committee of the Communist International to the regime of the Comintern and to the organisational methods of the leadership. Here is what the Kiangsu Committee resolution says on this point:

> After the conference of August 7 (1927), the Central Committee should have assumed the responsibility for the putschist tendencies, for it demanded rigorously of the local committees that the *new political line* be applied; if anybody was not in agreement with *the new line,* without further ceremony he was not permitted to renew his party card and even comrades who had already carried out this operation were expelled. . . . At this time, the putschist mood was making headway throughout the party; if anybody expressed doubts about the policy of uprisings, he was immediately called an opportunist and pitilessly attacked. This circumstance provoked great friction within the party organisations. (Page 6.)

All this took place with the accompaniment of pious academic warnings against the dangers of putschism 'in general'.

The policy of the sudden, hastily improvised armed insurrection demanded a speedy overhauling and a regrouping of the entire party. The Central Committee tolerated in the party only those who silently acknowledged the course of armed in-

surrection in the face of an obvious decline of the revolution.
It would be well to publish the instructions furnished by the
Executive Committee of the Communist International during
this period. They could be reduced to one: an instruction
for the organisation of defeat. The Kiangsu resolution sets
forth that

> The Central Committee continues not to take notice of the defeats
> and the depressed mood of the workers; it does not see that this
> situation is the result of the mistakes of its leadership. (Page 6.)

But that is not all:

> The Central Committee accuses someone or other [just so!—L.T.]
> for the fact that:

> (a) the local committees have not sufficiently well checked up on the
> reorganisation;

> (b) the worker and peasant elements are not *pushed ahead;*

> (c) the local organisations are not purged of opportunist elements, etc.

All this happens abruptly, by telegraph: somehow or other,
the mouth of the Opposition must be closed. But nevertheless
since matters are in a bad way, the Central Committee asserts
that

'. . . the disposition of the masses would be entirely
different if the signal for revolt had been given at least in one
single province. Does not this last indication bespeak a one
hundred per cent putschism of the Central Committee itself?'
(page 6) asks the Kiangsu Committee with full justice, passing
prudently over in silence that the Central Committee only
executed the instructions of the Executive Committee of the
Communist International.

For five years the party was led and educated in an
opportunist spirit. At the present moment, it is demanded of
it that it be ultra-radical and 'that it immediately put forward'
worker-leaders. How? . . . Very simply: by fixing a certain

percentage of them. The Kiangsu Committee complains:

1. No account is taken of the fact that the ones who are to supplement the leading cadres should be advanced in the course of the struggle. Whereas the Central Committee confines itself to a formal establishment of a percentage fixed in advance of workers and peasants in the leading organs of the various organisations.

2. In spite of the numerous failures, they do not examine the point to which our party is already restored, but they simply say formally that it is necessary to reorganise. . . .

3. The Central Committee simply says dictatorially that the local organisations do not put forward new elements, that they do not rid themselves of opportunism; at the same time, the Central Committee makes baseless attacks upon the militants of the cadres and replaces them light-mindedly.

4. Without paying attention to the mistakes of its own leadership, the Central Committee nevertheless demands the most severe party discipline from the rank-and-file militants.

Does it not seem as though all these paragraphs are copied from the *Platform of the Opposition?* No, they are copied from life. But since the *Platform* is also copied from life, there is no coincidence. Where then is the 'peculiarity' of Chinese conditions? Bureaucratism levels down each and every peculiarity. The policy as well as the regime are determined by the Executive Committee of the Communist International, more exactly by the Central Committee of the Communist Party of the Soviet Union. The Central Committee of the Chinese Communist Party drives both of them down into the lower organs. Here is how this takes place according to the Kiangsu resolution:

The following declaration made by a comrade of a district committee is very characteristic: 'At present it is very difficult to work; but the Central Committee shows that it has a very subjective manner of regarding the problem. It pounces down with accusations and says that the Provincial Committee is no good; the latter in its turn accuses the rank and file organisations and asserts that the district committee is bad. The latter also begins to accuse and asserts that it is the comrades working on the spot who are no good. And the comrades declare that the masses are not revolutionary.' (Page 8.)

There you really have a striking picture. Only, there is nothing peculiarly Chinese about it.

Every resolution of the Executive Committee of the Communist International, in registering new defeats, declares that on the one hand all had been foreseen and that on the other it is the 'executors' who are the cause of the defeats because they did not understand the line that had been pointed out to them from above. It remains unexplained how the perspicacious leadership was able to foresee everything save that the executors did not measure up to its instuctions. The essential thing in the leadership does not consist of presenting an abstract line, of writing a letter without an address, but of selecting and educating the executors. The correctness of the leadership is tested precisely in execution. The reliability and perspicacity of the leadership are confirmed only when words and deeds harmonise. But if chronically, from one stage to the other, in the course of many years, the leadership is obliged *post factum* to complain at every turn that it has not been understood, that its ideas have been deformed, that the executors have ruined its plan, that is a sure sign that the fault devolves entirely upon the leadership. This 'self-criticism' is all the more murderous by the fact that it is involuntary and unconscious. According to the Sixth Congress, the leadership of the Opposition must be held responsible for every group of turncoats; but *per contra* the leadership of the Communist International should in no wise have to answer for the Central Committee of all the national parties in the most decisive historical moments. But a leadership which is answerable for nothing is an irresponsible leadership. In that is to be found the root of all the evils.

In protecting itself against the criticism of the ranks, the Central Committee of the Chinese Communist Party bases itself on the Executive Committee of the Communist International, that is, it draws a chalk line on the floor which cannot be stepped over. Nor does the Kiangsu Committee overstep it.

But within the confines of this chalk line, it tells some bitter truths to its Central Committee which automatically extend to the Executive Committee of the Communist International. We are once more forced to quote an extract from the remarkable document of Kiangsu:

> The Central Committee says that the whole past leadership was exercised in accordance with the instructions of the Communist International. As if all these hesitations and errors depended only upon the rank and file militants. If one adopts such a manner of regarding the question, the Central Committee will itself be unable either to repair the mistakes or to educate the comrades to study this experience. It will not be able to strengthen its ties with the lower party apparatus. The Central Committee always says that its leadership was right; it charges the rank and file comrades with all the mistakes, always especially underscoring the hesitations of the rank and file party committees.

A little further on:

> If the leadership only attacks light-mindedly the local leading comrades or organs by pointing out their errors, but without actually analysing the source of these mistakes, this only produces friction within the party; such an attitude is disloyal ['rude and disloyal'.— L.T.] and can do no good to the revolution and to the party. If the leadership itself covers up its errors and throws the blame on others, such conduct will do no good to the party or to the revolution. (Page 10.)

A simple but classic characterisation of bureaucratic centrism's work of decaying and devastating the consciousness.

The Kiangsu resolution shows in an entirely exemplary manner how and by what methods the Chinese revolution was led to numerous defeats, and the Chinese party to the brink of catastrophe. For the imaginary hundred thousand members who figure on paper in the Chinese Communist Party only represent a gross self-deception. They would then constitute one-sixth of the total membership of the Communist parties of all the capitalist countries. The payments which Chinese Communism must make for the crime of the leadership are still far from completed.

Further decline is ahead. There will be great difficulty in rising again. Every false step will fling the party into a deeper ditch. The resolution of the Sixth Congress dooms the Chinese Communist Party to errors and false steps. With the present course of the Communist International, under its present regime, victory is impossible. The course must be changed. This is what the resolution of the Kiangsu Provincial Committee says once more.

Alma Ata, October 4, 1928.

What is Happening in China?

A QUESTION EVERY COMMUNIST MUST ASK HIMSELF

A MONG THE telegrams in *Pravda* there has been communicated several times during October, in the smallest type, that an armed Communist detachment under the command of comrade Chu-Deh is advancing successfully towards Chao-Cho (Kwangtung), that this detachment has grown from 5,000 to 20,000, etc. Thus we learn, as if incidentally, from the laconic telegrams in *Pravda* that the Chinese Communists are conducting an armed struggle against Chiang Kai-shek. What is the meaning of this struggle? Its origins? Its perspectives? Not a word is breathed to us about it. If the new revolution in China has matured to the point that the Communists have taken to arms, then it would seem necessary to mobilise the whole International in the face of events of such gigantic historical importance. Why then do we hear nothing of the sort? And if the situation in China is not such as puts on the order of the day the armed struggle of the Communists for power, then how and why has a Communist detachment begun an armed struggle against Chiang Kai-shek, that is, against the bourgeois military dictatorship?

Yes, why have the Chinese Communists risen in rebellion? Perhaps because the Chinese proletariat has already found the time to heal its wounds? Because the demoralised and debilitated Communist party has found the time to rise on the revolutionary wave? Have the city workers ensured their contact with the revolutionary masses of the country? Has the general strike pushed the proletariat to the insurrection? If such is the case, then everything is clear and in order. But then why does *Pravda* communicate these events in a few lines and in small type?

Or perhaps the Chinese Communists have risen in rebellion because they have received the latest comments of Molotov on the resolution on the 'third period'? It is no accident that Zinoviev who, in distinction to the other capitulators, still pretends to be alive, has come out in *Pravda* with an article which shows that the domination of Chiang Kai-shek is entirely similar to the temporary domination of Kolchak, that is, is only a simple episode in the process of the revolutionary rise. This analogy is of course bracing to the spirit. Unfortunately, it is not only false, but simply stupid. Kolchak organised an insurrection in one province against the dictatorship of the proletariat already established in the greater part of the country. In China, bourgeois counter-revolution rules in the country and it is the Communists who have stirred up an insurrection of a few thousand people in one of the provinces. We think, therefore, we have the right to pose this question: Does this insurrection spring from the situation in China or rather from the instructions concerning the 'third period'? We ask further, what is the political role of the Chinese Communist Party in all this? What are the slogans with which it mobilised the masses? What is the degree of its influence upon the workers? We hear nothing about all this. The rebellion of Chu-Deh appears to be a reproduction of the adventurist campaigns of Ho Lung and Yeh-Ting in 1927 and the Canton uprising timed for the moment of the expulsion of the Opposition from the Russian Communist Party.

Perhaps the rebellion broke out spontaneously? Well and good. But then what is the meaning of the Communist banner unfurled above it? What is the attitude of the official

Chinese Communist Party towards the insurrection? What is the position of the Comintern in this question? And why, finally, in communicating this fact to us, does the Moscow *Pravda* abstain from any comment?

But there is still another explanation possible, which is perhaps the most alarming one: Have the Chinese Communists risen in rebellion because of Chiang Kai-shek's seizure of the Chinese Eastern Railway? Has this insurrection, wholly partisan in character, as its aim to cause Chiang Kai-shek uneasiness at his rear? If that is what it is, we ask who has given such counsel to the Chinese Communists? Who bears the political responsibility for their passing over to guerilla warfare?

It was not long ago that we decisively condemned the ramblings on the necessity of handing over so important an instrument as the Chinese Eastern from the hands of the Russian revolution to those of the Chinese counter-revolution. We called to mind the elementary duty of the international proletariat in this conflict to defend the Republic of the Soviets against the Chinese bourgeoisie and all its possible instigators and allies. But on the other hand it is quite clear that the proletariat of the USSR, which has power and an army in its hands, cannot demand that the vanguard of the Chinese proletariat begin a war at once against Chiang Kai-shek, that is, that it apply the means which the Soviet government itself does not find possible, and correctly so, to apply. Had a war begun between the USSR and China, or rather between the USSR and the imperialist patrons of China, the duty of the Chinese Communists would be to transform this war in the shortest time into a civil war. But even in that case the launching of the civil war would have to be subordinated to general revolutionary policy; and even then the Chinese Communists would be unable to pass over arbitrarily, and at any moment at all, to the road of open insurrection, but only after having assured themselves of the necessary support of the worker and peasants masses. The rebellion in Chiang Kai-shek's rear, in this situation, would be an extension of the front of the Soviet workers and peasants; the fate of the insurgent Chinese workers would be intimately bound up with the fate of the Soviet republic; the tasks, the aims, the perspectives would be quite clear.

But what is the perspective opened up by this uprising of the today isolated Chinese Communists in the absence of war or revolution? The perspective of a terrific débâcle and of an adventurist degeneration of the remnants of the Communist party.

In the meantime, it must be said openly: calculations based upon guerilla adventure correspond entirely to the general nature of Stalinist policy. Two years ago, Stalin expected gigantic gains for the security of the Soviet state from the alliance with the imperialists of the General Council of the British trade unions. Today, he is quite capable of calculating that a rebellion of the Chinese Communists, even without any hope, would bring 'a little profit' in a precarious situation. In the first case, the calculation was grossly opportunist, in the second, openly adventurist, but in both cases, the calculation is made independently of the general tasks of the world labour movement, against these tasks and to the detriment of the correctly understood interests of the Soviet republic.

We have not at our disposal all the necessary data for a definite conclusion. That is why we ask:

What is happening in China? Let it be explained to us! The Communist who does not pose the question to himself and to the leadership of his party will be unworthy of the name of Communist. The leadership that would like to remain discreetly on the sidelines in order, in case of a defeat of the Chinese partisans, to wash its hands and transfer responsibility to the Central Committee of the Chinese Communist Party— such a leadership would dishonour itself—not for the first time, it is true—by the most abominable crime against the interests of the international revolution.

We ask: What is happening in China? We will continue to pose this question until we have forced a reply.

Prinkipo, November 9, 1929.

A Retreat in Full Disorder

MANUILSKY ON THE 'DEMOCRATIC DICTATORSHIP'

IN THE anniversary number of *Pravda* (November 7), Manuilsky once more shows the value of the present leadership of the Comintern. We will analyse briefly that part of his anniversary reflections devoted to China, and which amounts in essence to a cowardly, deliberately confused, and therefore all the more dangerous, semi-capitulation to the theory of the permanent revolution.

1. 'A revolutionary-democratic dictatorship of the peasantry and proletariat in China,' writes Manuilsky, 'will differ essentially from the democratic dictatorship outlined [!] by the Bolsheviks in the 1905-1906 revolution.'

The democratic dictatorship was 'outlined' by the Bolsheviks not only in 1905, but also in 1917 and in all the years between the two revolutions. But only *outlined*. Events served as a test. Manuilsky, like his teacher Stalin, does not reflect upon the points of resemblance and the points of difference of the Chinese revolution with the three Russian revolutions—no, with such comparison they would be unable to preserve the fiction of the democratic dictatorship, and along with it, the fiction of their theoretical reputations. Therefore these gentlemen do not compare the Chinese revolution with the real Russian revolution, but with the one that was 'outlined'. It is much easier in this way to confuse and to throw dust in the eyes.

2. In what respect then does the revolution taking place in China differ from the one 'outlined' in Russia? In the fact, we are taught by Manuilsky, that the Chinese revolution is directed against the 'whole system of world imperialism'! It is true that this was the basis upon which Manuilsky yesterday depended for the revolutionary role of the Chinese bourgeoisie as against the Bolshevik position 'outlined in 1905'. Today, however, Manuilsky's conclusions are different: 'The difficulties of the Chinese revolution are tremendous; and this is precisely why the victorious movement of the Chinese Red Army upon the industrial centres of China had to halt at Changsha.' It would have been much more simple and honest to say that the partisan peasant detachments, *in the absence of revolutionary uprisings in the cities,* found themselves powerless to take possession of the industrial and political centres of the country. Wasn't this clear to Marxists beforehand?

But Manuilsky must needs save Stalin's speech at the Sixteenth Congress. Here is how he fulfills this task:

> 'The Chinese revolution has at its disposal a Red army, it is in possession of a considerable territory, at this very moment it is creating on this territory a Soviet system of workers' and peasants' power in whose government the Communists are in the majority. And this condition permits the proletariat to realise not only an ideological but also *a state hegemony over the peasantry.* [Our emphasis.]

The fact that the Communists, as the revolutionary and most self-sacricing elements, appear at the head of the peasant movement and the armed peasant detachments, is quite natural in itself and is also exceptionally important in the symptomatic sense. But this does not change the fact that the Chinese workers find themselves throughout their vast country under the heel of the Chinese bourgeoisie and foreign imperialism. In what way can the proletariat realise 'state hegemony' over the peasantry, when the state power is not in its hands? It is absolutely impossible to understand this. The leading role of the isolated Communists and the isolated Communist groups in the peasant war does not decide the question of power. Classes decide and not parties. The peasant war may support the dictatorship of the proletariat, if they coincide in point of time, but under no circumstances can it be substituted for the dictatorship of the proletariat. Is it possible that the 'leaders' of the Comintern have not learned even this from the experiences of the three Russian revolutions?

3. Let us listen further to Manuilsky: 'All these [?] conditions lead to the fact that a revolutionary-democratic dictatorship in China will be confronted with the necessity of a *consistent confiscation of the enterprises belonging to foreign and Chinese capital.*' (Our emphasis.)

'All these conditions' is a commonplace whose purpose is to cover up the gap created in the old position. But the centre of gravity in the phrase quoted above is not in 'all these conditions' but in one single 'condition': Manuilsky has been instructed to manoeuvre away from the democratic dictatorship and to cover up the traces. This is why Manuilsky so diligently, but not very skilfully, wags his tail.

The democratic dictatorship can be contrasted only to the proletarian socialist dictatorship. The one differs from the other by the character of the class holding power and by the social content of its historical work. If the democratic dictatorship is to occupy itself not with clearing the road for capitalist development, as stated in the Bolshevik schema 'outlined in 1905', but on the contrary, with a 'consistent confiscation of the enterprises belonging to foreign and Chinese capital', as 'outlined' by Manuilsky, then we ask: wherein does this *democratic* dictatorship differ from the *socialist?* In no way. Then does it mean that Manuilsky, for the second time* after

---

* The reference is to the following passage from an article written by Manuilsky in 1918 and adduced to the latter's discomfiture at the

a lapse of twelve years, has bitten into the apple of the 'permanent' theory? He bit without really taking a bite: this will yet be seen.

4. We read one phrase after another. 'The presence of socialist elements will be the specific [!] peculiarity of the revolutionary-democratic dictatorship of the proletariat and peasantry in China.' Not a bad 'specific' peculiarity!

The democratic dictatorship was always thought of by the Bolsheviks as a *bourgeois*-democratic dictatorship, and not as a supra-class one, and was contrasted to the *socialist* dictatorship only in this—the only possible—sense. Now it appears that in China there will be a 'democratic dictatorship with socialist elements'. Between the bourgeois and socialist regimes, the class abyss thus disappears, everything is dissolved into pure democracy, and this pure democracy is supplemented gradually and planfully by 'socialist elements'.

Who did these people learn from? From Victor Chernov. It is precisely he who, in 1905-1906, outlined such a Russian revolution as would be neither bourgeois nor socialist, but democratic, and would gradually be supplemented by socialist elements. No, Manuilsky did not make much use of the apple of wisdom!

5. Further: the Chinese revolution in its transition from capitalism to socialism will have more intermediate stages than our October revolution: but the periods of its *growing over* into

---

November 1926 Plenum of the ECCI: 'Russian Bolshevism, born in the nationally-confined revolution of 1905-1906, had to go through the purification ritual of liberation from all the typical features of national peculiarity in order to receive full citizenship rights of an international ideology. Theoretically, this purging of Bolshevism of the national varnish that clung to it was carried through by Trotsky in 1905, who endeavoured to connect the Russian revolution with the whole international movement of the proletariat in the idea of the permanent revolution.'—Tr.

a socialist revolution will be considerably shorter than the periods outlined (!) by the Bolsheviks for the democratic dictatorship in 1905.

Our astrologer has drawn the balance to everything in advance: to the stages, the periods, and the length of the periods. He only forgot the A B C of Communism. It appears that under democracy, capitalism will *grow over* into socialism in a series of stages. And the power—will it remain the same in this process or will it change? What class will hold power under the democratic dictatorship and what class under the socialist? If different classes will hold power then they can supplant each other only by a new revolution, and not through the 'growing over' of the power of one class into the power of another. On the other hand, if it is assumed that in both periods one and the same class will dominate, that is, the proletariat, then what is the meaning of the democratic dictatorship as against the proletarian? To this there can be no answer. And there will not be. Manuilsky is ordered not to clear up the question but to cover up the traces.

In the October revolution, the democratic *tasks* grew over into socialist ones—under the unaltered domination of the proletariat. One can therefore draw a distinction (it is understood, only relatively) between the democratic period of the October revolution and the socialist period; but one cannot distinguish between the democratic and the socialist dictatorships because the democratic was—non-existent.

In addition, we have heard from Manuilsky that in China the democratic dictatorship, from the very beginning, will be confronted with a consistent confiscation of the enterprises, which means the expropriation of the bourgeoisie. This means that there will not even be a democratic stage of the proletarian dictatorship. Under these conditions, where will the democratic dictatorship come from?

Manuilsky's injudicious construction would be entirely impossible were he to compare the Chinese revolution with the Russian as it actually developed, and not with the one that was 'outlined', and at that, to confuse and distort the outline. And all this to what end? In order to retreat without retreating, in order to give up the reactionary formula of the democratic dictatorship, or, as they say in China, to save face. But on the face of Stalin-Manuilsky have already written, first, Chiang Kai-shek and then Wang Chin Wei! Enough! The face is already sufficiently descriptive. They cannot save it any more. Manuilsky's theoretical confusion is directed against the basic interests of the Chinese revolution. The Chinese Bolshevik-Leninists will reveal this.

Prinkipo, November 1930.

The Strangled Revolution

THE BOOK by André Malraux, *Les Conquérants,** was sent to me from various quarters and I think in four copies, but to my regret I read it after a delay of a year and a half or two. The book is devoted to the Chinese revolution, that is, to the greatest subject of the last five years. A fine and well-knit style, the discriminating eye of an artist, original and daring observation—all confer upon the novel an exceptional importance. If we write about it here it is not because the book is a work of talent, although this is not a negligible fact, but because it offers a source of political lessons of the highest value. Do they come from Malraux? No, they flow from the recital itself, unknown to the author, and they go against him. This does honour to the author as an observer and an artist, but not as a revolutionist. However, we have the right to evaluate Malraux too from this point of view; in his own name and above all in the name of Garine, his other self, the author does not hesitate with his judgments on the revolution.

This book is called a novel. As a matter of fact, we have before us a romanticised chronicle of the Chinese revolution, from its first period to the period of Canton. The chronicle is not complete. Social vigour is sometimes lacking from the picture. But for that there pass before the reader not only luminous episodes of the revolution but also clear-cut

---

* The Conquerors, by André Malraux. Harcourt, Brace and Co., New York, 1929.

silhouettes which are graven in the memory like social symbols.

By little coloured touches, following the method of *pointillisme,* Malraux gives an unforgettable picture of the general strike, not, to be sure, as it is below, not as it is carried out, but as it is observed from above: the Europeans do not get their breakfast, they swelter in the heat, the Chinese have ceased to work in the kitchens and to operate the ventilators. This is not a reproach to the author: the foreign artist could undoubtedly not have dealt with his theme otherwise. But there is a reproach to be made, and not a small one: the book is lacking in a congenital affinity between the writer, in spite of all he knows, understands and can do, and his heroine, the revolution.

The active sympathies of the author for insurgent China are unmistakeable. But chance bursts upon these sympathies. They are corroded by the excesses of individualism and by aesthetic caprice. In reading the book with sustained attention one sometimes experiences a feeling of vexation when in the tone of the persuasive recital one perceives a note of protective irony towards the barbarians capable of enthusiasm. That China is backward, that many of its political manifestations bear a primitive character—nobody asks that this be passed over in silence. But a correct perspective is needed which puts every object in its place. The Chinese events, on the basis of which Malraux's 'novel' unfolds itself, are incomparably more important for the future destiny of human culture than the vain and pitiful clamour of Europe parliaments and the mountain of literary products of stagnant civilization. Malraux seems to feel a certain fear to take this into account.

In the novel, there are pages, splendid in their intensity, which show how revolutionary hatred is born of the yoke, of ignorance, of slavery, and is tempered like steel. These pages might have entered into the Anthology of the Revolution if Malraux had approached the masses with greater freedom and intrepidity, if he had not introduced into his observations a small note of *blasé* superiority, seeming to excuse himself for his transient contact with the insurrection of the Chinese people, as much perhaps before himself as before the academic mandarins in France and the traffickers in spiritual opium.

*   *   *

Borodin represents the Comintern in the post of 'high counsellor' in the Canton government. Garine, the favourite of the author, is in charge of propaganda. All the work is done within the framework of the Kuomintang. Borodin, Garine, the Russian 'General' Galen, the Frenchman Gérard, the German Klein and others, constitute an original bureaucracy of the revolution raising itself above the insurgent people and conducting its own 'revolutionary' policy instead of the policy of the revolution.

The local organisations of the Kuomintang are defined as follows: 'groups of fanatics—brave . . . of a few plutocrats out for notoriety or for security—and crowds of students and coolies'. (Page 24.) Not only do bourgeois enter into every organisation but they completely lead the party. The Communists are subordinate to the Kuomintang. The workers and the peasants are persuaded to take no action that might rebuff the devoted friends of the bourgeoisie. 'Such are the societies that we control (more or less, do not fool yourself on this score).' An edifying avowal! The bureaucracy of the Comintern tried to 'control' the class struggle in China, like the international bankocracy controls the economic life of the backward countries. But a revolution cannot be controlled. One can only give a political expression to its internal forces. One must know to which of these forces to link one's destiny.

'Today coolies are beginning to discover that they exist, simply that they exist.' (Page 26.) That's well aimed. But to feel that they exist, the coolies, the industrial workers and the peasants must overthrow those who prevent them from existing. Foreign domination is indissolubly bound up with the domestic yoke. The coolies must not only drive out Baldwin or MacDonald but also overthrow the ruling classes. One cannot be accomplished without the other. Thus, the awakening of the human personality in the masses of China, who exceed ten times the population of France, is immediately transformed into the lava of the social revolution. A magnificent spectacle!

But here Borodin appears on the scene and declares: 'In the revolution the workers must do the coolie work for the bourgeoisie,' wrote Chen Du-Siu in an open letter to the Chinese Communists. The social enslavement from which they want to liberate themselves, the workers find transposed into the sphere of politics. To whom do they owe this perfidious operation? To the bureaucracy of the Comintern. In trying to 'control' the Kuomintang, it actually aids the bourgeoisie which seeks 'notoriety and security' in enslaving the coolies who want to exist.

Borodin, who remains in the background all the time, is characterised in the novel as a 'man of action', as a 'professional revolutionist', as a living incarnation of Bolshevism on the soil of China. Nothing is further from the truth! Here is the political biography of Borodin: in 1903, at the age of 19, he emigrated to America; in 1918, he returned to Moscow where, thanks to his knowledge of English, he 'ensured contact with the foreign parties'; he was arrested in Glasgow in 1922; then he was delegated to China as representative of the Comintern. Having quit Russia *before* the first revolution and having returned *after* the third, Borodin appeared as the consummate representative of that state and party bureaucracy which recognised the revolution only after its victory. When it is a question of young people, it is sometimes nothing more than a matter of chronology. With people of 40 or 50, it is already a political characterisation. If Borodin rallied successfully to the victorious revolution in Russia, it does not in the least signify that he was called upon to assure the victory of the revolution in China. People of this type assimilate without difficulty the gestures and intonations of 'professional revolutionists'. Many of them, by their protective coloration, not only deceive others but also themselves. The audacious inflexibility of the Bolshevik is most usually metamorphosed with them into that cynicism of the functionary ready for anything. Ah! to have a mandate from the Central Committee! This sacrosanct safeguard Borodin always had in his pocket.

Garine is not a functionary, he is more original than Borodin and perhaps even closer to the revolutionary type. But he is devoid of the indispensable formation; dilettante and theatrical, he gets hopelessly entangled in the great events and he reveals it at every step. With regard to the slogans of the Chinese revolution, he expresses himself thus: '. . . democratic chatter—"the rights of the proletariat", etc.' (Page 32.) This has a radical ring but it is a false radicalism. The slogans of democracy are execrable chatter in the mouth of Poincaré, Herriot, Léon Blum, sleight-of-hand artists of France and pailers of Indo-China, Algeria and Morocco. But when the Chinese rebel in the name of the 'rights of the proletariat', this has as little to do with chatter as the slogans of the French revolution in the eighteenth century. At Hong Kong, the British birds of prey threatened, during the strike, to re-establish corporal punishment. 'The rights of man and of the citizen' meant at Hong Kong the right of the Chinese not to be flogged by the British whip. To unmask the democratic rottenness of the imperialists is to serve the revolution: to call the slogans of the insurrection of the oppressed 'chatter', is involuntarily to aid the imperialists.

A good inoculation of Marxism would have preserved the author from fatal contempt of this sort. But Garine in general considers that revolutionary doctrine is 'doctrinaire rubbish' (*le fatras doctrinal*). He is, you see, one of those to whom the revolution is only a definite 'state of affairs'. Isn't this astonishing? But it is just because the revolution is a 'state of affairs', that is, a stage in the development of society conditioned by objective causes and subjected to definite laws, that a scientific mind can foresee the general direction of processes. Only the study of the anatomy of society and of its physiology permits one to react to the course of events by basing oneself upon scientific foresight and not upon a dilettante's conjectures. The revolutionist who 'despises' revolutionary doctrine is not a bit better than the healer who despises medical doctrine which he does not know, or than the engineer who rejects technology. People who without the aid of science, try to rectify the 'state of affairs' which is called a disease, are called sorcerers or charlatans and are prosecuted by law. Had there existed a tribunal to judge the sorcerers of the revolution, it is probable that Borodin, like his Muscovite inspirers, would have been severely condemned. I am afraid Garine himself would not have come out of it unscathed.

Two figures are contrasted to each other in the novel, like the two poles of the national revolution; old Chen-Dai, the spiritual authority of the Right wing of the Kuomintang, the prophet and saint of the bourgeoisie, and Hong, the young leader of the terrorists. Both are depicted with great force. Chen-Dai embodies the old Chinese culture translated into the language of European breeding; with this exquisite garment, he 'ennobles' the interests of all the ruling classes of China. To be sure, Chen-Dai wants national liberation, but he dreads the masses more than the imperialists; he hates the revolution more than the yoke placed upon the nation. If he marches towards it, it is only to pacify it, to subdue it, to exhaust it. He conducts a policy of passive resistance on two fronts, against imperialism and against the revolution, the policy of Gandhi in India, the policy which, in definite periods and in one form or another, the bourgeoisie has conducted at every longitude and latitude. Passive resistance flows from the tendency of the bourgeoisie to canalise the movement of the masses and to make off with it.

When Garine says that Chen-Dai's influence rises above politics, one can only shrug his shoulders. The masked policy of the 'upright man', in China as in India, expresses in the most sublime and abstractly moralising form the conservative interests of the possessors. The personal disinterestedness of Chen-Dai is in no sense in opposition to his political function: the exploiters need 'upright ment' as the corrupted ecclesiastical hierarchy needs saints.

Who gravitate around Chen-Dai? The novel replies with meritorious precision: a world of 'aged mandarins, smugglers of opium and of obscene photographs, of scholars turned bicycle dealers, of Parisian barristers, of intellectuals of every kind'. (Page 124.) Behind them stands a more solid bourgeoisie bound up with England, which arms General Tang against the revolution. In the expectation of victory, Tang prepares to make Chen-Dai the head of the government. Both of them, Chen-Dai and Tang, nevertheless continue to be members of the Kuomintang which Borodin and Garine serve.

When Tang has a village attacked by his armies, and when he prepares to butcher the revolutionists, beginning with Borodin and Garine, his party comrades, the latter with the aid of Hong, mobilise and arm the unemployed. But after the victory won over Tang, the leaders do not seek to change a thing that existed before. They cannot break the ambiguous bloc with Chen-Dai because they have no confidence in the workers, the coolies, the revolutionary masses, they are themselves contaminated with the prejudices of Chen-Dai whose qualified arm they are.

In order 'not to rebuff' the bourgeoisie they are forced to enter into struggle with Hong. Who is he and where does he come from? 'The lowest dregs.' (Page 36.) He is one of those who are making the revolution and not those who rally to it when it is victorious. Having come to the idea of killing the British gvernor of Hong Kong, Hong is concerned with only one thing: 'When I have been sentenced to capital punishment, you must tell the young to follow my example.' (Page 36.) To Hong a clear programme must be given: to arouse the workers, to assemble them, to arm them and to oppose them to Chen-Dai as to an enemy. But the bureaucracy of the Comintern seeks Chen-Dai's friendship, repulses Hong and exasperates him. Hong exterminates bankers and merchants one after another, the very ones who 'support' the Kuomintang, Hong kills missionaries: 'those who teach people to support misery must be punished, Christian priests or others. . . .' (Page 274.) If Hong does not find the right road, it is the fault of Borodin and Garine who have placed the revolution in the hands of the bankers and the merchants. Hong reflects the mass which is already rising but which has not yet rubbed its eyes or softened its hands. He tries by the revolver and the knife to act *for* the masses whom the agents of the Comintern are paralysing. Such is the un-varnished truth about the Chinese revolution.

*   *   *

Meanwhile, the Canton government is 'oscillating, in its attempt to stay straight, between Garine and Borodin, who control the police and the trade unions, on the one hand, and Chen-Dai, who controls nothing, but who exists all the same, on the other.' (Page 68.) We have an almost perfect picture of the duality of power. The representatives of the Comintern have in their hands the trade unions of Canton, the police, the cadet school of Whampoa, the sympathy of the masses ,the aid of the Soviet Union. Chen-Dai has a 'moral authority', that is, the prestige of the mortally distracted possessors. The friends of Chen-Dai sit in a powerless government willingly supported by the conciliators. But isn't this the regime of the February revolution, the Kerenskyist system, with the sole difference that the role of the Mensheviks is played by the pseudo-Bolsheviks? Borodin has no doubt of it even though he is made up as a Bolshevik and takes his make-up seriously.

The central idea of Garine and Borodin is to prohibit Chinese and foreign boats, cruising towards the port of Canton, from putting in at Hong Kong. By the commercial boycott these people, who consider themselves revolutionary realists, hope to shatter British domination in southern China. They never deem it necessary first of all to overthrow the government of the Canton bourgeoisie which only waits for the moment to surrender the revolution to England. No, Borodin and Garine knock every day at the door of the 'government', and hat in hand, beg that the saving decree be promulgated. One of them reminds Garine that at bottom the government is a phantom. Garine is not disconcerted. Phantom or not, he replies, let it go ahead while we need it. That is the way the priest needs relics which he himself fabricates with wax and cotton. What is concealed behind this policy which weakens and debases the revolution? The respect of a petty-bourgeois revolutionist for a solid conservative bourgeois. It is thus that the reddest of the French radicals is always ready to fall on his knees before Poincaré.

But perhaps the masses of Canton are not yet mature enough to overthrow the power of the bourgeoisie? From this whole atmosphere, the conviction arises that without the opposition of the Comintern the phantom government would long before have been overthrown under the pressure of the masses. But let us admit that the Cantonese workers were still too weak to establish their own power. What, generally speaking, is the weak spot of the masses? Their inclination to

follow the exploiters. In this case, the first duty of revolutionists is to help the workers liberate themselves from servile
confidence. Nevertheless, the work done by the bureaucracy
of the Comintern was diametrically opposed to his. It inculcated
in the masses the notion of the necessity to submit to the
bourgeoisie and it declared that the enemies of the bourgeoisie
were their own enemies.

Do not rebuff Chen-Dai! But if Chen-Dai withdraws in
spite of this, which is inevitable, it would not mean that Garine
and Borodin will be delivered of their voluntary vassaldom
towards the bourgeoisie. They will only choose as the new
focus of their activity, Chiang Kai-Shek, son of the same class
and younger brother of Chen-Dai. Head of the military school
of Whampoa, founded by the Bolsheviks, Chiang Kai-shek does
not confine himself to passive resistance; he is ready to resort
to bloody force, not in the plebeian form, the form of the
masses, but in the military form and only within limits that will
permit the bourgeoisie to retain an unlimited power over the
army. Borodin and Garine, by arming their enemies, disarm and
repulse their friends. This is the way they prepare the
catastrophe.

But are we not overestimating the influence of the revolutionary bureaucracy upon the events? No, it showed itself
stronger than it might have thought, if not for good then at
least for evil. The coolies who are only beginning to exist
politically require a courageous leadership. Hong requires a bold
programme. The revolution requires the energies of millions of
rising men. But Borodin and his bureaucrats require Chen-Dai
and Chiang Kai-shek. They strangle Hong and prevent the
worker from raising his head. In a few months, they will stifle
the agrarian insurrection of the peasantry so as not to repulse the
bourgeois army command. Their strength is that they represent
the Russian October, Bolshevism, the Communist International.

Having usurped authority, the banner and the material resources of the greatest of revolutions, the bureaucracy bars the road to another revolution which also had all chances of being great.

The dialogue between Borodin and Hong (pages 182-184) is the most terrific indictment of Borodin and his Moscow inspirers. Hong, as always, is after decisive action. He demands the punishment of the most prominent bourgeois. Borodin finds this sole objection: Those who are 'paying' must not be touched. 'Revolution is not so simple,' says Garine for his part. 'Revolution involves paying an army,' adds Borodin. These aphorisms contain all the elements of the noose in which the Chinese revolution was strangled. Borodin protected the bourgeoisie which, in recompense, made contributions to the 'revolution', the money going to the army of Chiang Kai-shek. The army of Chiang Kai-shek exterminated the proletariat and liquidated the revolution. Was it really impossible to foresee this? And wasn't it really foreseen? The bourgeoisie pays willingly only for the army which serves it against the people. The army of the revolution does not wait for donations: it makes them pay. This is called the revolutionary dictatorship. Hong comes forward successfully at workers' meetings and thunders against the 'Russians', the bearers of ruin for the revolution. The way of Hong himself does not lead to the goal but he is right as against Borodin. 'Had the Tai Ping leaders Russian advisers? Had the Boxers?' (Page 190.) Had the Chinese revolution of 1924-1927 been left to itself it would perhaps not have come to victory immediately but it would not have resorted to the methods of hara-kiri, it would not have known shameful capitulations and it would have trained revolutionary cadres. Between the dual power of Canton and that of Petrograd there is the tragic difference that in China there was no Bolshevism in evidence; under the name of Trotskyism, it was declared a counter-revolutionary doctrine and was persecuted by every method of calumny and repression. Where Kerensky did not succeed during the July days, Stalin succeeded ten years later in China.

Borodin and 'all the Bolsheviks of his generation', Garine assures us, were distinguished by their struggle against the anarchists. This remark was needed by the author so as to prepare the reader for the struggle of Borodin against Hong's group. Historically it is false. Anarchism was unable to raise its head in Russia not because the Bolsheviks fought successfully against it but because they had first dug up the ground under its feet. Anarchism, if it does not live within the four walls of intellectuals' cafes and editorial offices, but has penetrated more deeply, translates the psychology of despair in the masses and signifies the political punishment for the deceptions of democracy and the treachery of opportunism. The boldness of Bolshevism in posing the revolutionary problems and in teaching their solution left no room for the development of anarchism in Russia. But if the historical investigation of Malraux is not exact, his recital shows admirably how the opportunist policy of Stalin-Borodin prepared the ground for anarchist terrorism in China.

Driven by the logic of this policy, Borodin consents to adopt a decree against the terrorists. The firm revolutionists, driven on to the road of adventurism by the crimes of the Moscow leaders, the bourgeoisie of Canton, with the benediction of the Comintern, declares them outlaws. They reply with acts of terrorism against the pseudo-revolutionary bureaucrats who protect the monied bourgeoisie. Borodin and Garine seize the terrorists and destroy them, no longer defending the bourgeois alone but also their own heads. It is thus that the policy of conciliation inexorably slips down to the lowest degree of treachery.

The book is called *Les Conquérants*. With this title, which has a double meaning when the revolution paints itself with imperialism, the author refers to the Russian Bolsheviks, or more exactly, to a certain part of them. The conquerors? The Chinese masses rose for a revolutionary insurrection, with the influence of the October upheaval as their example and with Bolshevism as their banner. But the 'conquerors' conquered nothing. On the contrary, they surrendered everything to the enemy. If the Russian revolution called forth the Chinese revolution, the Russian epigones strangled it. Malraux does not make these deductions. He does not even suspect their existence. All the more clearly do they emerge upon the background of his remarkable book.

Prinkipo, February 9, 1931.

A Strangled Revolution and Its Stranglers

URGENT WORK prevented me from reading sooner the article by Malraux in which he defends, against my criticism, the Communist International, Borodin, Garine, and himself. As a political publicist, Malraux is at a still greater distance from the proletariat and from the revolution than as an artist. By itself, this fact would not justify these lines, for it is nowhere said that a talented writer must necessarily be a proletarian revolutionist. If I nevertheless return to the same question again, it is for the sake of the subject, and not of Malraux.

The best figures of the novel, I said, attained the stature of social symbols. I must add: Borodin, Garine and all their 'collaborators' constitute symbols of the quasi-revolutionary bureaucracy, of that new 'social type' which was born thanks to the existence of the Soviet state on the one hand, and on the other to a definite regime in the Comintern.

I declined to classify Borodin among the 'professional revolutionists', as he is characterised in the novel. Malraux endeavours to show me that Garine has enough mandarin's buttons to give him the right to this title. Here, Malraux finds it in place to add that Trotsky has a greater quantity of buttons. Isn't it ridiculous? The type of the professional revolutionist is not at all some sort of an ideal type. But in all events, it is a *definite* type, with a definite political biography and with salient traits.

Only Russia created this type during the last decades; in Russia, the most perfect of this type was created by the Bolshevik party. The professional revolutionists of the generation to which Borodin belonged began to take shape on the eve of the first revolution, they were put to the test in 1905, they tempered and educated (or decomposed) themselves during the years of the counter-revolution; they stood the supreme test in 1917. From 1903 up to 1918, that is, during the whole period when, in Russia, was being formed the type of professional revolutionist, Borodin, and hundreds, thousands of Borodins, remained outside of the struggle. In 1918, after the victory, Borodin arrived to offer his services. This does him honour: it is worthier to serve the proletarian state than the bourgeois state. Borodin charged himself with perilous missions. But the agents of bourgeois states in foreign countries, especially in colonial countries also and that quite frequently, accomplish perilous tasks. Yet they do not become revolutionists because of that. The type of the functionary-adventurer and the type of the professional revolutionist, at certain moments and by certain qualities, can find points of similarity. But by their psychological formation as much as by their historical function, they are two opposite types.

The revolution pursues its course together with its class. If the proletariat is weak, if it is backward, the revolution confines itself to the modest, patient and persevering work of the creation of propaganda circles, of the preparation of cadres; supporting itself upon the first cadres, it passes over to mass agitation, legal or illegal, according to the circumstances. It always distinguishes its class from the enemy class, and conducts only such a policy as corresponds to the strength of its class and consolidates this strength. The French, the Russian or the Chinese proletarian revolutionist, will look upon the Chinese workers as his own army, of today or of tomorrow. The functionary-adventurer raises himself above all the classes of the

Chinese nation. He considers himself predestined to dominate, to give orders, to command, independently of the internal relationship of forces in China. Since the Chinese proletariat is weak today and cannot assure the commanding positions, the functionary conciliates and joins together the different classes. He acts as the inspector of the nation, as the viceroy for the affairs of the colonial revolution. He arranges combinations between the conservative bourgeois and the anarchist, he improvises a programme *ad hoc*, he erects policies upon ambiguities, he creates a bloc of four classes, he swallows swords and scoffs at principles. With what result? The bourgeoisie is richer, more influential, more experienced. The functionary-adventurer does not succeed in deceiving it. But for all that, he deceives the workers, filled with the spirit of abnegation, but not experienced, by turning them over to the hands of the bourgeoisie. Such was the role of the bureaucracy of the Comintern in the Chinese revolution.

Considering as natural the right of the 'revolutionary' bureaucracy to command independently of the forces of the proletariat, Malraux informs us that one could not participate in the Chinese revolution without participating in the war, and one could not participate in the war without participating in the Kuomintang, etc. . . . To this, he adds: the break with the Kuomintang would have meant, for the Communist party, the necessity of passing into illegality. When one thinks that these arguments sum up the philosophy of the representatives of the Comintern in China, he cannot refrain from saying: Indeed, the dialectic of the historical process sometimes plays bad jokes upon organisations, upon men and upon ideas! How easy it is to solve the problem: in order to participate successfully in the events directed by the enemy class, one must submit to this class; in order to avoid repressions on the part of the Kuomintang, one must paint oneself up in its colours! There you have the secret of Borodin-Garine.

Malraux's political estimate of the situation, of the possibilities and the tasks in China in 1925, is entirely false; it hardly reaches the border line where the real problems of the revolution begin. I have said elsewhere all that had to be said on this subject, and Malraux's article gives no ground for a re-examination of what has been said. But even by standing on the ground of the false estimate Malraux gives of the situation, one can in no case justify the policy of Stalin-Borodin-Garine. In order to protest in 1925 against this policy, certain things had to be foreseen. In order to defend it in 1931, one must be incurably blind.

Did the strategy of the functionaries of the Comintern bring the Chinese proletariat anything but humiliations, the extermination of its cadres and above all, a terrific confusion in the mind? Did the shameful capitulation before the Kuomintang avert repression for the party? On the contrary, it only accumulated and concentrated the repressions. Was not the Communist party compelled to pass into illegality? And when? In the period of the crushing of the revolution! If the Communists had begun by illegal work, at the beginning of the revolutionary tide, they would have emerged upon the open arena at the head of the masses. By effacing and demoralising the party with the aid of the Borodins and Garines, Chiang Kai-shek compelled it later, with all the greater success to take refuge in illegality during the years of the counter-revolution. The policy of Borodin-Garine entirely served the Chinese bourgeoisie. The Chinese Communist Party must begin all over again at the beginning, and that on an arena encumbered with debris, with prejudices, with uncomprehended mistakes and with the distrusts of the advanced workers. Those are the results.

The criminal character of this whole policy reveals itself with particular acuteness in isolated questions. Malraux presents as a merit of Borodin and Company the fact that in turning over the terrorists to the hands of the bourgeoisie, he deliberately pushed under the knife of the terror the leader of the bourgeoisie, Chen-Dai. This machination is worthy of a bureaucratic Borgia or of the 'revolutionary' Polish *szlachta* (gentry and nobility) who always preferred to fire with the hands of others behind the backs of the people. No, the task was not to kill Chen-Dai in ambush, but to prepare the overthrow of the bourgeoisie. When the party of the revolution is obliged to kill, it does it on its open responsibility, in the name of tasks and immediate aims understood by the masses.

Revolutionary morals are not abstract Kantian norms, but rules of conduct which place the revolutionist under the control of the tasks and aims of his class. Borodin and Garine were not bound up with the masses, they did not absorb the spirit of responsibility before the class. They are bureaucratic supermen who consider that 'everything is permitted' . . . within the limits of the mandate received from above. The activity of such men, effective as it may be at certain moments, can only be directed, in the last instance, against the interests of the revolution.

After having killed Chen-Dai with the hands of Hong, Borodin and Garine then turn over Hong and his group to the hands of the executioners. This stamps their whole policy with the brand of Cain. Here too Malraux poses as a defender. What is his argument? Lenin and Trotsky also punished the anarchists. It is hard to believe that this is said by a man who came near the revolution, even if but for a moment. Malraux forgets or does not understand that the revolution takes place in the name of the domination of one class over another, that it is only from this task that revolutionists draw their right to violence. The bourgeoisie exterminates the revolutionists, sometimes also the anarchists (more and more infrequently, because they become ever more obedient) in the name of safeguarding the regime of exploitation and baseness. Under the domination of the bourgeoisie, the Bolsheviks always defend the anarchists against the Chiappes.* After having conquered power, the Bolsheviks did everything to draw the anarchists over to the side of the dictatorship of the proletariat. They succeeded in actuality in drawing the majority of the anarchists behind them. Yes, the Bolsheviks severely punished those anarchists who undermined the dictatorship of the proletariat. Were we right or weren't we? That depends upon the manner in which one evaluates our revolution and the regime instituted by it. But can one imagine for a single instant that the Bolsheviks—under Prince Lvov or under Kerensky, under the bourgeois regime— would act as its agents in the extermination of anarchists? It is enough to formulate the question clearly, to turn aside in disgust. Just as Brid'oison interests himself only in the form and ignores the essence, so the quasi-revolutionary bureaucracy and its literary attorney interest themselves only in the mechanics of the revolution, ignoring the question of what class and what regime they should serve. Here lies the abyss between the revolutionist and the functionary of the revolution.

What Malraux says about Marxism is a joke. The Marxian policy was not applicable in China because, you see, the proletariat was not class-conscious. It would seem then that from this flows the task of awakening this class-consciousness. But Malraux deduces a justification of the policy directed against the interests of the proletariat.

The other argument is no more convincing and still less amusing: Trotsky speaks of the need of Marxism for revolutionary politics; but isn't Borodin a Marxist? And Stalin, isn't he a Marxist? Then it is not a question of Marxism. I defend, against Garine, the revolutionary doctrine, just as I would defend, against a sorcerer, the medical sciences. The sorcerer will say

---

* Chiappe was the head of the police forces in Paris and was noted for his violent procedure against revolutionists.—Tr.

to me in his defence that diplomaed doctors also very often kill their patients. It is an argument unworthy of a moderately educated burgher, and not only of a revolutionist. The fact that medicine is not omnipotent, that the doctors do not always effect cures, that one finds among them ignoramuses, block-heads and even poisoners—can this fact serve as an argument for giving the right to practise medicine to sorcerers, who have never studied medicine and who deny its significance?

I must make one correction, after having read Malraux's article. In my article I expressed the idea that an inoculation of Marxism would do Garine good. I don't think so any more.

Kadikoy, June 13, 1931.

Stalin and the Chinese Revolution

FACTS AND DOCUMENTS

THE CHINESE revolution of 1925-1927 remains the greatest event of modern history after the 1917 revolution in Russia. Over the problems of the Chinese revolution the basic currents of Communism come to clash. The present official leader of the Comintern, Stalin, has revealed his true stature in the events of the Chinese revolution. The basic documents pertaining to the Chinese revolution are dispersed, scattered, forgotten. Some are carefully concealed.

On these pages we want to reproduce the basic stages of the Chinese revolution in the light of articles and speeches by Stalin and his closest assistants, as well as decisions of the Comintern dictated by Stalin. For this purpose we use genuine texts from our archives. We especially present excerpts from the speech of Khitarov, a young Stalinist, at the 15th Congress of the Communist Party of the Soviet Union, which were concealed from the party by Stalin. The readers will convince themselves of the tremendous significance of the testimony of Khitarov, a young Stalinist functionary-careerist, a participant in the Chinese events, and at the present time one of the leaders of the Young Communist International.

In order to make the facts and citations more comprehensible, we think it useful to remind the readers of the sequence of the most important events in the Chinese revolution.

March 20th, 1926—Chiang Kai-shek's first coup in Canton.

Autumn 1926—the Seventh Plenum of the ECCI, with the participation of a Chiang Kai-shek delegate from the Kuomintang.

April 13, 1927 — *coup d'état* by Chiang Kai-shek in Shanghai.

The end of May 1927—the counter-revolutionary coup of the 'Left' Kuomintang in Wuhan.

The end of May 1927—the Eighth Plenum of the ECCI proclaims it the duty of Communists to remain within the 'Left' Kuomintang.

August 1927—the Chinese Communist Party proclaims a course toward an uprising.

December 1927—the Canton insurrection.

February 1928—the Ninth Plenum of the ECCI proclaims for China the course towards armed insurrection and Soviets.

July 1928—the Sixth Congress of the Comintern renounces the slogan of armed insurrection as a practical slogan.

1.   THE BLOC OF FOUR CLASSES

Stalin's Chinese policy was based on a bloc of four classes. Here is how the Berlin organ of the Mensheviks appraised this policy:

On April 10 [1927], Martinov, in *Pravda,* most effectively and . . . in a quite Menshevik manner, showed the correctness of the official position which insists on the necessity of retaining the bloc of four classes, on not hastening to overthrow the coalition government, in which the workers sit side by side with the big bourgeoisie, not to impose 'socialist tasks' upon it prematurely. (*Sotsialistichesky Vestnik,* No. 8, April 23, 1927, page 4.)

What did the policy of coalition with the bourgeoisie look like? Let us quote an excerpt from the official organ of the Executive Committee of the Comintern:

> On January 5, 1927, the Canton government made public a new strike law in which the workers are prohibited from carrying weapons at demonstrations, from arresting merchants and industrialists, from confiscating their goods, and which establishes compulsory arbitration for a series of conflicts. This law contains a number of paragraphs protecting the interests of the workers. . . . But along with these paragraphs there are others, which limit the freedom to strike more than is required by the interests of defence during a revolutionary war. (*Die Kommunistische Internationale,* March 1, 1927, No. 9, page 408.)

In the rope placed around the workers by the bourgeoisie the threads ('paragraphs') favourable to the workers are traced. The shortcoming of the noose is that it is tightened more than is required 'by the interests of defence' (of the Chinese bourgeoisie). This is written in the central organ of the Comintern. Who does the writing? Martinov. When does he write? On February 25, six weeks before the Shanghai blood-bath.

2. THE PERSPECTIVES OF THE REVOLUTION ACCORDING TO STALIN

How did Stalin evaluate the perspectives of the revolution led by his ally, Chiang Kai-shek? Here are the least scandalous parts of Stalin's declaration (the most scandalous parts of it were never made public):

> The revolutionary armies in China [that is, the armies of Chiang Kai-shek] are the most important factor in the struggle of the Chinese workers and peasants for their liberation. For the advance of the Cantonese means a blow at imperialism, a blow at its agents in China, and freedom of assembly, freedom of press, freedom of organisation for all the revolutionary elements in China in general and for the workers in particular. (*On the Perspectives of the Chinese Revolution,* page 46.)

The army of Chiang Kai-shek is the army of workers and peasants. It bears freedom for the whole population, 'for the workers in particular'.

What is needed for the success of the revolution? Very little:

> The student youth (the revolutionary youth), the working youth, the peasant youth—all these are a force that can advance the revolution with seven league boots, if it should be subordinated to the ideological and political influence of the Kuomintang. (*Ibid.,* page 55.)

In this manner, the task of the Comintern consisted not of liberating the workers and peasants from the influence of the bourgeoisie but, on the contrary, of subordinating them to its influence. This was written in the days when Chiang Kai-shek, armed by Stalin, marched at the head of the workers and peasants subordinated to him, 'with seven-league boots', towards . . . the Shanghai *coup d'état.*

3. STALIN AND CHIANG KAI-SHEK

After the Canton *coup d'état,* engineered by Chiang Kai-shek in March 1926, and which our press passed over in silence, when the Communists were reduced to the role of miserable appendices of the Kuomintang and even signed an obligation not to criticise Sun-Yat-Senism, Chiang Kai-shek—a remarkable detail indeed!—came forward to insist on the acceptance of the Kuomintang into the Comintern: in preparing himself for the role of an executioner, he wanted to have the cover of world Communism and—he got it. The Kuomintang, led by Chiang Kai-shek and Hu Han Min, was accepted into the Comintern (as a 'sympathising' party). While engaged in the preparation of a decisive counter-revolutionary action in April 1927, Chiang Kai-shek at the same time took care to exchange portraits with Stalin. This strengthening of the ties of friendship was prepared by the journey of Bubnov, a member of the Central Committee and one of Stalin's agents, to Chiang Kai-shek. Another 'detail': Bubnov's journey to Canton coincided with the March *coup d'état* of Chiang Kai-shek. What about Bubnov? He made the Chinese Communists submit and keep quiet.

After the Shanghai overturn, the bureaux of the Comintern, upon Stalin's order, attempted to deny that the executioner Chiang Kai-shek still remained a member of the Comintern. They had forgotten the vote at the Political Bureau, when everybody, against the vote of one (Trotsky), sanctioned the admission of the Kuomintang into the Comintern with a consultative voice. They had forgotten that at the Seventh Plenum of the ECCI, which condemned the Left Opposition, 'comrade Shao Li-tse', a delegate from the Kuomintang, participated. Among other things he said:

> Comrade Chiang Kai-shek in his speech to the members of the Kuomintang, declared that the Chinese revolution would be inconceivable if it could not correctly solve the agrarian, that is, the peasant question. What the Kuomintang strives for is that there should not be created a bourgeois domination after the nationalist revolution in China, as happened in the West, as we see it now in all countries except the USSR. . . . We are all convinced, that under the leadership of the Communist party and the Comintern, the Kuomintang will fulfil its historic task. (*Minutes of the Enlarged Executive of the Communist International*, [German Edition], November 30, 1926, pages 403-404.)

This is how matters stood at the Seventh Plenum in the autumn of 1926. After the member of the Comintern, 'comrade Chiang Kai-shek', who had promised to solve all the tasks under the leadership of the Comintern, solved only one: precisely the task of a bloody crushing of the revolution, the Eighth Plenum in May 1927 declared in the resolution on the Chinese question:

> The ECCI states that the events fully justified the prognosis of the Seventh Plenum.

Justified, and right to the very end! If this is humour, it is at any rate not arbitrary. However, let us not forget that this humour is thickly coloured with Shanghai blood.

4. THE STRATEGY OF LENIN AND THE STRATEGY OF STALIN

What tasks did Lenin set before the Comintern with regard to the backward countries?

> It is necessary to carry on a determined struggle against the attempt to surround the bourgeois democratic liberation movements in the backward countries with a Communist cloak.

In carrying this out, the Kuomintang, which had promised to establish in China 'not a bourgeois regime', was admitted into the Comintern.

Lenin, it is understood, recognised the necessity of a temporary alliance with the bourgeois-democratic movement, but he understood by this, of course, not an alliance with the bourgeois parties, duping and betraying the petty-bourgeois revolutionary democracy (the peasants and the small city folk), but an alliance with the organisations and groupings of the masses themselves—against the national bourgeoisie. In what form, then, did Lenin visualise the alliance with the bourgeois democracy of the colonies? To these, too, he gives an answer in his thesis written for the Second Congress:

> The Communist International should enter into a temporary alliance with the democratic bourgeoisie of the colonies and backward countries, but should not fuse with it and must unconditionally maintain the independent character of the proletarian movement—even in its embryonic form.

It seems that in executing the decisions of the Second Congress, the Communist party was made to join the Kuomintang and the Kuomintang was admitted into the Comintern. All this summed up is called Leninism.

5. THE GOVERNMENT OF CHIANG KAI-SHEK AS A LIVING REFUTATION OF THE STATE

How the leaders of the Communist Party of the Soviet Union appraised the government of Chiang Kai-shek one year after the first Canton *coup d'état* (March 20, 1926) may be seen clearly from the public speeches of the members of the party Political Bureau.

Here is how Kalinin spoke in March 1927, at the Moscow factory *Goshnak*:

> All the classes of China, beginning with the proletariat and ending with the bourgeoisie, hate the militarists as the puppets of foreign capital; all the classes of China look upon the Canton government as the national government of the whole of China in the same way. (*Izvestia*, March 6, 1927.)

Another member of the Political Bureau, Rudzutak, spoke a few days later at a gathering of the street car workers. The *Pravda* report states:

> Pausing further on the situation in China, comrade Rudzutak pointed out that the revolutionary government has behind it all the classes of China. (*Pravda*, March 9, 1927.)

Voroshilov spoke in the same spirit more than once.

Truly in vain did Lenin clear the Marxian theory of the state from the petty-bourgeois garbage. The epigones succeeded in a short time in covering it with twice as much refuse.

As late as April 5, Stalin spoke in the Hall of the Columns in defence of the Communists remaining inside the party of Chiang Kai-shek, and what is more, he denied the danger of a betrayal by his ally. 'Borodin is on guard!' The coup occurred exactly one week later.

6.   How the Shanghai Coup Took Place

In this connection we have the exceptionally valuable testimony of a witness and participant, the Stalinist Khitarov, who arrived from China on the eve of the Fifteenth Congress and appeared there with his information. The most important points of his narrative have been deleted by Stalin from the Minutes with the consent of Khitarov himself; the truth cannot be made public if it so crushingly proves all the accusations the Opposition directed against Stalin. Let us give the floor to Khitarov (Sixteenth session of the XV Congress of the CPSU, December 11, 1927):

The first bloody wound has been inflicted upon the Chinese revolution in Shanghai by the execution of the Shanghai workers on April 11-12.

I would like to speak in greater detail about this coup because I know that in our party little is known about it. In Shanghai there existed for a period of 21 days the so-called People's Government in which the Communists had a majority. We can therefore say that for 21 days Shanghai had a Communist government. This Communist government, however, showed complete inactivity in spite of the fact that the coup by Chiang Kai-shek was expected any day.

The Communist government, in the first place, did not begin to work for a long time under the excuse that, on the one hand, the bourgeois part of the government did not want to get to work, sabotaging it, and, on the other hand, because the Wuhan government did not approve of the composition of the Shanghai government. Of the activity of this government three decrees are known, and one of them, by the way, speaks of the preparation of a triumphal reception to Chiang Kai-shek who was expected to arrive in Shanghai.

In Shanghai, at this time, the relations between the army and the workers became acute. It is known, for instance, that the army [that is, Chiang Kai-shek's officers—L.T.] deliberately drove the workers into slaughter. The army for a period of several days stood at the gates of Shanghai and did not want to enter the city because they knew that the workers were battling against the Shantungese, and they wanted the workers to be bled in this struggle. They expected to enter later. Afterwards the army did enter Shanghai. But among these troops there was one division that sympathised with the workers —the First Division of the Canton army. The commander, Say-O, was in disfavour with Chiang Kai-shek, who knew about his sympathies for the mass movement, because this Say-O himself came from the ranks. He was at first the commander of a company and later commanded a division.

Say-O came to the comrades in Shanghai and told them that there was a military coup in preparation, that Chiang Kai-shek had summoned him to headquarters, had given him an unusually cold reception and that he, Say-O, would not go there any longer because he feared a trap. Chiang Kai-shek proposed to Say-O that he get out of the city with his division and to go to the front; and he, Say-O, proposed to the Central Committee of the Communist party that they agree that he should not submit to Chiang Kai-shek's order. He was ready to remain in Shanghai and fight together with the Shanghai workers against the military overthrow that was in preparation. To all this, our responsible leaders of the Chinese Communist Party, Chen Du-Siu included, declared that they knew about the coup being prepared, but that they did not want a premature conflict with Chiang Kai-shek. The First Division was let out of Shanghai, the city was occupied by the Second Division of Bai-Sung Gee and, two days later, the Shanghai workers were massacred.

Why was this truly stirring narrative left out of the Minutes (page 32)? Because it was not at all a question of the Chinese Communist Party but of the Political Bureau of the Soviet Union.

On May 24, 1927, Stalin spoke at the Plenum of the ECCI:

The Opposition is dissatisfied because the Shanghai workers did not enter into a decisive battle against the imperialists and their myrmidons. But it does not understand that the revolution in China cannot develop at a fast tempo. It does not understand that one cannot take up a decisive struggle under unfavourable conditions. The Opposition does not understand that not to avoid a decisive struggle under unfavourable conditions (when it can be avoided), means to make easier the work of the enemies of the revolution. . . .

This section of Stalin's speech is entitled: 'The Mistakes of the Opposition'. In the Shanghai tragedy Stalin found mistakes . . . by the Opposition. In reality the Opposition at that time did not yet know the concrete circumstances of the situation in Shanghai, that is, it did not know how much more favourable the situation still was for the workers in March and the beginning of April, in spite of all the mistakes and crimes of the leadership of the Comintern. Even from the deliberately concealed story of Khitarov it is clear that the situation could have been saved even at that time. The workers in Shanghai are in power. They are partly armed. There is all the possibility of arming them far more extensively. Chiang Kai-shek's army is unreliable. There are sections of it where even the commanding staff is on the side of the workers. But everything and everyone is paralysed at the top. We must not prepare for the decisive struggle against Chiang Kai-shek, but for a triumphal reception to him. Because Stalin gave his categorical instructions from Moscow: not only do not resist the ally, Chiang Kai-shek, but on the contrary, show your loyalty to him. How? Lie down on your back and play dead.

At the May Plenum of the ECCI, Stalin still defended on technical, tactical grounds this terrible surrender of positions without a struggle, which led to the crushing of the proletariat in the revolution. Half a year later, at the Fifteenth Congress of the CPSU, Stalin was already silent. The delegates at the Congress extended Khitarov's time so as to give him a chance to end his narrative which gripped even them. But Stalin found a simple way out of it by deleting Khitarov's narrative from the Minutes. We publish this truly historic document here for the first time.

Let us note in addition one interesting circumstance: While smearing up the course of events as much as possible and concealing the really guilty one, Khitarov singles out for responsibility Chen Du-siu whom the Stalinists had until then defended in every way against the Opposition, because he had merely carried out their instructions. But at that time it was already becoming clear that comrade Chen Du-siu would not agree to play the role of a silent scapegoat, that he wanted openly to analyse the reasons for this catastrophe. All the hounds of the Comintern were let loose upon him, not for mistakes fatal to the revolution but because he would not agree to deceive the workers and to be a cover for Stalin.

7. The Organisers of the 'Infusion of Workers' and Peasants' Blood'

The leading organ of the Comintern wrote on March 18, 1927, about three weeks prior to the Shanghai overturn:

The leadership of the Kuomintang is at present ill with a lack of revolutionary workers' and peasants' blood. The Chinese Communist

Party must aid in the infusion of this blood, and then the situation will radically change.

What an ominous play on words! The Kuomintang is in 'need of workers' and peasants' blood'. The 'aid' was rendered in the fullest measure: in April-May, Chiang Kai-shek and Wang Chin Wei received a sufficient 'infusion' of workers' and peasants' blood.

With regard to the Chiang Kai-shek chapter of Stalin's policy, the Eighth Plenum (May 1927) declared:

> The ECCI assumes that the tactic of the bloc with the national bourgeoisie in the already declining period of the revolution was absolutely correct. The Northern expedition alone [!] serves as historic justification for this tactic. . . .

And how it serves!

Here is Stalin all the way through. The Northern expedition, which incidentally proved to be an expedition against the proletariat, serves as a justification of his friendship with Chiang Kai-shek. The ECCI has done everything it could to make it impossible to draw the lessons of the blood-bath of the Chinese workers.

8. STALIN REPEATS HIS EXPERIMENT WITH THE 'LEFT' KUOMINTANG

Further on, the following remarkable point is left out of Khitarov's speech:

> After the Shanghai *coup,* it has become clear to everyone that a new epoch is beginning in the Chinese revolution; that the bourgeoisie is retreating from the revolution. This was recognised and immediately so stated. But one thing was left out of sight in connection with this— that while the bourgeoisie was retreating from the revolution, the Wuhan government did not even think of leaving the bourgeoisie. Unfortunately, among the majority of our comrades, this was not understood; they had illusions with regard to the Wuhan government. They considered the Wuhan government almost an image, a prototype of the democratic dictatorship of the proletariat and peasantry.

The omission is on page 33.

After the Wuhan coup, it became clear that the bourgeoisie is retreating. . . .

This would be ridiculous if it were not so tragic. After Chiang Kai-shek slew the revolution in the face of the workers disarmed by Stalin, the penetrating strategists finally 'understood' that the bourgeoisie is 'retreating'. But having recognised that his friend Chiang Kai-shek was retreating, Stalin ordered the Chinese Communists to subordinate themselves to that same Wuhan government which, according to Khitarov's information at the Fifteenth Congress, 'did not even think of leaving the bourgeoisie'. Unfortunately 'our comrades did not understand this'. What comrades? Borodin, who clung to Stalin's telegraph wires? Khitarov does not mention any names. The Chinese revolution is dear to him, but his hide—is still dearer.

However, let us listen to Stalin :

Chiang Kai-shek's *coup d'état* means that there will now be two camps, two armies, two centres in the South : a revolutionary centre in Wuhan and a counter-revolutionary centre in Nanking.

Is it clear where the centre of the revolution is located? In Wuhan !

This means that the revolutionary Kuomintang in Wuhan, leading a decisive struggle against militarism and imperialism, will in reality be transformed into an organ of the revolutionary democratic dictatorship of the proletariat and peasantry. . . .

Now we finally know what the democratic dictatorship of the proletariat and peasantry looks like !

From this it follows further [Stalin continues], that the policy of close collaboration of the Lefts and the Communists inside the Kuomintang acquires a particular force and a particular significance at the present stage . . . that without such a collaboration the victory of the revolution is impossible. (*Problems of the Chinese Revolution,* pages 125-127.)

Without the collaboration of the counter-revolutionary bandits of the 'Left' Kuomintang, 'the victory of the revolution is impossible'!   That is how Stalin, step after step—in Canton, in Shanghai, in Hankow—assured the victory of the revolution.

9.   AGAINST THE OPPOSITION—FOR THE KUOMINTANG!

How did the Comintern regard the 'Left' Kuomintang?   The Eighth Plenum of the ECCI gave a clear answer to this question in its struggle against the Opposition.

> The ECCI rejects most determinedly the demand to leave the Kuomintang. . . .   The Kuomintang in China is precisely that specific form of organisation where the proletariat collaborates directly with the petty bourgeoisie and the peasantry.

In this manner the ECCI quite correctly saw in the Kuomintang the realisation of the Stalinist idea of the 'two-class workers' and peasants' party'.

The not unknown Rafes, who was at first a minister under Petlura and afterward carried out Stalin's instructions in China, wrote in May 1927 in the theoretical organ of the Central Committee of the CPSU:

> Our Russian Opposition, as is known, also considers it necessary for the Communists to leave the Kuomintang.   A consistent defence of this viewpoint would lead the adherents of the policy to leave the Kuomintang, to the famous formula proclaimed by comrade Trotsky in 1917: 'Without a Tsar, but a labour government!', which, for China, might have been changed in form: 'Without the militarists, but a labour government!'   We have no reason to listen to such consistent defenders of leaving the Kuomintang.   (*Proletarskaia Revolutsia,* page 54.)

The slogan of Stalin-Rafes was: 'Without the workers, but with Chiang Kai-shek!'   'Without the peasants, but with Wang Chin Wei!'   'Against the Opposition, but for the Kuomintang!'

10.   STALIN AGAIN DISARMS THE CHINESE WORKERS AND PEASANTS

What was the policy of the leadership during the Wuhan period of the revolution?   Let us listen to the Stalinist Khitarov on this question. Here is what we read in the Minutes of the Fifteenth Congress:

> What was the policy of the CC of the Communist party at this time, during this whole [Wuhan] period? The policy of the CC of the Communist party was carried on under the slogan of *retreat*. . . .
>
> . . . .
>
> Under the slogan of retreat—in the revolutionary period, at the moment of the highest tension of the revolutionary struggles—the Communist party carries on its work, and under this slogan surrenders one position after another without a battle: To this surrender of positions belongs: the agreement to subordinate all the trade unions, all the peasant unions and other revolutionary organisations to the Kuomintang; the rejection of independent action without the permission of the Central Committee of the Kuomintang; the decision on the voluntary disarming of the workers' pickets in Hankow; the dissolution of the pioneer organisations in Wuhan; the actual crushing of all the peasant unions in the territory of the national government, etc.

Here is pictured quite frankly the policy of the Chinese Communist Party, the leadership of which actually helps the 'national' bourgeoisie to crush the people's uprising and to annihilate the best fighters of the proletariat and the peasantry.

But the frankness here is treacherous: the above citation is printed in the Minutes after the omission cited above by the line of periods. Here is what the section concealed by Stalin says:

> At the same time, some responsible comrades, Chinese and *non-Chinese*, invented the so-called theory of retreat. They declared: the reaction is advancing upon us from all sides. We must therefore immediately retreat in order to save the possibility of legal work, and if we retreat, we will save this possibility, but if we defend ourselves or attempt to advance, we will lose everything.

Precisely in those days (end of May 1927), when the Wuhan counter-revolution began to crush the workers and peasants, in the face of the Left Kuomintang, Stalin declared at the Plenum of the ECCI (May 24, 1927):

> The agrarian revolution is the basis and content of the bourgeois democratic revolution in China. *The Kuomintang in Hankow and the Hankow government are the centre of the bourgeois-democratic revolutionary movement.* (*Minutes* [German edition], page 71.)

To a written question of a worker as to why no Soviets were being formed in Wuhan, Stalin replied:

> It is clear that whoever calls at present for the immediate creation of Soviets of workers' deputies in this [Wuhan] district, is attempting to jump [!] over the *Kuomintang phase of the Chinese revolution,* and he risks putting the Chinese revolution in a most difficult position.

Precisely: In a 'most difficult' position! On May 13, 1927, in a conversation with students, Stalin declared:

> Should Soviets of workers' and peasants' deputies, in general, be created in China? Yes, they should, absolutely they should. They will have to be created *after the strengthening of the Wuhan revolutionary government,* after the unfolding of the agrarian revolution, in the transformation of the agrarian revolution, of the bourgeois-democratic revolution into the revolution of the proletariat.

In this manner, Stalin did not consider it permissible to strengthen the position of the workers and peasants through Soviets, so long as the positions of the Wuhan government, of the counter-revolutionary bourgeoisie, were not strengthened.

Referring to the famous theses of Stalin which justified his Wuhan policy, the organ of the Russian Mensheviks wrote at that time:

> Very little can be said against the essence of the 'line' traced there [in Stalin's theses]. As much as possible to remain in the Kuomintang, and to cling to its Left wing and to the Wuhan government to the last possible moment: 'to avoid a decisive struggle under unfavourable conditions'; not to issue the slogan 'All power to the Soviets' so as not to 'give new weapons into the hands of the enemies of the Chinese people for the struggle against the revolution, for creating new legends that it is not a national revolution that is taking place in China, but an artificial transplanting of Moscow Sovietisation'— what can actually be more sensible? . . . (*Sotsialistichesky Vestnik,* No. 9 [151], page 1.)

On its part, the Eighth Plenum of the ECCI, which was in session at the end of May 1927, that is, at a time when the crushing of the workers' and peasants' organisations in Wuhan had already begun, adopted the following decision:

> The ECCI insistently calls the attention of the Chinese Communist Party to the necessity of taking all possible measures for the streng-

thening and development of all mass organisations of workers and peasants . . . within all these organisations it is necessary to carry on an agitation *to enter the Kuomintang*, transforming the latter into a mighty mass organisation of the revolutionary petty-bourgeois democracy and the working class.

'To enter the Kuomintang' meant to bring one's head voluntarily to the slaughter. The bloody lesson of Shanghai passed without leaving a trace. The Communists, as before, were being transformed into cattle herders for the party of the bourgeois executioners (the Kuomintang), into suppliers of 'workers' and peasants' blood' for Wang Chin Wei and company.

11. THE STALINIST EXPERIMENT WITH MINISTERIALISM

In spite of the experience of the Russian Kerenskiad and the protests of the Left Opposition, Stalin wound up his Kuomintang policy with an experiment in ministerialism: two Communists entered the bourgeois government in the capacity of ministers of labour and agriculture—the classic posts of hostages!—under the direct instructions of the Comintern: to paralyse the class struggle with the aim of retaining the united front. Such directives were constantly given from Moscow by telegraph until August 1927.

Let us hear how Khitarov depicted Communist 'ministerialism' in practice before the audience of delegates at the Fifteenth Congress of the CPSU:

'You know that there were two Communist ministers in the government,' says Khitarov. The rest of this passage is deleted from the Minutes:

Afterwards, they [the Communist ministers] stopped coming around to the ministries altogether, failed to appear themselves and put in their places a hundred functionaries. During the activity of these ministers not a single law was promulgated which would ease the position of the workers and peasants. This reprehensible activity was wound up with a still more reprehensible, shameful end. These ministers declared that one of them was ill and the other wished to go abroad, etc., and therefore asked to be released. They did not resign with a political declaration in which they would have declared: You are counter-revolutionists, you are traitors, you are betrayers— we will no longer go along with you. No. They declared that one was allegedly ill. In addition, *Tang Ping Shan* wrote that *he could not cope with the magnitude of the peasant movement,* therefore he asked that his release be granted. Can a greater disgrace be imagined? A Communist minister declares that he cannot cope with the peasant movement. Then who can? It is clear, the military, and nobody else. This was an open legalisation of the rigorous suppression of the peasant movement, undertaken by the Wuhan government.

This is what the participation of the Communists in the 'democratic dictatorship' of the workers and peasants looked like. In December 1927, when Stalin's speeches and articles were still fresh in the minds of all, Khitarov's narrative could not be printed, even though the latter—young but precocious!— in looking after his own welfare, did not say a word about the Moscow leaders of Chinese ministerialism and even referred to Borodin only as 'a certain non-Chinese comrade'.

Tang Ping Shan complained—Khitarov raged hypocritically— that he could not cope with the peasant movement. But Khitarov could not help knowing that this was just the task that Stalin set before Tang Ping Shan. Tang Ping Shan came to Moscow at the end of 1926 for instructions and reported to the Plenum of the ECCI how well he coped with the 'Trotskyists', that is, with those Communists who wanted to leave the Kuomintang in order to organise the workers and peasants. Stalin was sending Tang Ping Shan telegraphic instructions to curb the peasant movement in order not to antagonise Chiang Kai-shek and the bourgeois military staff. At the same time, Stalin accused the Opposition of . . . underestimating the peasantry.

The Eighth Plenum even adopted a special 'Resolution on the Speeches of comrades Trotsky and Vuyovich at the Plenary Session of the ECCI'. It read:

Comrade Trotsky . . . demanded at the Plenary Session the immediate establishment of the dual power in the form of Soviets and the immediate adoption of a course towards the overthrow of the Left Kuomintang government. This apparently [!] ultra-Left [!!] but in reality opportunist [!!!!] demand is nothing but the repetition of the old Trotskyist position of jumping over the petty-bourgeois, peasant stage of the revolution.

We see here in all its nakedness the essence of the struggle against Trotskyism: the defence of the bourgeoisie against the revolution of the workers and peasants.

12. LEADERS AND MASSES

All the organisations of the working class were utilised by the 'leaders' in order to restrain, to curb, to paralyse the struggle of the revolutionary masses. Here is what Khitarov related:

The congress of the trade unions [in Wuhan] was postponed from day to day and when it was finally convened no attempt whatsoever was made to utilise it for the organisation of resistance. On the contrary, on the last day of the congress, it was decided to stage a demonstration before the building of the National government with the object of expressing their sentiment of loyalty to the government. (*Lozovsky :* I scared them there with my speech.)

Lozovsky was not ashamed at that moment to bring himself forward. 'Scaring' the same Chinese trade unionists whom he had thrown into confusion, with bold phrases, Lozovsky succeeded on the spot, in China, in not seeing anything, not understanding anything, and not foreseeing anything. Returning from China, this 'leader' wrote:

The proletariat has become the dominant force in the struggle for the national emancipation of China. (*Workers' China,* page 6.)

This was said about a proletariat whose head was being squeezed in the iron manacles of Chiang Kai-shek. This is how the general secretary of the Red International of Labour Unions deceived the workers of the whole world. And after the crushing of the Chinese workers (with the aid of all sorts of 'general secretaries'), Lozovsky derides the Chinese trade unionists: those 'cowards' got scared, you see, by the intrepid speeches of the most intrepid Lozovsky. In this little episode lies the art of the present 'leaders', their whole mechanism, the whole of their morals!

The might of the revolutionary movement of the masses of the people was truly incomparable. We have seen that in spite of three years of mistakes the situation could still have been saved in Shanghai by receiving Chiang Kai-shek not as a liberator but as a mortal foe. Moreover, even after the Shanghai *coup d'état* the Communists could still have strengthened themselves in the provinces. But they were ordered to submit themselves to the 'Left' Kuomintang. Khitarov gives a description of one of the most illuminating episodes of the second counter-revolution carried out by the Left Kuomintang:

> The coup in Wuhan occurred on May 21-22. . . . The coup took place under simply unbelieveable circumstances. In Changsha the army consisted of 1,700 soldiers, and the peasants made up a majority of the armed detachments gathered around Changsha to the number of 20,000. In spite of this, the military command succeeded in seizing power, in shooting all the active peasants, in dispersing all revolutionary organisations and in establishing its dictatorship only because of the cowardly, irresolute, conciliatory policy of the leaders in Changsha and Wuhan. When the peasants learned of the coup in Changsha they began to prepare themselves, to gather around Changsha in order to undertake a march on it. This march was set for May 21. The peasants started to draw up their detachments in increasing numbers towards Changsha. It was clear that they would seize the city without great effort. But at this point *a letter arrived from the Central Committee of the Chinese Communist Party in which Chen Du-Siu wrote that they should presumably avoid an open conflict and transfer the question to Wuhan.* On the basis of this letter, the District Committee dispatched to the peasant detachments an order to retreat, not to advance any further; but this order failed to reach two detachments. Two peasant detachments advanced on Wuhan and were there annihilated by the soldiers. (*Minutes*, page 34.)

This is approximately how matters proceeded in the rest of the provinces. Under Borodin's guidance—'Borodin is on guard!'—the Chinese Communists carried out very punctiliously the instructions of Stalin: not to break with the Left Kuomintang, the chosen leaders of the democratic revolution. The capitulation at Changsha took place on May 31, that is, a few days after the decisions of the Eighth Plenum of the ECCI and in full conformity with these decisions.

The leaders indeed did everything in order to destroy the cause of the masses!

In that same speech of his, Khitarov declares:

> I consider it my duty to declare that in spite of the fact that the Chinese Communist Party has for a long time committed unheard-of opportunist errors . . . we do not, however, need to blame the party masses for them. . . . To my deep conviction (I have seen many sections of the Comintern), there isn't another such section so devoted to the cause of Communism, so courageous in its fight for our cause as are the Chinese Communists. There are no other Communists as courageous as the Chinese comrades. (*Minutes*, page 36.)

Undoubtedly, the revolutionary Chinese workers and peasants revealed exceptional self-sacrifice in the struggle. Together with the revolution, they were crushed by the opportunist leadership. Not the one that had its seat in Canton, Shanghai and Wuhan but the one that was commanding from Moscow. Such will be the verdict of history!

13. THE CANTON UPRISING

On August 7, 1927, the special conference of the Chinese Communist Party condemned, according to previous instructions from Moscow, the opportunist policy of its leadership, that is, its whole past, and decided: to prepare for an armed insurrection. Stalin's special emissaries had the task of preparing an insurrection in Canton timed for the Fifteenth Congress of the Communist Party of the Soviet Union, in order to cover up the physical extermination of the Russian Opposition with the political triumph of the Stalinist tactic in China.

On the declining wave, while the depression still prevailed among the urban masses, the Canton 'Soviet' uprising was hurriedly organised, heroic in the conduct of the workers, criminal in the adventurism of the leadership. The news of the new crushing of the Canton proletariat arrived exactly at the moment of the Fifteenth Congress. In this manner, Stalin was smashing the Bolshevik-Leninists exactly at the moment when his ally of yesterday, Chiang Kai-shek, was crushing the Chinese Communists.

It was necessary to draw up new balance sheets, that is, once more to shift the responsibility on to the executors. On February 7, 1928, *Pravda* wrote:

> The provincial armies fought undividedly against Red Canton and this proved to be the greatest and *oldest shortcoming of the Chinese Communist Party, precisely insufficient political work for the decomposition of the reactionary armies.*

'The oldest shortcoming'! Does this mean that it was the task of the Chinese Communist Party to decompose the armies of the Kuomintang? Since when?

On February 25, 1927, a month and a half prior to the crushing of Shanghai, the central organ of the Comintern wrote:

> The Chinese Communist Party and the conscious Chinese workers must not *under any circumstances* pursue a tactic which would disorganise the revolutionary armies just because the influence of the bourgeoisie is to a certain degree strong there. . . . (*Die Kommunististische Internationale*, February 25, 1927, page 19.)

And here is what Stalin said—and repeated on every occasion—at the Plenum of the ECCI on May 24, 1927:

> Not unarmed people stand against the armies of the old regime in China, but an armed people in the form of the revolutionary army. In China, an armed revolution is fighting against armed counter-revolution.

In the summer and autumn of 1927, the armies of the Kuomintang were depicted as an armed people. But when these armies crushed the Canton insurrection, *Pravda* declared the 'oldest [!] shortcoming' of the Chinese Communists to be their inability to decompose the 'reactionary armies', the very ones that were proclaimed 'the revolutionary people' on the very eve of Canton.

Shameless mountebanks! Was anything like it ever seen among real revolutionists?

14. THE PERIOD OF PUTSCHISM

The Ninth Plenum of the ECCI met in February 1928, less than two months after the Canton insurrection. How did it estimate the situation? Here are the exact words of its resolution:

> The ECCI makes it the duty of all its sections to fight against the slanders of the social-democrats and the Trotskyists who assert that the Chinese revolution has been liquidated.

What a treacherous and at the same time miserable subterfuge! Social-democracy considers in reality that the victory of Chiang Kai-shek is the *victory* of the national revolution (the confused Urbahns went astray on this very same position). The Left Opposition considers that the victory of Chiang Kai-shek is the *defeat* of the national revolution.

The Opposition never said and never could have said that the Chinese revolution *in general* is liquidated. What was liquidated, confused, deceived and crushed was 'only' the *second* Chinese revolution (1925-1927). That alone would be enough of an accomplishment for the gentlemen of the leadership!

We maintained, beginning with the autumn of 1927, that a period of ebb is ahead in China, of the retreat of the proletariat, the triumph of the counter-revolution. What was Stalin's position?

On February 7, 1928, *Pravda* wrote:

> The Chinese Communist Party is heading towards an armed insurrection. The whole situation in China speaks for the fact that this is

the correct course. . . . Experience proves that the Chinese Communist Party must concentrate all its efforts on the task of the day-to-day and widespread careful preparation of the armed insurrection.

The Ninth Plenum of the ECCI, with ambiguous bureaucratic reservations on putschism, approved this adventurist line. The object of these reservations is known: to create holes for the 'leaders' to crawl into in the event of a new retreat.

The criminally lightminded resolution of the Ninth Plenum meant for China: new adventures, new skirmishes, breaking away from the masses, the loss of positions, the consuming of the best revolutionary elements in the fire of adventurism, the demoralisation of the remnants of the party. The whole period between the conference of the Chinese party on August 7, 1927, and the Sixth Congress of the Comintern on July 8, 1928, is permeated through and through with the theory and practice of putschism. This is how the Stalinist leadership was dealing with final blows to the Chinese revolution and the Communist party.

Only at the Sixth Congress did the leadership of the Comintern recognise that

> The Canton uprising was objectively already a 'rear-guard battle' of the receding revolution. (*Pravda*, July 27, 1928.)

'Objectively'! And subjectively? That is, in the consciousness of its initiators, the leaders? Such is the masked recognition of the adventurist character of the Canton insurrection. However that may be, one year after the Opposition, and what is more important, after a series of cruel defeats, the Comintern recognised that the second Chinese revolution had terminated together with the Wuhan period, and that it cannot be revived through adventurism. At the Sixth Congress the Chinese delegate, Chan Fi-Yun, reported:

> The defeat of the Canton insurrection has delivered a still heavier blow to the Chinese proletariat. The first stage of the revolution was

in this manner ended with a series of defeats. In the industrial centres, a depression is being felt in the labour movement. (*Pravda*, July 17, 1928, No. 164.)

Facts are stubborn things! This had to be recognised also by the Sixth Congress. The slogan of armed insurrection was eliminated. The only thing that remained was the name 'second Chinese revolution' (1925-1927), 'the first stage' of which is separated from the future second stage by an undefined period. This was a terminological attempt to save at least a part of the prestige.

15. AFTER THE SIXTH CONGRESS

The delegate of the Chinese Communist Party, Siu, declared at the Sixteenth Congress of the CPSU:

Only Trotskyist renegades and Chinese Chen Du-Siuists say that the Chinese national bourgeoisie has a perspective of independent [?] development [?] and stabilisation [?].

Let us leave aside the abuse: these unfortunate people would never be in the Lux boarding house* if they did not address their abuse to the Opposition. This is their only resource. Tang Ping Shan thundered in exactly the same manner against the 'Trotskyists' at the Seventh Plenum of the ECCI before he went over to the enemy. What is curious in its naked shamelessness is the attempt to father us, Left Oppositionists, with the idealisation of the Chinese 'national bourgeoisie' and its 'independent development'. Stalin's agents, as well as their leader, fulminate because the period after the Sixth Congress once more revealed their complete incapacity to understand the change in circumstances and the direction of its further development.

---

* Hotel Lux in Moscow, where many of the foreign and Russian officials of the Comintern had their residence.—Tr.

After the Canton defeat, at a time when the ECCI in February 1928—was steering the course towards an armed insurrection, we declared in opposition to this:

The situation will now change in the exactly opposite direction; the working masses will temporarily retreat from politics; the party will grow weak which does not exclude the continuation of peasant uprisings. The weakening of the war of the generals as well as the weakening of the strikes and uprisings of the proletariat will inevitably lead in the meantime to some sort of an establishment of elementary processes of economic life in the country and consequently to somewhat of an, even though very weak, commercial and industrial rise. The latter will revive the strike struggles of the workers and permit the Communist party, under the condition of correct tactics, once more to establish its contact and its influence in order that later, already on a higher plane, the insurrection of the workers may be interlocked with the peasant war. That is what our so-called 'liquidationism' consisted of.

But, apart from abuse, what did Siu say about China in the last two years? First of all, he stated, after the fact:

In Chinese industry and commerce a certain revival was to be marked in 1928.

And further:

In 1928, 400,000 workers went on strike, in 1929, the number of strikers had already reached 750,000. In the first half of 1930, the labour movement was still further fortified in the tempo of development.

It is understood that we must be very cautious with the figures of the Comintern, including Siu's. But regardless of the possible exaggeration of the figures, Siu's exposition bears out entirely our prognosis at the end 1927 and the beginning of 1928.

Unfortunately, the leadership of the ECCI and the Chinese Communist Party took their point of departure from the directly opposite prognosis. The slogan of armed insurrection was dropped only at the Sixth Congress, that is, in the middle of 1928. But aside from this purely negative decision the party did not receive any new orientation. The possibility of economic revival was not taken into consideration by it. The strike movement went on to a considerable extent apart from it. Can one doubt for an instant that if the leadership of the Comintern had not occupied itself with stupid accusations of liquidationism against the Opposition and had understood the situation in time, as we did, the Chinese Communist Party would have been considerably stronger, primarily in the trade union movement? Let us recall that during the highest ascent of the second revolution, in the first half of 1927, there were 2,800,000 workers organised in trade unions under the influence of the Communist party. At the present time, there are, according to Siu, around 60,000. This in the whole of China!

And these miserable 'leaders', who have worked their way into a hopeless corner, who have done terrific damage, speak about the 'Trotskyist renegades' and think that by this slander they can make good the damage. Such is the school of Stalin! Such are its fruits!

16. THE SOVIETS AND THE CLASS CHARACTER OF THE REVOLUTION

What, according to Stalin, is the role of the Soviets in the Chinese revolution? What place has been assigned to them in the alternation of its stages? With the rule of what class are they bound up?

During the Northern Expedition, as well as in the Wuhan period, we heard from Stalin that Soviets can be created only *after* the completion of the bourgeois-democratic revolution, only on the *threshold* of the proletarian revolution. Precisely because of this the Political Bureau, following right behind Stalin, stubbornly rejected the slogan of Soviets advanced by the Opposition:

> The slogan of Soviets means nothing but an immediate skipping over the stage of the bourgeois-democratic revolution and the organisation of the power of the proletariat. (From the written *Reply of the Political Bureau* to the Opposition theses, April 1927.)

On May 24, after the Shanghai *coup d'état* and during the Wuhan coup, Stalin proved the incompatibility of Soviets with bourgeois-democratic revolution in this manner:

> But the workers will not stop at this if they have Soviets of workers' deputies. They will say to the Communists—and they will be right: If we are the Soviets, and the Soviets are the organs of power, then can we not squeeze the bourgeoisie a little, and expropriate 'a little'? The Communists will be empty windbags if they do not take the road of expropriation of the bourgeoisie with the existence of Soviets of workers' and peasants' deputies. Is it possible to and should we take this road at present, at the present phase of the revolution? No, we should not.

And what will become of the Kuomintang after passing over to the proletarian revolution? Stalin had it all figured out. In his discourse to the students on May 13, 1927 which we already quoted, Stalin replied:

> I think that in the period of the creation of Soviets of workers' and peasants' deputies and the preparation for the Chinese October, the Chinese Communist Party will have to substitute for the present bloc inside the Kuomintang the bloc outside the Kuomintang.

Our great strategists foresaw everything—decidedly they forsaw everything, except the class struggle. Even in the matter of going over to the proletarian revolution Stalin solicitously supplied the Chinese Communist Party with an ally, with the same Kuomintang. In order to carry out the socialist revolution, the Communists were only permitted to get out of the ranks of the Kuomintang, but by no means to break the bloc with it. As is known, the alliance with the bourgeoisie was the best condition for the preparation of the 'Chinese October'. And all this was called Leninism. . . .

Be that as it may, in 1925-1927 Stalin posed the question of Soviets very categorically, connecting the formation of Soviets with the immediate socialist expropriation of the bourgeoisie. It is true he needed this 'radicalism' at that time not in defence of the expropriation of the bourgeoisie but on the contrary in defence of the bourgeoisie from expropriation. But the principled posing of the question was at any rate clear: *the Soviets can be only and exclusively organs of the socialist revolution.* Such was the position of the Political Bureau of the CPSU, such was the position of the ECCI.

But at the end of 1927 an insurrection was carried out in Canton to which a Soviet character was given. The Communists had the power. They decreed measures of a purely socialist character (nationalization of the land, banks, dwellings, industrial enterprises, etc.) It would seem we were confronted with a proletarian revolution. But no. At the end of February 1928, the Ninth Plenum of the ECCI drew up the balance of the Canton insurrection. And what was the result?

> The current year in the Chinese revolution is a period of bourgeois-democratic revolution, which has not been completed . . . The tendency towards jumping over the bourgeois-democratic stage of the revolution with the simultaneous appraisal of the revolution as a 'permanent' revolution is a mistake similar to the one made by Trotsky in 1905.

But ten months before that (April 1927) the Political Bureau declared that the very slogan of Soviets (not Trotskyism, but the slogan of Soviets!) means the inadmissible skipping of the bourgeois-democratic stage. But now, after a complete exhaustion of all the variations of the Kuomintang, when it was necessary to sanction the slogan of Soviets, we were told that only Trotskyists can connect this slogan with the proletarian dictatorship. This is how it was revealed that Stalin, during 1925-1927, was a . . . 'Trotskyist', even though the other way around.

It is true that the programme of the Comintern also made a decisive turn in this question. Among the most important tasks of the colonial countries, the programme mentioned: 'The establishment of a democratic dictatorship of the proletariat and peasantry based on the Soviets.' Truly miraculous! What was yesterday incompatible with the democratic revolution was today proclaimed to be its foundation base. One would seek in vain for any theoretical explanation of this complete somersault. Everything was done in a strictly administrative manner.

In what instance was Stalin wrong? When he declared the Soviets incompatible with the democratic revolution or when he declared the Soviets to be the basis of the democratic revolution? In both instances. Because Stalin does not understand the meaning of the democratic dictatorship, the meaning of the proletarian dictatorship, their mutual relationship, and what rôle the Soviets play in connection with them.

He once more revealed it best, even though in a few words, at the Sixteenth Congress of the CPSU.

17. THE CHINESE QUESTION AT THE SIXTEENTH CONGRESS OF THE CPSU.

In his ten-hour report Stalin, however anxious he was to do so, could not completely ignore the question of the Chinese revolution. He devoted to it exactly five phrases. And what phrases! Indeed, 'a lot in a little', as the Latinists say (*multum in parvo*). Desiring to avoid all sharp corners, to refrain from risking generalisations and still more from concrete prognoses, Stalin in five phrases succeeded in making all the mistakes still left for him to make.

> It would be ridiculous to think, [Stalin said] that this misconduct of
> of the imperialists will pass for them unpunished. The Chinese
> workers and peasants have already replied to this by the creation of
> Soviets and a Red army. It is said that a Soviet government has

already been created there. I think that if this is true then there is nothing surprising in it. There is no doubt that only Soviets can save China from complete dismemberment and impoverishment. (*Pravda,* June 29, 1930.)

'It would be ridiculous to think.' Here is the basis for all the further conclusions. If the misconduct of the imperialists will inevitably provoke a reply in the form of Soviets and a Red army, then how is it that imperialism still exists in the world?

'It is said that a Soviet government has already been created there.' What does it mean: 'It is said'? Who says so? And what's most important, what does the Chinese Communist Party say about it? It is part of the Comintern and its representative spoke at the Congress. Does it mean that the 'Soviet government' was created in China without the Communist party and without its knowledge? Then who is leading this government? Who are its members? What party holds power? Not only does Stalin fail to give a reply, but he does not even put the question.

'I think that if [!] this is true then [!] there is nothing surprising in it.' There is nothing surprising in the fact that in China a Soviet government was created about which the Chinese Communist Party knows nothing and about whose political physiognomy the highest leader of the Chinese revolution can give us no information. Then what is there left in the world to be surprised at?

'There is no doubt that only Soviets can save China from dismemberment and improverishment.' Which Soviets? Up to now, we have seen all sorts of Soviets: Tseretelli's Soviets Otto Bauer's and Scheidemann's, on the one hand, Bolshevik Soviets on the other. Tseretelli's Soviets could not save Russia from dismemberment and improverishment. On the contrary, their whole policy went in the direction of transforming Russia into a colony of the Entente. Only the Bolsheviks transformed the Soviets into a weapon for the liberation of the toiling masses. What kind of Soviets are the Chinese? If the Chinese Communist Party can say nothing about them, then it means that it is not leading them. Then who is? Apart from the Communists, only accidental, intermediate elements, people of a 'third party', in a word, fragments of the Kuomintang of the second and third sort, can come to the head of the Soviets and create a Soviet government.

Only yesterday Stalin thought that 'it would be ridiculous to think' of the creation of Soviets in China prior to the completion of the democratic revolution. Now he seems to think—if his five phrases have any meaning at all—that in the democratic revolution the Soviets can save the country even without the leadership of the Communists.

To speak of a Soviet government without speaking of the dictatorship of the proletariat means to deceive the workers and to help the bourgeoisie deceive the peasants. But to speak of the dictatorship of the proletariat without speaking of the leading role of the Communist party means once more to convert the dictatorship of the proletariat into a trap for the proletariat. The Chinese Communist Party, however, is now extremely weak. The number of its worker-members is limited to a few thousand. There are about fifty thousand workers in the Red trade unions. Under these conditions, to speak of the dictatorship of the proletariat as an *immediate* task is obviously unthinkable. On the other hand, in South China a broad peasant movement is unfolding itself in which partisan bands participate. The influence of the October revolution, in spite of the years of epigone leadership, is still so great in China that the peasants call their movement 'Soviet' and their partisan bands—'Red armies'. This shows once more the depths of Stalin's philistinism in the period when, coming out against Soviets, he said that we must not scare off the masses of the Chinese people by 'artificial Sovietisation'. Only Chiang Kai-shek could have been scared off by it, but not the workers, not the peasants, to whom, after 1917, the Soviets had become symbols of emancipation. The Chinese peasants, it is understood, inject no few illusions into the slogan of Soviets. It is pardonable in them. But is it pardonable in the leading *khvostists* who confine themselves to a cowardly and ambiguous generalisation of the illusions of the Chinese peasantry, without explaining to the proletariat the real meaning of events?

'There is nothing surprising in it,' says Stalin, if the Chinese peasants, without the participation of the industrial centres and without the leadership of the Communist party, created a Soviet government. But we say that the appearance of the Soviet government under these circumstances is absolutely impossible. Not only the Bolsheviks but even the Tseretelli government or half-government of the Soviets could make its appearance only on the basis of the cities. To think that the peasantry is capable of creating its Soviet government *independently*, means to believe in miracles. It would be the same miracle to create a peasant Red army. The peasant partisans played a great revolutionary role in the Russian revolution, but under the existence of centres of proletarian dictatorship and a centralised proletarian Red army. With the weakness of the Chinese labour movement at the present moment, and with the still greater weakness of the Communist party, it is difficult to speak of a dictatorship of the proletariat as the *task of the day* in China. This is why Stalin, swimming in the wake of the peasant uprising, is compelled, in spite of all his earlier declarations, to link the peasant Soviets and the peasant Red army with the bourgeois-democratic dictatorship. The leadership of this dictatorship, which is too heavy a task for the Communist party, is delivered to some other political party, to some sort of a revolutionary *x*. Being that Stalin hindered the Chinese workers and peasants from conducting their struggle for the dictatorship of the proletariat, then somebody must now help Stalin by taking in hand the Soviet government as the organ of the bourgeois democratic dictatorship. As a motivation for this new perspective we are presented with five arguments in five phrases. Here they are: (1) 'It would be ridiculous to think'; (2) 'it is said'; (3) 'if it is true'; (4) 'there is nothing surprising in it'; (5) 'there is no doubt'. Here it is, administrative argumentation in all its power and splendour!

We warn: the Chinese proletariat will again have to pay for this whole shameful concoction.

18. THE CHARACTER OF STALIN'S 'MISTAKES'

There are mistakes and mistakes. In the various spheres of human thought, there can be very considerable mistakes which flow from the insufficient examination of the object, from insufficient factual data, from a too great complexity of the factors to be considered, etc. Among these we may consider, let us say, the mistakes of meteorologists in foretelling the weather, which are typical of a whole series of mistakes in the sphere of politics. However, the mistakes of a learned, quick-witted meteorologist are often more useful to science than the conjecture of an empiric, even though it is accidentally substantiated by facts. But what should we say of a learned geographer, of a leader of a polar expedition who would take as his point of departure that the earth rests on three whales? Yet the mistakes of Stalin are almost completely of this last category. Never rising to Marxism as a method, making use of one or the other 'Marxian-like' formulae in a ritualistic manner, Stalin in his practical actions takes as his point of departure the crassest empirical prejudices. But such is the dialectic of the process: these prejudices became Stalin's main strength in the period of revolutionary decline. They were the ones that permitted him to play the role which subjectively he did not want. The cumbersome bureaucracy, separating itself from the revolutionary class that conquered power, seized upon Stalin's empiricism for his mercenariness, for his complete cynicism in the sphere of principles, in order to make him its leader and in order to create the legend of Stalin which is the holiday legend of the bureaucracy itself. This is the explanation of how and why the strong but absolutely mediocre person who occupied third and fourth roles in the years of the rise of the revolution proved called upon to play the leading role in the years of its ebb, in the years of the stabilisation of the world bourgeoisie, the regeneration of social-democracy, the weakening of the Comintern and the conservative degeneration of the broadest circles of the Soviet bureaucracy.

The French say about a man: His defects are his virtues. Of Stalin it can be said: his defects proved to be to his advantage. The gear-teeth of the class struggle meshed into his theoretical limitedness, his political adaptibility, his moral indiscriminateness, in a word, into his defects as a proletarian revolutionist, in order to make him a statesman of the period of the petty-bourgeois emancipation from October, from Marxism, from Bolshevism.

The Chinese revolution was an examination of the new role of Stalin—by the inverse method. Having conquered power in the USSR with the aid of the strata who have been breaking away from the international revolution and with the indirect but very real aid of the hostile classes, Stalin automatically became the leader of the Comintern and by that alone the leader of the Chinese revolution. The passive hero of the behind-the-scenes apparatus mechanism had to show his method and quality in the events of the great revolutionary flow. Within this lies the tragic paradox of Stalin's role in China. Having subordinated the Chinese workers to the bourgeoisie, put the brakes on the agrarian movement, supported the reactionary generals, disarmed the workers, prevented the appearance of Soviets and liquidated those that did appear, Stalin carried out to the end that historic role which Tseretelli only attempted to carry out in Russia. The difference is that Tseretelli acted on the open arena, having arrayed against him the Bolsheviks— and he immediately and on the spot had to bear the responsibility for his attempt to betray to the bourgeoisie a fettered and duped working class. Stalin, however, acted in China primarily behind the scenes, defended by a powerful apparatus and draped in the banner of Bolshevism. Tseretelli supported himself on the repressions of the power of the Bolsheviks by the bourgeoisie. Stalin, however, himself applied these repressions against the Bolshevik-Leninists (Opposition). The repressions of the bourgeoisie were shattered by the rising wave. Stalin's repressions were fostered by the ebbing wave. This is why it was possible for Stalin to carry out the experiment with the purely Menshevik policy in the Chinese revolution to the end, that is, to the most tragic catastrophe.

But what about the present Left paroxysm of the Stalinist policy? To see in this episode—and the Left zig-zag with all its significance will nevertheless go down into history as an episode —a contradiction to what has been said, can be done only by very near-sighted people who are foreign to an understanding of the dialectic of human consciousness in connection with the dialectic of the historic process. The decline of the revolution as well as its rise does not move along a straight line. The empirical leader of the down-sliding of the revolution—'You think that you are moving but you are being moved' (Goethe)— could not help at a certain moment but take fright at that abyss of social betrayal to the very edge of which he was pushed in 1925-1927 by his own qualities, utilised by forces half-hostile and hostile to the proletariat. And since the degeneration of the apparatus is not an even process, since the revolutionary tendencies within the masses are strong, then for the turn to the Left from the edge of the Thermidorian abyss there were sufficient points of support and reserve forces already at hand.

The turn assumed a character of panicky jumps, precisely because this empiric foresaw nothing until he had reached the very brink of the precipice. The ideology of the jump to the Left was prepared by the Left Opposition—it only remained to utilise its work in bits and fragments, as befits an empiric. But the acute paroxysm of Leftism does not change the basic processes of the evolution of the bureaucracy, nor the nature of Stalin himself.

The absence in Stalin of theoretical preparation, of a broad outlook and creative imagination—those features without which there can be no independent work on a large scale—fully explains why Lenin, who valued Stalin as a practical assistant, nevertheless recommended that the party remove him from the post of general secretary when it became clear that this post might assume independent significance. Lenin never saw in Stalin a political leader.

Left to himself, Stalin always and invariably took up an opportunistic position on all big questions. If Stalin had no important theoretical or political conflicts with Lenin, like Bukharin, Kamenev, Zinoviev and even Rykov, it is because Stalin never held on to his principal views and in all cases of serious disagreement simply kept quiet, retreated to one side and waited. But for all that, Lenin very often had practical organisational-moral conflicts with Stalin, frequently very sharp ones, precisely for those Stalinist defects which Lenin, so carefully in form but so mercilessly in essence, characterised in his 'testament'.

To all that has been said we must add the fact that Lenin worked hand in hand with a group of collaborators, each of whom brought into the work knowledge, personal initiative, distinct talent. Stalin is surrounded, particularly after the liquidation of the Right wing group, by accomplished mediocrities, devoid of any international outlook and incapable of producing an independent opinion on a single question of the world labour movement.

In the meantime, the significance of the apparatus has grown immeasurably since Lenin's time. Stalin's leadership in the Chinese revolution is just the fruit of the combination of theoretical, political and national limitedness with huge apparatus power. Stalin has proved himself incapable of learning. His five phrases on China at the Sixteenth Congress are permeated through and through with that same organic opportunism which governed Stalin's policy at all the earlier stages of the struggle of the Chinese people. The undertaker of the second Chinese revolution is preparing before our very eyes to strangle the third Chinese revolution at its inception.

Prinkipo, August 26, 1930.

Appendices

G. Zinoviev

V. Vuyovich

N. Nassonov

N. Fokine

A. Albrecht

Zinoviev's Theses on the Chinese Revolution

To the Political Bureau of the Central Committee of the CPSU

In view of the exceptional importance and complexity of the question of the Chinese revolution, I have formulated my views on it in writing. I considered this all the more necessary because comrades Stalin and Bukharin, at the meeting of the Moscow functionaries which was devoted to the Chinese question, attributed to me views which, in reality, I do not share. I request that my theses be distributed to the members of the Plenum, since I intend to ask that they reject the decision presented by the CC on the situation created in China after the capture of Shanghai and the other events of recent date.

Moscow, April 15, 1927.

G. Zinoviev.

* * *

The events taking place in China at the present time have as great a significance as the events that occurred in October 1923 in Germany. And if at that time the entire attention of our party was turned to Germany, so this must now be done with China, all the more so because the international situation has become more complicated and more disturbing to us.

As a result of the 1923 events in Germany, the CC of our party called together a special conference of representatives of the local party organisations (together with the Plenum), adopted special theses, mobilised the whole party, called a special international conference through its representatives in the ECCI, etc.

The same thing must also be done now.

1. THE PRINCIPLES OF LENINISM AND THE NATIONAL LIBERATION MOVEMENTS

The revolution in China is of world historical importance. To comprehend and correctly estimate the Chinese events, one must be thoroughly clear on the standpoint of Leninism on the character of the national liberation movement in colonial and semi-colonial countries in general.

Lenin wrote :

> The social revolution can be accomplished only in an epoch that embraces the civil war of the proletariat against the bourgeoisie in the advanced countries and a whole series of democratic and revolutionary as well as national liberation movements in the undeveloped, backward and oppressed nations.
>
> Why? Because capitalism develops unevenly and objective reality shows us, side by side with highly developed capitalist countries, a whole series of very weakly, or economically not at all developed nations. (Volume XIII, pages 369-370.)

The national liberation movements of the oppressed nations are, therefore, according to Lenin a *component part* of the socialist world revolution, although Lenin himself defines them as democratic and revolutionary, that is, so far as their immediate aims are concerned, bourgeois movements. The national liberation movements of the oppressed peoples are an element of the international socialist revolution. This does not, however, mean that *any* national movement, at *every moment,* in *every* situation, is a revolutionary factor. It only means that in the *last analysis,* the national liberation movement *as a whole* is such a factor.

A national liberation movement can pass through various stages. When the Finnish people (the bourgeoisie included) conducted its struggle against Tsarism (that is, against Russian imperialism of that time), it was a national liberation struggle. At one time, the Finnish bourgeoisie, led by Svinhufvud (he himself was exiled by Tsarism), fought against the imperialist government of Kerensky. Objectively, this undermined the power of the Russian bourgeoisie and served to prepare the victory of the Russian proletariat in October 1917. On the morrow of the the October revolution, the Svinhufvuds, to whom the Soviets had just granted independence, did no less for 'their' workers, who were preparing an October revolution, than to give them the butcher Mannerheim, who drowned in blood the proletarian revolution in Finland. The Finnish bourgeoisie today still conducts, to a certain extent, a struggle for its national independence. It cannot be said that Finland is an imperialist state, it can only be a 'tool' of imperialism. In spite of this, one cannot speak at this time of the revolutionary import of the Finnish national movement. The national liberation movement in Finland has grown over into bourgeois reaction, because the proletariat, all things considered, did not have enough power to raise the movement to a higher plane, that is, to lead to a victorious proletarian state in Finland.

Another example: the national liberation movement in Poland. The best spirits of Russia—Herzen, Chernyshevsky—sympathised with the Polish rebellion. Marx and Engels, in the period of the First International, correctly considered the national liberation movement in Poland as worthy of the support of the international proletariat. The hatred of Tsarism, born in Poland out of the oppression of the Polish people by the great Russian landowners, had a revolutionary significance. Nevertheless, the Polish bourgeoisie, from the inception of the imperialist war, converted the national movement, with Pilsudski at its head, into a plaything of German imperialism, and later on, into an instrument of French and English imperialism.

Turkey furnishes us with a still more interesting example. The national movement in Turkey, led by Kemal Pasha, for a long time had an indubitably revolutionary character, and thoroughly deserved to be called a national revolutionary movement. It was directed against the old feudal regime in the country, against the Sultanate, as well as against imperialism, primarily against British imperialism. This movement swept along with it a tremendous mass of the peasants and to a certain degree the Turkish working class. The Kemalist party *of that time* resembled *to a certain extent* the Kuomintang of today. (But it must not be forgotten for a single moment that the working class in Turkey was of course far weaker than in China.) The Kemalist party had its 'council of People's Commissars', it stressed its solidarity with Soviet Russia, etc., etc. In a telegram from Kemal to Chicherin, dated November 29, 1920, it says literally: 'I am deeply convinced that on the day that the toilers of the West, on the one side, and the oppressed peoples of Asia and Africa, on the other, will understand that international capital uses them for mutual destruction and enslavement, solely for the benefit of their masters, on the day when the consciousness of the crimes of colonial policy will imbue the hearts of the toiling masses of the world—*then the power of the bourgeoisie will be at an end!'* This did not prevent the same Kemal from cutting the throats of the Communist leaders some time later, from driving the labour movement into illegality, from reducing agrarian reform to a minimum, and in his domestic policy, from following a road to the bourgeoisie and the rich peasants. This happened because the Turkish proletariat was too weak to create an independent class power and to help the peasantry, under the hegemony of the proletariat, to create a directing centre of the Turkish revolution which would not depend upon the liberal bourgeoisie, upon the bourgeois officers, etc., etc. Now, Kemalism is not a national revolutionary movement, it is not a sector of the socialist world revolution. The national unification of Turkey proceeded—but 'in the Kemalist manner', i.e., in the bourgeois manner, just as the national unification of Germany was achieved in its day 'in the Bismarckian manner'. The national movement in Turkey did not grow directly into a revolutionary movement linked up with the international proletarian movement.

In Persia, the slogans of the national liberation movement were in the beginning also given lip service by the possessing classes, but were then transformed into their opposite, into the military and fascist monarchy of Reza Shah, which to a great extent is really an instrument of Britain. Under the cloak of the slogan of 'national unification' and of 'progress' ('centralisation', 'modernisation') a régime of serfdom is really being maintained in the village and the slightest expression of political dissatisfaction by the toilers is suppressed.

Numerous such examples could be drawn from the history of the national movements in India, Egypt, etc., especially in the period of imperialist war and in the years that immediately followed.

The history of the revolution has demonstrated that every bourgeois-democratic revolution that is not transformed into a socialist revolution inevitably goes the way of bourgeois reaction. Either it goes forward or it goes backward, but it does not remain standing one one spot. Either a rising line or else a falling line. This law runs like a red thread through all the great revolutions, beginning with the great French revolution, through the revolutions of 1848 and the Russian revolution of 1905, up to the German revolution of 1918.

When Lenin raised the slogan 'dictatorship of the proletariat and the peasantry' for the first Russian revolution of 1905, and defended the view that the radical victory of the bourgeois revolution could be realised only by a revolutionary dictatorship of the proletariat and the peasantry, he wrote at the same time that 'this dictatorship will inevitably be a temporary phenomenon (namely, it is either a transition to a bourgeois dictatorship and to the defeat of the proletariat, or else to the socialist dictatorship)'. (Lenin, *Collected Works*, Volume V, page 123.)

The same law applies essentially to national liberation movements. Insofar as a national liberation movement and national unification proceed under the bourgeoisie, to that extent the national liberation movements, even if they gain wide scope, will at a certain time go the way of bourgeois reaction. The national liberation movements of the last decade as a whole have contributed not a little to the shaking of the foundations of imperialism. In spite of this, the concrete course and conclusion of these national movements of the past years must bring the vanguard of the international proletariat to realise in all soberness the fact that national movements in no wise always bear the same character and that so long as they remain under the leadership of the bourgeoisie, they will absolutely play an anti-proletarian role at certain periods, that they will become instruments of imperialism.

2. BOURGEOIS DEMOCRACY AND THE NATIONAL REVOLUTIONARY MOVEMENT

Every national revolutionary movement is a bourgeois movement, but not every bourgeois-democratic movement is a national revolutionary movement, just as every peasants' revolution is a bourgeois revolution but not every bourgeois revolution is a peasant revolution. Lenin distinguished between 'bourgeois-democratic' movements in backward countries and 'national liberation movements' in those countries. In his report to the Second Congress of the Comintern, Lenin said in the discussion on the national and colonial question:

> Thirdly, I should especially like to emphasise the question of the bourgeois-democratic movements in backward countries. That is

the point which has aroused some differences of opinion. We debated whether it was correct theoretically and in principle to declare that the CI and the Communist parties should support the bourgeois-democratic movement in backward countries. The result of the discussion was that we came to a unanimous decision to speak only of nationalist-revolutionary movements instead of 'bourgeois-democratic' movements. There is no doubt that every national movement in the backward countries can only be a bourgeois-democratic movement, since the great mass of the population there consist of peasants who represent the capitalist middle class. It would be Utopian to think that proletarian parties, insofar as it is at all possible for them to arise in such countries, could carry out Communist tactics and Communist policies in backward countries without having a definite attitude towards the peasants' movements, without actually supporting it. But the objections raised were that if we say bourgeois-democratic, the distinction is lost between the revolutionary and the reformist movements, which have become quite clear in recent times in the backward countries and the colonies, for the imperialist bourgeoisie has done everything possible to create a reformist movement among the oppressed peoples also. *A certain understanding has been arrived at between the bourgeoisie of the exploiting and of the colonial countries, so that very often, perhaps even in most cases, the bourgeoisie of the oppressed countries, despite its support even of national movements, nevertheless fights against all revolutionary movements and revolutionary classes in agreement with the imperialist bourgeoisie, that is, together with it.* This was completely demonstrated in the Commission and we believed that the only correct thing to do would be to take this distinction into consideration and to substitute almost everywhere the words 'nationalist-revolutionary' for 'bourgeois-democratic'. *The sense of it is that as Communists we will support the bourgeois liberation movements in the colonial countries only if these movements are really revolutionary, that is, if their representatives do not prevent us from educating and organising the peasantry and the great masses of the exploited in a revolutionary sense. If this cannot be done, the Communists are obliged to fight there also against the reformist bourgeoisie, to whom the heroes of the Second International belong.* There already exist reformist parties in the colonial countries and sometimes their representatives call themselves social democrats or socialists. (*Minutes of the Second World Congress,* pages 139-140.)

We already have in these theses of Lenin the key to all the tactical problems of the Chinese revolution. Taking advantage even of an opportunist movement of the bourgeoisie and the petty-bourgeoisie in the interests of the proletariat, as Communists, we do not support every single national movement, but only those whose representatives do not hinder us from educating and organising the peasantry and the broad masses of the exploited. The bourgeoisie of the oppressed countries has learned very well to 'support' the national movement with one hand, and to fight in alliance with the imperialist bourgeoisie against all revolutionary movements of the revolutionary classes with the other hand.

If we apply this to present-day China, we must say: the Right Kuomintang, which has been and remains the leading Kuomintang, also 'supports' the national movement with one hand, while with the other it allies itself with the imperialists (American, Japanese, and British) against the revolutionary classes (the proletariat and the peasantry).

These fundamental directives of Lenin, which were approved at the Second Congress of the Comintern, must be kept in mind when we proceed to the solution of the problems of the Chinese revolution.

3. The General Perspectives of the Chinese Revolution

The development of capitalism in China has made tremendous progress in the last two decades. It would be wrong to believe that the native Chinese capitalist bourgeoisie owns only a very small part of Chinese industry. Sixty per cent of the capital in the coal industry, twenty per cent in the iron industry, sixty-seven per cent in the textile industry, seventy per cent in the match industry, twenty-five in the sugar industry, fifty-eight of the railroads, twenty-six of the river and sea transports, belong to Chinese capitalists. Twenty-seven Chinese banks have a capital of 250,000,000 Chinese dollars. Besides this, the trading capital of the native Chinese bourgeoisie also amounts to a large sum. In comparison, we recall the fact that at the end of the nineteenth century Russian industry also lived chiefly on foreign capital, that only twenty-one per cent of its total capital was Russian (M. N. Pokrovsky's figures). The sum total of foreign capital invested in Russian industry, trade and banks up to 1917 was estimated at approximately two and one-half billion rubles. The investment of foreign capital in China is appreciably greater.

'The conquest of China by capitalism will give an impetus to the overthrow of capitalism in Europe and America,' wrote Engels in 1895.

'The next uprising of the people of Europe will in all probability depend more upon what happens in the Celestial Kingdom [that is, in China] than upon any other cause,' wrote Marx even earlier.

One can safely prophesy that the Chinese revolution will fling a spark into the powder barrel of the present industrial system, that it will provoke an explosion of the general crisis which is being prepared and which, once it has extended over the foreign countries, will follow on the heels of the political revolution on the continent.'

Marx was generally of the opinion (cf. Class Struggles in France) that 'violent upheavals happen sooner at the extremities of the bourgeois organism than at its heart, where the regulation of its functions is easier than elsewhere'. In this sense he attributed a tremendous world historical significance to the revolution in China as well as to the revolution in Russia.

The proletarian dictatorship has now triumphed in Russia, while in China the revolutionary democratic dictatorship under the leadership of the proletariat can triumph and begin to grow into a socialist dictatorship providing a correct tactic is pursued by the Chinese proletariat and the vanguard of the international working class. Then the socialist revolution on the continent and in Europe will take a huge step forward.

In China today we have almost five million wage workers, including three million industrial workers employed in the mines, on the railroads, the textile and silk factories, in the big iron mills, etc.

These workers are joined by a great number of artisans and small employees who can and will go along with the working class under present conditions.

Sixty-three per cent of the peasantry consists of poor peasants who do not possess more than two hectares of land and are exploited and enslaved by the large landowners and the kulaks. This sixty-three per cent of poor peasants possesses only one-fourth of all the cultivated land. Five per cent of the rich kulaks and large landowners has thirty per cent of the total cultivated land; ten per cent owns twenty per cent of the landed property; the middle peasants— twenty per cent of the total—have twenty-six per cent of the cultivated land in their hands.

The poor and middle peasantry are burdened by taxes, by high rent payments, by the despotism of the authorities, etc. Hundreds of millions of peasants can become allies of the proletariat.

If we add to this that the national bourgeoisie of China is still relatively weak, that the compradores are hated by the people; that the usurers, gentry and kulaks in the village have repeatedly provoked outbreaks of peasant uprisings (because of their suppressive measures); that numerous technical petty bourgeois, tens of millions of the poor city population and small tradesmen on the one side, and an important part of the intellectuals, students, on the other, are in their overwhelming majority dissatisfied with the present situation; if we remember further what great strength the Chinese proletariat has in such decisive points as Shanghai, Hong Kong, Tientsin, Hankow, etc., it becomes clear that the hegemony of the proletariat in the developing bourgeois-democratic Chinese revolution is quite possible.

The Chinese revolution will be victorious under the leadership of the working class or not at all. Otherwise, the bourgeoisie will take the whole affair in its hands, in one way or another it will come to an agreement with foreign imperialism (with one group of countries or another, or with a single country) and then it will lead China for a certain period of time on the bourgeois road, wiping out the vanguard of the working class more cruelly than did Kemal Pasha.

The perspective of a non-capitalist (i.e., a socialist) development of China is not excluded and has much in its favour, given a correct policy, Imperialism has not developed the productive forces of China in recent years, and it is not inclined to do it in the next few years :

(1) because its own productive apparatus at home is not being completely utilized;

(2) because imperialism is afraid of the growth of the native proletariat and

(3) because the whole situation in China is not 'secure' enough for imperialism, not 'safe' enough.

The development of the productive forces in China can follow the non-capitalist road in the epoch of world revolution in which we live. Since the USSR exists, covering one-sixth on the earth's surface, and already has an enormous influence of the Chinese revolution; since the proletarian revolution in the USSR has already existed for ten years; since the CI exists, uniting the vanguard of the world proletariat in its ranks; since national liberation movements are growing throughout the world; since serious contradictions still divide the camp of the imperialists and since a lusty, young, rapidly revolutionised working class, comprising millions of people, exists in China—the non-capitalist road of development of China is possible.

'The question was,' said Lenin at the Second Congress, 'can we acknowledge as correct that the capitalist development of economy is necessary for the backward peoples who are now liberating themselves, among whom progressive movements have now arisen after the war? We came to the conclusion that we must answer in the negative. If the revolutionary victorious proletariat organizes a systematic propaganda and the Soviet governments come to its aid with all means it is wrong to assume that the capitalist stage of development is necessary for such peoples.' (*Minutes of the Second Congress,* page 142.)

The non-capitalist (socialist) road of development for China is possible *if*:

(a) the working class really becomes a class fighting for itself, an independent class force, if it builds a strong Communist party capable of drawing the masses of the peasantry behind it, if it does not permit the large and petty bourgeoisie to absorb the working class into a petty-bourgeois bloc 'comprising the whole nation', in short, if it understands how to become in reality the leader and director of the whole revolutionary movement in China, if it takes the leadership in the unification of China into its own hands;

(b) the USSR supports the Chinese working class with all its strength;

(c) the proletarian revolutions in the advanced capitalist countries (Britain, France, Japan, America) grow to maturity and if the workers of these countries understand how to prevent their bourgeoisie from strangling the Chinese revolution with military force:

(4) the Chinese revolution finds a favourable echo in the other oppressed countries like India, Indo-China.

The successful struggle for the non-capitalist (socialist) road of development for China is possible only if we first of all throw aside energetically and irrevocably the basic Menshevik formula: The working class must subordinate its policy in the revolution to the consideration that the liberal bourgeoisie shall not recoil from the revolution since that would weaken the impetus of the revolution.

'From the fact that the content of our revolution is bourgeois,' Lenin wrote in 1907, 'the superficial deduction is made among us that the bourgeoisie is the motive power of the revolution, that the proletariat has only secondary tasks to fulfil in this revolution, that a proletarian leadership of the revolution is impossible.'

There is no doubt that in its present stage, the Chinese revolution is still a bourgeois-democratic revolution in a semi-colonial country. To complete this bourgeois-democratic revolution, to give it the greatest possible scope, to help it carry through to the end the struggle against the imperialists, and to complete a real unification of China, to lead it to the stage where the bourgeois-democratic national revolution begins to grow into a socialist revolution—all this is possible only when the working class succeeds in tearing the leadership of the movement completely out of the hands of the bourgeoisie, under the slogan of the agrarian revolution, and in general in drawing the petty bourgeoisie with it.

In other words, all this is possible only with a radical class differentiation in the camp of the national liberation movement in China, a differentiation that has begun and will from now on move forward everyday. To fear this differentiation, to insist on the united front with the national bourgeoisie, to endeavour 'not to frighten' the leaders of this bourgeoisie, to construe the tactic of the united front in the Chinese revolution as an alliance of the proletariat with the bourgeoisie, and the Kuomintang as a government of the 'bloc of four classes' (Martinov, *Pravda,* April 10, 1927) is to extinguish the revolutionary spirit of the masses, to restrict the programme of the revolution, to force it into the Procrustean bed of bourgeois-Menshevik slogans—in other words, to abandon the perspective of a non-capitalist, socialist development of China.

When Lenin, at the Second Congress of the Comintern, outlined the perspective of a non-capitalist development of the backward countries, he immediately combined the perspective with *the slogan of Soviets for the East*, and along with it preached the creation at all costs of independent Communist organisation in these countries. Lenin said: 'We must not only build independent nuclei and parties in all colonial and backward countries, we must not only immediately propagate the idea of peasants' Soviets and seek to adapt the Soviet organisation to pre-capitalist conditions, but the CI must also explain theoretically that with the aid of the proletariat of the advanced countries, the backward countries can reach the Soviet form of organisation, and through a series of stages, avoiding the capitalist system, also to Communism.' (*Minutes of the Second Congress,* page 142.)

Further on:

The idea of Soviet organisation is simple and can be applied not only to proletarian relationships but also to feudal and semi-feudal peasant relationships. Our experiences on this field are not yet extensive. But the discussions in the Commission, where present, very decisively showed us that we must incorporate in the principles of the Communist International that peasant Soviets, Soviets of the exploited, are not only an appropriate means for capitalist countries, but are also suitable for pre-capitalist conditions, and that it is the absolute duty of the Communist parties and of those elements ready to create Communist parties, to propagate everywhere the idea of peasant Soviets, of Soviets of the toilers, also in the backward countries and in the colonies, and to make the practical attempt to form Soviets of the toiling people as soon as the conditions allow. (*Ibid.*, page 141.)

In the thesis on the national and colonial questions adopted at the Second World Congress of the Comintern, after the report by Lenin, it says literally:

Especially necessary is the support of the peasant movement in the backward countries against the land-owners and against all forms and remnants of feudalism. Above all, we must strive wherever possible *to give the peasant movement the most revolutionary character possible, to organise the peasants and all the exploited into Soviets* and thereby to establish the closest possible union between the West European Communist proletariat and the East, in the colonies and the backward countries. (*Ibid.*, page 230.)

If we keep in mind this highly important directive of Lenin and the Second Congress of the CI, and if we take into consideration the tremendous movement that has now arisen among the Chinese working masses and led to the capture of Shanghai and the unification of a territory with twenty million people under the power of the national government, *it becomes immediately necessary to raise the slogan of Soviets for China.*

The Chinese revolution has reached the point where the slogan of Soviets becomes the essential slogan.

Whoever speaks of a non-capitalist development of China and now (after the capture of Shanghai) rejects the slogan of Soviets, does not take seriously his own words on the non-capitalist development of China.

4. On the Class Independence of the Proletarian Movement in the Backward Countries

The idea of the class independence of the proletarian movement and above all the idea of the creation of independent proletarian parties in the backward countries, the colonies and the semi-colonies, is one of Lenin's basic teachings on the world revolution. It is most closely connected with the idea of the possibility for these countries to avoid the stage of capitalist development under favourable conditions. The struggle of the backward countries, colonies and semi-colonies against imperialism, which has of course a tremendous significance for the general balance of forces of the revolutionary world movement, creates for a certain time the conditions for common action of the proletariat with the non-proletarian sections of the population, for certain blocs and agreements against the common imperialist enemy. *But just because of that, the Communists must underline with special emphasis the need for the complete independence of the proletarian movement or of the proletarian elements in the movement,* to say nothing of the independence of the Communist party. In Lenin's thesis approved by the Second Congress of the CI, which retains its full force to the present day, it says on the question:

It is necessary to wage a determined war against the attempt to cloak the not really Communist revolutionary liberation movements in the backward countries with a Communist mantle. It is the duty of the Communist International to support the revolutionary movement in the colonies and the backward countries for the sole purpose of assembling the units of the future proletarian parties—Communist in reality and not only in name—in all the backward countries and of educating them to the consciousness of their specific tasks, that is, to the tasks of the struggle against the bourgeois democratic tendencies within their own countries. The Communist International should establish a temporary agreement, even an alliance, with the revolutionary movement of the colonies and the backward countries; it must not however fuse with it but must absolutely preserve the independent character of the proletarian movement—even if this is still in embryonic form. (*Minutes of the Second Congress of the Communist International* [German edition], page 231.)

The basis of the dispute between the Bolsheviks and the Mensheviks, in the last analysis, proceeded for a long time from the question: Should a completely independent Marxian proletarian party be created in backward Tsarist Russia and could the working class and its party assume the leading role in the revolution? The policy of the Mensheviks rejected this in deeds. And precisely this rejection led the Mensheviks more and more into the camp of the enemies of the proletarian revolution.

The Bolshevik party, said Lenin, 'need not be afraid of inflicting blows upon the enemy hand in hand with the revolutionary bourgeois democracy under the absolute provision: not to amalgamate the organisations; to march separately and strike together; not to conceal the conflict of interests; to watch its allies as closely as its enemy,' etc., etc. (Volume VI, page 130.)

It is just this 'absolute provision' that we have no right to forget in China now, otherwise we leave the road of Bolshevism.

Of the Kuomintang as a party we can say now, with the necessary modifications, what was said by Marx and Engels of petty bourgeois democratic party of Germany and on the attitude of the working class to it:

> The relationship of the revolutionary workers' party to the petty-bourgeois democracy is: it marches together with it against the faction whose overturn it aims at; it opposes it in everything with which this fraction seeks to consolidate itself.' (Karl Marx, *Enthüllungen über den Kommunistenprozess in Köln*, page 129.) By the side of the new official governments, they [the workers] must at the same time set up their own revolutionary workers' governments, be it in the form of communal committees, communal councils, by means of workers' clubs or workers' committees, so that the bourgeois-democratic governments not only instantly lose the backing of the workers but find themselves from the very beginning under the supervision and threats of authorities behind whom stands the whole mass of the workers. In a word: from the first moment of victory our distrust must no longer be directed against the vanquished reactionary party but against our former allies, against the party which seeks to exploit the common victory for itself. . . . The arming of the whole proletariat with rifles, guns, arms and ammunition must be carried out immediately, the revival of the old bourgeois militia, directed against the workers, must be opposed . . . In this connection [the nomination of candidates against the bourgeois democrats] they should not permit themselves to be duped by the phrases of the democrats as, for example, that the democratic party is thereby being split and the reaction is being given the possibility to triumph. All these phrases are calculated, in the last analysis, to trick the proletariat . . . But they [the workers] themselves must do the greater part of the work for their final victory by enlightening themselves on their class interests, by

adopting as quickly as possible their independent party position, by refusing to be diverted for an instant from the independent organisation of the party of the proletariat by the hypocritical phrases of the democratic petty bourgeoisie.' (*Ibid.*, pages 133, 134, 137.)

Such are the general principles which the Communists must adopt in order to solve the most important questions of the Chinese revolution, especially of the questions of the relations of the Chinese Communist Party and the Kuomintang.

5. The Chinese Bourgeoisie and Its Present Role in the Revolution.

The basic problem of the Chinese revolution is the question: which class shall lead the peasantry?

Can the Chinese bourgeoisie lead the peasantry behind it?

The Chinese bourgeoisie is not homogeneous: It is above all a trading bourgeoisie plus the usurers. Thanks to a whole series of reasons, in the first place thanks to the fact that foreign capital has applied the brakes to an appreciable degree to the development of this bourgeoisie, the capital accumulated in trade has been concentrated in landed property and has thereby preserved the feudal roots of the exploitation of the Chinese peasantry.

In certain districts, seventy-five per cent of the total cultivated land belongs to merchants. The usurers take from one hundred and twenty per cent. to three hundred and sixty per cent. annual interest from the peasants. Trading capital has completely subordinated home work and hand work in the village, above all textile home work which plays a colossal role in China. The Chinese landowner who applies feudal forms of exploitation to the peasantry appears in the city as a merchant who is connected with the other sections of the Chinese bourgeoisie. But the civil war has begun in the village. The peasantry is organising itself into Peasants' Leagues which already embrace five million people, it is creating its armed defence detachments, and has already entered into armed struggles against the usually firmly organized large landowners and gentry and their armed brigades, the Min Tuan.

The civil war in the village is thus already a fact and there is no doubt that the front of this war will rapidly be extended and that in this war, important sections of the city trading bourgeoisie, not to speak of the large landowners in their pure form, *are already to be found on the other side of the revolutionary barricades and are grouping themselves around the Right Kuomintang.*

In the city, an ever more intense struggle of the proletariat against the native industrial bourgeoisie is taking place, which has burst out in an unusually broad strike wave. In the first two and a half months since the occupation of Wuhan by the national revolutionary army, 200,000 workers struck there, achieving only a thirteen-hour working day instead of seventeen, and a ten and a half hour working day instead of eleven. In Canton the development of the strike struggle almost reached the calling of a general strike.

Under the pressure of the working class, which is organising ever more strongly into trade unions, the Chinese bourgeoisie moves away from the national revolution, makes alliances with the large landowners and agrees to compromises with foreign imperialism in which it strives to unite with it for the suppression of the working class and the peasant movement.

The Chinese big bourgeoisie cannot solve the agrarian question, it cannot lead the peasantry behind it, because it is itself in large measure connected with landed property, it is leagued politically with the class of large landowners, which means that the Chinese bourgeoisie cannot lead the peasantry, that it cannot advance the revolution. The Chinese bourgeoisie is being transformed, with the development of the workers' and peasants' movement, into a counter-revolutionary factor.

The crisis in the government and in the CC of the Kuomintang is only the beginning of the political appearance of the civil war in the village and class struggle in town. The national revolutionary government can only be partisan in this civil war, i.e., either a government of the working class, the peasantry, and the city poor (and to that extent an anti-imperialist government) or else a government of the big landlords and the bourgeoisie, that is, of agreements with foreign imperialism.

6.   WHAT IS THE KUOMINTANG?

What is the Kuomintang? We must be completely clear on this score, otherwise enormous mistakes are possible.

The organisation of the party dates back to 1922, when the

Communists entered the Kuomintang. It found expression at the Reorganisation Convention of the Kuomintang in January 1924. Already at that time, the Leftward development of the Kuomintang, expressed in the attempt to base itself on the masses of workers, peasants and city poor, provoked an uprising of the Canton bourgeoisie (uprising of the 'Paper Tigers') against this line of the Kuomintang. The suppression of the Canton bourgeoisie in 1924 with the aid of workers and peasants brought about an influx of these elements into the party. These elements at present form the majority of the Kuomintang. The organisation in Canton numbered 150,000 members in December 1926, including 32,000 workers, 30,000 students and 64,000 peasants. If we cross out about 25 per cent from the figure for the peasants, under whose flag gentry and large landowners have smuggled their way in, we still obtain an absolute majority of radical Left elements. But this Left majority does not lead the party. It is led by the Right bourgeois minority which bases itself on the commanding staff of the national revolutionary army, thanks to which the Right Kuomintang continues to rule over all the territory occupied by the Southern troops. The bourgeoisie and the large landowners not only take the state apparatus in their hands with the aid of the army staff, but they go so far as to disperse Kuomintang committees that do not pursue a purely bourgeois line (Li Ti Sin's *coup de force* in Canton). This is how the Kuomintang becomes an amorphous organisation under the right-wing leadership. Meetings are almost never called together by the organisations, and questions of political action and the building up of the state are not discussed. Since there are no meetings, the members have no means of influencing the policies of the authorities. These circumstances have led to a situation where the Kuomintang is largely a party that stands objectively in opposition to the Right wing which keeps the party leadership in its hands and has the supreme power locally. The Chinese Communists base themselves to a large degree on this Left majority of the party. Together with the Left majority they must overthrow the Right elements and remove them from the party as well as from the government. Such a purging is connected with the arming of the workers and peasants, since the Right Kuomintang, which is supported by the staff of the national revolutionary army, will undoubtedly oppose with arms any attempt of the Left to take power in the state or the party. To this day the worker pickets are either unarmed or they are being disarmed by the authorities

(Canton). The peasants' leagues are armed chiefly with bamboo sticks. To arm them requires time. Therefore manoeuvres from above are necessary until the revolution is better armed. At present they assume the form of giving support to Tan Shen Shi against Chiang Kai-shek. Such manoeuvres are unavoidable. But even Tan Shen Shi will solve nothing in the question of the Leftward development of the government, for he is an even more reactionary general than Chiang Kai-shek, a large landowner attached to Japanese imperialism, who hooked up with the Kuomintang in 1926.

The official ideology of the Kuomintang is the doctrine of Sun Yat Sen. Lenin characterised Sun Yat Senism as a peculiarly Chinese populism. In actuality, Sun Yat Senism 'in its pure form' is a peculiar populism adapted to Chinese conditions, plus nationalism. Lenin called Sun Yat Sen's party a liberal party. Sun Yat Senism is the Chinese doctrine of Social Revolutionism as it existed in Russia, plus nationalism, plus Cadetism. In distinction from the Mensheviks, Lenin perceived in Russian populism not only its petty bourgeois and reactionary nature (it was a petty bourgeois 'Russian socialism') but also its progressive bourgeois democratic essence, in so far as it was an expression of the maturing agrarian revolution in Russia. We must see not only its petty bourgeois national 'socialist', reactionary content but also its progressive and democratic essence. Sun Yat Senism expresses primarily the striving for the national unification of China, thence also to a certain degree the tendency toward the peasants' revolution. This national movement becomes in even larger measure a peasants' movement. But in Sun Yat Senism (as in the Russian populist movement in its time) the intellectuals play an important role, and in the present Kuomintang they form a strong and influential wing that represents the interests of the national bourgeoisie.

In 1894, Sun Yat Sen founded the 'League for the Renovation of China' (Sing Hun Fu). The party was almost exclusively bourgeois. In 1905, Sun Yat Sen organised a new party, the Tung Men Fu, which already looked for support, up to a certain point, among the peasants. In 1911, shortly before the first Chinese revolution, Sun Yat Sen laid the foundation for the present people's revolutionary party, the Kuomintang. He drew in the liberal bourgeoisie, the intellectuals, broad sections of the city petty bourgeoisie and the home workers, and at the same time sought connections with the working class and the peasantry.

An honest democrat, a sincere friend of the oppressed masses, Sun Yat Sen nevertheless accorded the working class a very insignificant role in his teachings. For many years he was an enthusiastic admirer of American democracy, saw in President Lincoln his ideal and declared the social order established in the Hawaiian Islands by American imperialism to be a sort of paradise.

Just as little elaborated in the teaching of Sun Yat Sen is the peasant question.

Only in the last two years of his life, under the influence of the Russian revolution and the growth of the working class in China, did Sun Yat Sen begin to devote more attention to the labour movement and to be convinced that the working class would play a great role in the Chinese revolution.

The three main slogans of Sun Yat Senism are, as is known: 1, Nationalism; 2, Democracy; 3, State Socialism. Taken together they represent a nebulous petty-bourgeois 'socialism'.

It is obvious that this petty-bourgeois ideology can in no case be the ideology of the Chinese proletariat, whose vanguard already stands on the foundation of Marxism-Leninism. The memory of Sun Yat Sen as a sincere revolutionist who rendered inestimable services to the national liberation movement of China, can and should be honoured. Sun Yat Sen can and should be regarded as an ally of the proletarian revolution at a certain stage of the movement in China. But it must be clearly seen that Sun Yat Senism cannot be the ideology of the Chinese proletariat, only Marxism-Leninism can and should be that. Marxism or Sun Yat Senism? That is the question.

What is the Kuomintang as a political organisation? What is the national government? What are the national armies?

It is often said that the present national armies are Red armies. But that is not the case. They should be compared neither to the Red Guard in our revolution nor to the Red Army, for they are neither purely proletarian detachments, as were our Red Guards, nor a peasant army, led by workers and the proletarian party, as is the case with our Red Army. The national armies are extremely heterogeneous. Their Canton nucleus has been increased by various badly organised detachments that joined it. Of the 40 corps at present, 35 are composed of those who went over to the side of the South during the struggle. These armies consist of mercenaries with only a small percentage of volunteers.

But the general situation transforms them into an excellent peasant army, revolutionary and eager for the struggle. The role of the commanding staff is unusually great. But the staff is very little to be relied on. The commanders of the national armies are mostly elements alien not only to the workers, but also to the peasants' movements, belonging to the bourgeoisie and the large landowners. A whole host of commanders in the national army were only a short time ago in the service of the North. The Communists are a very small handful in the Army. The generalissimo Chiang Kai-shek belongs to the Rights, that is, to the bourgeois elements of the Kuomintang, and has already repeatedly shown himself to be an open enemy of the proletarian movement, a man capable of betraying the Chinese revolution. His last declaration (March 1927), which was extolled as a 'victory' of the Communists and the Left wing of the Kuomintang, is in reality a diplomatic chess move. It is the same language that Kerensky used for a long time towards the Central Committee of the Social Revolutionists, when this Central Committee still sought to maintain a Centrist position, with this difference, that there is now much more real power in the hands of Chiang Kai-shek than there was then in the hands of Kerensky. The first *coup d'état* made by Chiang Kai-shek on March 20, 1926 was not a 'struggle of ambition' between Chiang Kai-shek and Wang Chin Wei (as the political philistines picture it) but a reflection of the class struggle. The victory of Chiang Kai-Shek led to the victory of reaction in Kwangtung. The armed counter-revolutionary detachments (the so-called Min Tuan) hastened to break up the peasant leagues and to disarm the peasants. The old officials were brought back into the government. Very serious blows were inflicted upon the workers.

The national government, up to very recently, was a tool in the hands of the generals. Only the pressure of the masses tempered the Right tendencies of the government and made some more or less radical elements enter the government (the minister for foreign affairs, Eugene Chen, is a sort of Fabian). The national government frequently comes out openly against the workers' and peasants' movement: in a whole series of places it has suppressed workers' strikes and strangled the peasants' movement, does not permit it to grow, restricts it, resorts to dissolutions and arrests and endeavours to throw the movement of the peasants and the bandits' 'movement' into one pot, supports strike-breakers' organisations against the workers. It rejects the most just and most elementary demands of the peasantry. Without granting the peasantry anything serious 'from above', at the same time it does not permit this movement to develop from below. Up to 1925, the big bourgeoisie played first fiddle in the national movement.

Canton was, up to a very short time ago, the main point of support of the national movement. The national government was located here for a long time. That is why it is especially important to know the attitude of the national government to the labour movement in Canton. The real wages of the Canton worker have fallen about fifty per cent since 1917. The average wage of the worker in Canton varies between three and ten dollars a month. Only a small number of skilled industrial workers who form the labour aristocracy (a small handful of the 200,000 workers in Canton) receive between 15 and 27 dollars a month. It is just this group of the labour aristocracy that has formed the Mechanics' Union, which does not affiliate to the class trade unions but follows the Right Kuomintang.

Under the slogan of 'civil peace', the national government demands of the workers that they refrain from striking 'behind the front of the national-revolutionary armies', and submit all economic conflicts to the decision of governmental arbitration commissions. The workers did this readily; but in the vast majority of cases the arbitration of the government operated in the interests of the employers. The government labour bureau draws out its arbitration decisions, subjecting the workers to starvation, save where it ranges itself deliberately on the side of the capitalists. In the Kuomintang there is a 'workers' department' and in addition a 'merchants' department'. The bourgeoisie exerts its pressure on the merchants' department and in the vast majority of cases draws the official organs of the Kuomintang over to its side.

It was like this while Sun Yat San lived and it is all the more so now.

On the pretext of resisting an alleged 'Red terror', the bourgeoisie organises its armed bands. In recent times it has even reached the point of the lynching of workers by employers, not to speak at all of those who are sacked from their jobs. The national government of Canton has not only frequently closed its eyes to these exploits of the employers, but even encouraged the building of yellow labour organisations under the leadership of former labour leaders who went over to the side of the employers. The government opposes arming the workers. On August 6, 1926, the generalissimo of the national-revolutionary army, Chiang Kai-shek, ordered the disarming of the workers, their arrest and the court martial for those workers who would use their arms against the mercenary bands of the employers. In December 1926, after the departure of the government and the Central Committee of the Kuomintang for Wuhan, a similar order was issued, and the workers were energetically disarmed by a mobilisation of the troops for this purpose.

After the departure of the government from Canton, the 'revolutionary' general Li Ti Sin dispersed the Canton committee of the Kuomintang where the 'Left' had a 'far too great' influence, and he actually installed a right-wing committee. Of the 50,000 members of the Kuoumintang there remained only 13,000; the workers dropped away. But there are Communists in this committee also. And in spite of that, this 'revolutionary general' arranges ceremonial receptions for the delegation of the Communist International that comes to Canton. By their participation, however, the Communists cover up all these exploits of Li Ti Sin, who is the real master of Canton.

The police of the national government have continually defended the strike-breakers' unions against the real labour unions. Under the protection of the police, the employers have repeatedly suppressed strikes. In October 1926, a detachment of armed soldiers of the 25th regiment of the 3rd army swarmed into the railway car shops late at night and opened fire upon the workers, leaving a number of dead and wounded. This 'incident' took place in connection with a peaceful industrial conflict on the railroads in which the provocation of the Right Kuomintang people played no small part.

What is happening in Canton is also taking place all over the territory occupied by the national armies. The provincial governments imitate the Canton central government. In July 1926, the shooting of workers and arrest of Communists took place in Wuchow, Kwangsi province. The pretext was that the striking workers were disorganising the rear of the Northern Expedition. Among those shot were three workers who had participated in the Hong-Kong strike.

The same things happen to the peasant organisations. In

Tun Yang Sen, a detachment of the peasant guard was mercilessly destroyed.

In the province of Hupeh, there were a series of cases in October and November 1926 where peasants' organisations were dissolved. In Ma Chin Tan, for example, ten men were fatally wounded in the dispersal of a demonstration of workers and peasants. In Hunan, during the dissolution of a peasant organisation, one of the leaders of this organisation was hanged. The Right Kuomintang people actually direct the most important governmental organs and army corps and utilise them to smash the workers' and peasants' movement. The district captains and commanders of the army corps in various localities act in concert against the workers and peasants, while the courts and the press of the Kuomintang wink at it.

The official government demands that all politics shall be excluded from the programme of the peasant leagues. The peasant organisations are labelled 'robber bands'. In the organs of the Kuomintang the following declarations can be read: In June 1926, the journal *The Rights of Man* wrote: 'What is the present misfortune. . . . We believe it lies in the robber bands and the organisations of the peasantry mixed up with them. That is the greatest misfortune, and we strongly hope that firm measures to annihilate them will be adopted.'

The Republican Gazette writes in the leading article of its issue for July 17, 1926 'The peasant organisations continue to incite only unrest, they destroy the peace of the villages.' The *Go Hua* likewise assails the peasant organisations.

The reduction of farm rents by 25 per cent was 'decided' while Sun Yat Sen was still alive. But it has not yet been carried through, for the whole apparatus of the national government and the Kuomintang is connected by a thousand threads with the bourgeoisie, and through it with the large landowners.

The national government has pursued an impermissible policy towards the workers in the most recent times. On January 5, 1927, the Canton government, in accordance with a decision of the Central Committee of the Kuomintang, published a new law on strikes which forbids the workers to carry weapons during demonstrations, prohibits special strike pickets, and sets up compulsory arbitration for the workers in almost every trade. The representatives of the national government have repeatedly decided directly in favour of the bourgeoisie against the workers, the merchants against the commercial employees, and so forth, in the proceedings of the complsory arbitration commissions. A whole series of cases are known where the followers of Chiang Kai-shek dispersed workers' meetings (in Hankow) which did not suit him, etc. Even the existence of the trade unions has not yet been recognised, and the workers' organisations in Canton and elsewhere under the national government can be considered to this day as 'illegal organisations'.

The revolution has not only not assured the working class the eight-hour day, but has not even assured it one day of rest in the week, nor labour insurance, nor broad social legislation. The master and the factory owner can still subject the coolie and the worker to corporal punishment. The position of the industrial worker in China is even now still extremely miserable, only very little better than that of the coolie.

That is how matters stand with the labour question.

The Kuomintang formally numbers 300,000 members. The government officials enter the party 'out of reasons of service'. Its organisation is indefinite in the extreme. No one can say exactly what is the basic unit of the party, or where the party begins and where it ends. The influence of the average party member on the policy of his leaders is extremely weak but the Central Committee has extensive powers and is at the same time politically unreliable in the extreme.

Actually, an almost unlimited power rests in the hands of Chiang Kai-shek and the other generals.

Perhaps the reorganisation of the Central Committee under-taken at the last Plenum of the Kuomingtang will mean a few improvements. But the fact is that besides the Political Bureau there has been created a 'special committee' with very far-reaching and little-defined full powers.

In social questions, the Central Committee of the Kuomintang has frequently had a policy that recalls the policy of the Cadet party in old Russia. The government has granted few real economic improvements to the workers and peasants. The political legislation of the Kuomintang is equally niggardly and steeped in bourgeois principles.

In our Communist press, especially in the press of our party. the real essence of the Kuomintang, unfortunately, has up to now been painted in glowing colours. The Kuomintang government has been explained among us and continues to be explained as a 'government of the whole population of China' or as a 'bloc of the four classes', etc.

As though Marxism no longer applied to China, and as though a government 'standing above the classes' could exist there! The average reader of our press must have received the impression that the Kuomingtang people are 'almost' Communists (who differ with us only on 'details') and that what is taking place in China at present is already all but a socialist revolution. Even the putsch of Chiang Kai-shek on March 20, 1926, when the Russian Communists were arrested in China, was not mentioned by a single word in our press, and the workers of the USSR, just as the whole international proletariat, knew nothing about this event. Only very recently, in March 1927, did the first article appear, in the review of the ECCI, which lifts the curtain a bit over what is happening in the Kuomintang. In this editorial article, we read:

> The national government is already in the hands of the Centre, which has lately been tending in most cases outspokenly toward the Right. To an even higher degree is this the case with the provincial governments of the South China state. . . . To the Right Kuomintang belong important statesmen, representatives of the bourgeois strata of China and the like. By their past, their present, their social and political connections, the Right Kuomintang people are pre-destined to reach agreements with the imperialists, to reject thoroughgoing social reforms, to stem a further development of the revolutionary workers' and peasants' movement (*die Kommunistische Internationale,* No. 12, March 22, 1927, page 554.)

In the same article we read that the Kuomintang and the national government are seriously concerned over the growth of the labour movement and are issuing laws which are really directed against the right to strike.

When, after all this, the leading article of *die Kommunistische Internationale* declares that 'the Kuomintang is now suffering from a lack of revolutionary workers' and peasants' blood. The Chinese Communist Party must concern itself with an appropriate blood supply, then the situation will change radically' (*Ibid.,* page 557)—such a unique diagnosis and peculiar manner of treating anaemia only attests the profoundly erroneous attitude of the editors of the review themselves.

The recent victories of the national armies have greatly extended the territory of the Kuomintang, by including Hankow and Shanghai, two centres of large working-class populations. Under favourable circumstances, this can lead to a strengthening of the Left wing of the Kuomintang. But even now there is also noticeable a parallel strengthening of the Right wing. One part of the Chinese bourgeoisie, doubtlessly with the full approval of the foreign imperialists, is revising its attitude to the Kuomintang, is going over to its side, endeavours to enter it with the aim of getting at the head of the organisation in order to behead the organisation.

> The bourgeoisie is streaming into the ranks of the Kuomintang, which is also gaining other new members from the commanders of the new troops that flow into the national army. These two sources lead to the strong growth of the right wing. Without having the masses at their disposal, the Rights are strong through their close connection with the whole state and military apparatus. (From an article by L. Heller, the official representative of the RILU in China).

'At the present moment, the forces of the Left wing of the movement are greater than those of the Right. But one must not lose sight of the fact that *in the process of the victories of the Canton armies they have been joined by many camp-followers who can easily be utilised against the interests of the worker and peasant masses,* if the Communist party and the revolutionary Left wing of the Kuomintang are not constantly on guard for the interests of the revolution,' writes Rafes (*The Revolution in China,* page 131), even Rafes, who together with Martinov, sinks back most obviously into Menshevism in the problems of the Chinese revolution.

To compare the present Kuomintang to the workers' and peasants' Soviets, even if only of the February 1917 period, and the remaining of the Chinese Communists within it to the participation of the Russian Communists in the Soviets of that time, is to make a gross error. In the first place, the Kuomintang has in its ranks only 300,000 members (out of a population of 400,000,000) while tens of millions of people were represented in the February Soviets. In the second place, the Bolsheviks, when they went into the February Soviets, maintained the complete independence of their own party, which is not the case in China. In the third place, if the Kuomintang is the same thing as the Soviets were, then why raise objections to the slogan of Soviets in China?

'The Kuomintang is *a cross between party and Soviets'*, said comrade Bukharin in the meeting of the Moscow functionaries on April 4, 1927.

"The Kuomintang is a sort of revolutionary parliament, with its Praesidium, the Central Committee', said comrade Stalin in the same meeting, and added: 'Chiang Kai-shek is a head higher than Tseretelli and Kerensky, for by force of circumstances he is leading a war against the imperialists.'

The one assertion is as false as the other!

If the Kuomintang is a cross between party and Soviets, then why would it not accept the slogan of Soviets? The present leaders of the Kuomintang will certainly be against this slogan.

If the Kuomintang is a revolutionary parliament, the struggle of the parties there is inevitable and necessary. Then why does not the Chinese Communist Party enjoy complete political and organisational independence in this revolutionary parliament?

To 'speak Russian', the Kuomintang can sooner be compared to the old party of the Social Revolutionists (plus part of the 'Left' Cadets) of the days when this party was still progressive.

But it would be more correct to compare the present Kuomintang to the Kemalist party of 1920. At that time, the Kemalist party posed strenuously as a revolutionary, 'almost' Bolshevik party, coquetted with the workers, called the peasant masses to its side, permitted collaboration with the Communists, called its government a 'Council of People's Commissars', etc. But after it had bided its time, it drove the Communists into illegality, slit the throats of a number of their leaders (the murder of comrade Soubkhi and others) and formed a bourgeois national government with a conservative internal policy.

Naturally, Turkey is not to be compared in everything to China. Above all, there exists a numerous working class in China which is capable of playing a great revolutionary role. This basic difference must not be forgotten for a moment. But the working class of China will be able to play this role politically only when it becomes an independent force, when it ceases to be an appendage to the Kuomintang. Then the fate of the Kuomintang also with a correct tactic on our part, will be different from the fate of the Kemalist party. There are many honest supporters of an alliance of the proletariat and the peasantry among the Left Kuomintang people. With a more correct tactic, the Left Kuomintang people would make the final break with the Right, and thereby be enabled to create a mass organisation capable of playing a great revolutionary role. But the historical experience with the development of the Kemalist party should not be lost upon us.

'Will China go the road of Turkey and Kemal Pasha or the road of Lenin and the Bolshevik revolution?' That is how the imperialists put the question (*Peking-Tientsin Times*, March 6, 1927). The greatest danger for the world revolution, especially for the USSR, would be such an evolution of the Kuomintang, that is, a victory of its right wing and a compromise of this 'Kemalist' wing, under the leadership of Chiang Kai-shek or some one else, with American or Anglo-American imperialism. Such a conclusion would be worse than the situation we had before the taking of Shanghai. It would open the Chinese markets to 'peaceful' conquest by international imperialism, which would serve to consolidate capitalist stabilisation. It would free the hands of imperialist England and hasten the moment of a possible expedition of international imperialism against the USSR. The danger of such a conclusion must absolutely be seen.

On this ground alone, we absolutely have the duty: *to tell ourselves and the whole working class the whole truth about the present Kuomintang, to keep the whole international proletariat well informed on this matter, to make no attempt to give diplomatic solutions to questions arising in reality out of the class struggle.* The utilisation of one general against another, in the interest of the revolution, is necessary. But this game with the antagonisms and rivalries among generals cannot replace a class line. Our orientation is towards the masses. Just as the struggle between the Right and Left Social Revolutionists had a tremendous significance at a certain stage of our revolution, so the present struggle between the Left and Right Kuomintang also possesses no small significance. But in any case, we need a *Chinese Communist Party which is independent of both the Right and the Left Kuomintang.*

7.   THE CHINESE COMMUNIST PARTY

The Chinese party is comparatively young. Only after the four month political strike in Shanghai (June to October 1924) and the almost one and a half year boycott strike of the Hong Kong workers (beginning in June 1925), did the Chinese Communist Party begin to grow till it reached 15,000 members (and about as many in the Young Communist League). In the Chinese trade unions, however, there are about one and a half million workers and the young Communist party exerts a strong influence upon them. The Chinese Communist Party also has a certain influence upon the peasants' leagues, which, under somewhat favourable conditions and a correct policy, will grown even more rapidly.

The Chinese Communist Party is a component part of the Kuomintang under exceedingly ambiguous conditions. It assumes the obligation not to criticise Sun Yat Senism, a teaching that has nothing in common with Marxism.

As a TASS telegram of March 23, 1927 reports (this telegram was not made public in our press) the Plenum of the Kuomintang of March 13, 1927 decided among other things 'Nothing shall be published in the organs of the Communist Party that disturbs the collaboration of the Chinese Communist Party with the Kuomintang'. Such a formulation signifies in reality the prohibition of criticism of the Kuomintang by the Communist Party of China. Such obligations must never be assumed by any Communist party.

The Communist organisations are really pretty amorphous. In the eyes of the people, the Communists share the responsibility for all the actions of the Kuomintang, including those directed against the workers and against the peasants, for they abstain from any sharp criticism of the Kuomintang. In their agitation among the masses of the people the Communists never, or almost never, appear in the name of their own party but in the name of the Kuomintang. In this manner the Communist face of the party is frequently lost in its contact with the masses. Despite the colossal scope of events, the Communist Party does not possess its own daily paper to this very day, or, in general, any widely circulated Bolshevist press, although it already has ministers in the National government. The lack of a Communist daily paper really signifies the lack of a Communist organising centre. In a word, the Communist party is really transformed into an annex of the Kuomintang. This is so true, that even in the Chinese party 'there are people who do not consider it possible to kindle the revolution in the village, since they are afraid that to draw the peasantry into the revolution will disrupt the anti-imperialist united front' (Stalin at the Seventh Plenum of the ECCI).

The political and organisational dependence of the Communist Party of China on the Kuomintang makes it impossible for the party to fulfil its duty either to the working class or the peasantry.

The political line of the Communist Party of China is an extreme zigzag. Its basic orientation is neither clear nor stable. The June 1926 Plenum of the CC of the Communist Party of China, for example, adopted the following resolution:

> The alleviation of all these sufferings is an urgent demand of the Chinese people. This is not Bolshevism. It can however be said that this is a Bolshevism in the name of our people but not in the name of Communism. . . .
> They [the bourgeoisie] do not understand that such a minimum of class struggle as is expressed in workers' organisation and strikes in no way weakens the fighting capacity of the anti-imperialist and anti-militarist forces. What is more, they do not understand that the welfare of the Chinese bourgeoisie depends upon the success of the war carried on together with the proletariat against the imperialists and militarists, and not upon the continuation of the class struggle of the proletariat.

This viewpoint is absolutely non-Bolshevik; it is really a Menshevik standpoint. With such a policy of the Communist party the defeat of the working class in the Chinese revolution is guaranteed. But simultaneous with this ultra-Right deviation we also observe ultra-Left moods among the Chinese communists. Declarations something like this: 'The Kuomintang died on March 20, 1926, and since May 15 it has putrefied. So why should we support this rotting corpse with our hands?' (*die Kommunistische Internationale*, March 1, 1927, page 409) are naturally false. As a Communist organisation the Kuomintang could not die, for it never was one. As a petty-bourgeois organisation, which has a strong bourgeois kernel at its centre, it is by no means dead. Such ultra-Left moods are explicable only as a reaction to the false ultra-Right, almost Menshevik policy, to which the erroneous political attitude of the Communist Party of China is leading.

Above all the Communist Party of China must apply in their entirety the theses of Lenin adopted by the Second Congress of the CI, for they alone give a correct orientation which assures the victory.

The Communist Party of China must be legalised in the territory occupied by the national army. For the most part the Communist party is illegal even here, for the leaders of the army suppress the Communists at every opportunity. A Communist mass press must be created. The Communists must speak to the masses in their own name.

8.   The Communist Party of China and the Kuomintang

For the Communist Party of China to remain in the Kuomintang at all costs radically contradicts the theses by Lenin adopted by the Second Congress of the CI. The advocates of this course apparently imagine the line of development as follows: first we will drive ahead to the complete victory of the national army, i.e., to the unification of China, then we will begin to separate the Communist party from the Kuomintang. In other words: first let us make the bourgeois revolution in alliance with the bourgeoisie, and then the proletariat will start acting as an independent class force with a fully independent working class party, etc. This is a Menshevik conception through and through.

One national unification can be entirely different from another. It is well known that after the revolution of 1911 China was unified under Yuan Shi Kai (a cross between a Chinese Stolypin and a Witte). Then, China was unified under Wu Pei Fu (the Chihli period), the present ally of Chang Tso Lin. It is well known how ephemeral was the unification of China under Sun Yat Sen at the beginning of the revolution of 1921, for there were not yet any real class forces capable of assuring this unification.

In the course of the struggle for unification itself, the Chinese proletariat must conquer the leading role. For if the unification is to proceed under the leadership of the bourgeoisie (even the most democratic) the conditions for the further struggle of the proletariat will become much worse. The entrenched national bourgeoisie can impose far more unfavourable conditions upon the proletariat than at present. The proletariat must serve the cause of China's unification—that is the formula of the Chinese bourgeoisie. The national unification of China must serve the cause of the Chinese and international proletariat—that should be the formula of the working class. For the proletariat cannot free itself without freeing the whole world.

The bourgeois revolution and the socialist revolution in China are not separated by a 'Chinese wall'. But the bourgeois revolution can grow and finally develop into a socialist revolution only if the proletariat conquers an ever greater leading role in the bourgeois revolution itself. Lenin insisted on this point:

> The CI should establish temporary agreements, even an alliance, with the revolutionary movement in the colonies and the backward countries, but it must not merge with it, rather it must absolutely maintain the independent character of the proletarian movement— be it only in its embryonic form.

Moreover, in China the proletarian movement is no longer in an embryonic form. The internal contradictions in China, as in every great revolution, are maturing very swiftly.

The Communists can and must support the national armies and the National government. The Communists can and must, under certain conditions, even enter the National government. Lenin was for the entry of the Bolsheviks into a provisional revolutionary government but naturally he was against entry into a provisional government like that of Prince Lvov or Kerensky.

The Chinese Communists can enter the National government upon the following conditions

1. Complete political and organizational independence of the Communist Party of China; full opportunity for it to carry on its agitation, propaganda, organisational work, arming of the workers, etc.

2. Full opportunity for the Communists to criticise the half-measures and mistakes of the Kuomintang before the masses.

3. Strictest control by the Communist party itself and the Communist International over its representatives in the National Government.

4. Full opportunity for the Chinese Communists to raise the *slogan of Soviets* and to defend this slogan before the masses the moment the party judges it opportune.

5. The platform of the government must be of a kind that does not hinder us in the 'education and organisation of the peasantry and the broad masses of the exploited in a revolutionary spirit' (Lenin).

The participation of the Communists in the National government *without these conditions* is pregnant with enormous dangers and may positively break the backbone of the young Communist Party of China.

If we have a few ministers in the Kuomintang movement, but

not a single daily party paper, then such a situation is more than dangerous for the young Communist Party of China, and forces one to doubt that the Communist ministers will accomplish their responsible task. It can be said with certainty that the participation of the Communist ministers in the National government will compromise the party if it remains an annex to the Kuomintang.

It is from the leading article in Number 12 of the journal *die Kommunistische Internationale* (March 1927) that our party learns for the first time that

The June Plenum of the Central Committee of the Chinese Communist Party decided on the following tasks with regard to the Kuomintang:

(1) to pass over from the policy of an alliance from within to the policy of a bloc; (2) to work out a clear independent political line; (3) to strive towards having the urban petty-bourgeois democracy become the foundation of the Kuomintang; (4) to see to it that the Kuomintang is not built up as a centralised party, that its local organisations should rather take on the form of clubs. (March 22, 1927, page 555.)

Further on it is reported that the Communist Party of China considers indispensable the organisation of a Left faction in the Kuomintang. The editorial of *die Kommunistische Internationale* is of the opinion that 'all these decisions must be revised'. Yet the basic tendency of these decisions is undeniably correct. A 'revision' is rather needed of the line that allows the Communist Party of China to remain *an annex of the Kuomintang*.

Is the entry of a Communist party into a non-Communist organization permissible in general? There are cases where it is admissible, where the peculiarity of the situation even makes such a participation necessary. We had such a situation, for example, with regard to the British Labour Party. The Comintern decided at its Second Congress that the British Communists must enter the Labour Party. Lenin motivated this necessity by the peculiarity of the situation. He said

It must be borne in mind that the British Labour Party is in a particularly peculiar position: it is a very original sort of party, or more correctly, it is not a party at all in the ordinary sense of the word. It is made up of the members of trade unions with a membership of about four million, and allows sufficient liberty to all the affiliated political parties.

The British Communists, Lenin continued:

> enjoy sufficient liberty to write that such and such leaders of the
> Labour Party are traitors, that these old leaders represent the interests
> of the bourgeoisie, that they are agents of the bourgeoisie in the
> labour movement . . . when Communists enjoy such liberty . . . it is
> their duty to join the Labour Party.

But only under such conditions.

Besides this, the following must not be lost sight of: Lenin
did not express himself for the participation of the British Communist Party in the Labour Party at a time when a revolution
was already under way in Britain, but in a relatively 'peaceful'
period in British life. The example of the recent British general
strike has shown that the relations between the Labour Party
and the Communists immediately sharpen as soon as the movement rises.

China, however, is passing through a period of revolutionary
rise. The movement is growing and the contradictions between
the working class and the bourgeois section of the Kuomintang
are also growing.

Naturally, the Kuomintang cannot simply be compared with
the British Labour Party. On the one hand, workers predominate
in the English Labour Party. There it is a question of the united
front tactic with members of our own class. Despite this, we
ought not to forget the following words of Lenin on the British
Labour Party:

> Of course, the bulk of the members of the Labour Party are workers;
> however, whether a party is really a political party of the workers
> or not depends not only upon whether it consists of workers but
> also upon who leads it, upon the content of its activities and of its
> political tactics. Only the latter determines whether we have before
> us really a political party of the proletariat. From this point of view,
> the only correct one, the Labour Party is a thoroughly bourgeois
> party, because although it consists of workers, it is led by reaction-
> aries, and the worst reactionaries at that, who act fully in the
> spirit of the bourgeoisie.

The leaders of the British Labour Party are accomplices of
the imperialists and are frequently themselves 'labour' imperialists.

On the other hand, the Left Kuomintang, in so far as it works
together with the Communists, objectively plays the role of an
anti-imperialist factor in the present period. Herein lies naturally

a colossal difference. At the same time, however, it must also not be forgotten that worker elements do not predominate in the Kuomintang. Up to now, bourgeois elements have played a great rôle in the leadership of the Kuomintang, elements who are capable even tomorrow of becoming allies and accomplices of imperialism in one form or another, to one degree or another. The Right Kuomintang leaders are already the allies of imperialism.

It must be remembered that the Kuomintang as a whole fights against imperialism only up to a certain point. The Kuomintang demands the annulment of the unequal treaties imposed upon China, the abolition of the crassest forms of customs dependence, but no more. It must be remembered that so far as customs dependence is concerned, Britain for example considered it possible to meet India half way, and thereby disarmed a section of the Indian national bourgeoisie. It must be clearly seen that the Right and the Centre of the Kuomintang are passionately steering towards a compromise with America, Japan and even Britain, that they will attempt to get loans from them, etc. It is entirely possible that the present struggle of the leading kernel of the Kuomintang against imperialism will quickly give way to an agreement with imperialism.

We should also have no illusions about the 'Left' leaders of the Kuomintang, especially about Wang Chin Wei. At the decisive moment, they may prove to be not one whit better than the 'Left' leaders of the British Trade Union Council. But everything possible must be done to lead the Left Kuomintang people on the revolutionary road, without being transformed into a tail of the Lefts, who are themselves the tail of the Rights.

In principle the question must stand so: the Chinese Communists can and must adhere to the Kuomintang, *but only under the conditions which Lenin agreed to for the entry of the British Communist Party into the Labour Party.* Up till now, this has not been the case.

In the present military and political situation, the Communist Party of China can and must remain in the Kuomintang, but only in order to gather its forces, to begin immediately to rally the masses under its banner, to conduct a relentless struggle against the Right Kuomintang and to strive for their expulsion and destruction. Our slogan under the present circumstances is not withdrawal from the Kuomintang, but the *immediate announcement and realisation of the complete and unconditional political and organi-*

*sational independence of the Communist Party of China from the
Kuomintang, that is, the complete political and organisational
autonomy of the Communist Party of China.*

*The Communist Party of China must declare openly that it
no longer assumes any obligations which restrict its political and
organisational independence in the slightest, and that so far as it
has previously assumed such obligations it now annuls them.
The Communist Party of China, in a manifesto and in a series of
leaflets to the people, must set forth the grounds for such a
declaration. The Communist Party of China must immediately
create its daily press.*

The line for the Communist party remaining in the Kuomintang at any price leads not only to uncritical eulogies of the Kuomintang, not only to cloaking the class struggle in the Kuomintang,
not only to the suppression of facts that cry to high heaven about
the shooting of workers and peasants and the worsening of the
material position of the workers, but also to the direct disorienta-
tion of the parties of the Comintern, including also the Communist
Party of China.

A big meeting called by the French Communists in Paris on
March 23, 1927, at which the leaders of the Communist Party of
France, Semard, Monmousseau, Cachin and others appeared, sent
the following telegram to the Kuomintang:

> The workers of Paris greet the entry of the revolutionary Chinese
> army into Shanghai. Fifty-six years after the Paris Commune and
> ten years after the Russian, the Chinese Commune marks a new
> stage in the development of the world revolution.

The French Communist workers are apparently being told
that the present Kuomintang is the Chinese Commune!

The organ of the German Communists, *die Rote Fahne*, prints
a picture of Chiang Kai-shek on March 17, 1927, and presents him
as the leader of the revolutionary workers of China, without explaining to the German worker who Chiang Kai-shek really is.

Die Rote Fahne of March 18, 1927, reports that 'three million
Chinese workers are in the ranks of the Red International of
Labour Unions'.

One of the largest papers of our Russian party, *Worker of
Baku*, interprets the position of our party in the Chinese question
in such a way that it gives the National government the advice
'to carry on temporarily the policy of Brest-Litovsk on the field

of international policy'. (*Worker of Baku,* April 5, 1927.)

The *Worker of Baku* forgets that the 'policy of Brest' was correct *after the seizure of power by the proletariat, after the establishment of the Soviet republic.* But our party could in no case have proposed the policy of Brest to the government of Kerensky, for example. The government of Scheidemann and Haase, after the overthrow of Wilhelm, also embarked upon a 'policy of Brest', but this does not lead to the victory of the proletarian revolution but to the victory of the bourgeoisie. The policy of Brest practised by social democrats signifies Versailles, and at the same time the victory of the bourgeoisie over the proletarian revolution. The policy of Brest carried through by Chiang Kai-shek would signify the alliance with Anglo-American imperialism. The *Worker of Baku* makes the 'little' mistake of identifying the government of the Kuomintang with a proletarian government. Of course, if this 'little' mistake is permitted, then the Kuomintang may be allowed to crush workers' strikes, and it may also be called the 'Chinese Commune'. The Right and the moderate Kuomintang people will be quite able to come to an agreement with Anglo-American imperialism without the Communists.

But the climax of the mistake is reached by the secretary of the Communist Party of China, comrade Chen Du-Siu, when he signs the joint declaration of the Kuomintang and the Communist Party of China on April 5, 1927. It says:

'Even if our basic views *are not alike in all details,* we must be united.' The suppression of workers' strikes, the disarming of the workers and the shooting down of workers and peasants are merely 'details'!

The document denies the rumours that 'the Communist party is preparing to organise a workers' government, that it wants to invade the concessions by force, and overthrow the government of the Kuomintang'. As if the occupation of the imperialist concessions by the workers were the same thing as the overthrow of the Kuomintang government. It is absolutely false. In Hankow the workers occupied the concessions and that did not at all signify the overthrow of the Kuomintang government. Instead of elevating the revolutionary elements of the Kuomintang to the level of the vanguard of the working class, the Communist Party of China itself sinks in this appeal to the ideological level of the Kuomintang leaders. Such a way of putting the question is pregnant with the greatest dangers.

At the same time the appeal expresses the idea that the present form of collaboration of the Communist party inside the Kuomintang may be replaced by the form of *'alliance' of the two parties.* Obviously a section of the Communists insisted on that.

Our position is not at all the one of converting the Kuomintang into a 'workers' and peasants'' party which is to replace and absorb the Communist party. The idea that we do not need workers' parties in the East, but workers' and peasants' parties, is a complete break with the ideas of Marx and Lenin. There never were any 'workers' and peasants'' parties that could defend the cause of the workers. The ideal of a 'workers' and peasants'' party was realised in Georgia by Noa Jordania, but everyone knows what role Georgian Menshevism actually played. The Kuomintang is a petty bourgeois organisation which we are now supporting *in so far as it fights imperialism.* The peculiarity of the situation even permits our collaboration within the Kuomintang, *if only our political and organisational independence is assured one hundred per cent.* But if the Kuomintang leaders force things to a point where the Communist Party of China is not given the possibility of working together with the Kuomintang under such conditions (that is, under the conditions of complete organisational and political independence), that is, if they expel the Communists from the Kuomintang, *the Communist party must not draw back in fear even from that.* Even then, of course, it will apply the policy of a bloc towards the Kuomintang, so long as the Kuomintang fights against the imperialists. *But the complete political and organisational independence of the workers' party is something that must not be lost sight of for a single moment.*

It is however entirely possible that with a correct tactic of the Comintern and the Communist Party of China, the Left Kuomintang elements will be sufficiently strong to repel the Rights and create the possibility for the Communists to remain within the Kuomintang under the conditions specified above. But if the Communists do not immediately raise the question openly of their complete organizational and political independence, if the Communists relinquish aiding the Left Kuomintang people to create their own faction against the Right, then the political victory of the Right Kuomintang is not out of the question. This victory would have the most ruinous consequences for the whole Chinese revolution, and would do the greatest damage to the cause of the world revolution in general.

Only such a policy can ensure the leading rôle of the working class in the Chinese revolution, and the drawing over to its side of the peasantry and the whole petty bourgeoisie.

> To the question whether the leading role of the proletariat in the bourgeois Russian revolution is possible, we answer: Yes, if the petty bourgeoisie inclines to the Left, not only by our propaganda but by a series of objective factors of an economic, financial (the burdens of the war), military and political nature, etc. (Lenin, *Against the Stream.*)

That is how Lenin wrote in the year 1915.

Only with a correct, independent class policy can the Communist Party of China help the petty bourgeoisie incline to the Left in the Chinese revolution, to the side of the proletariat.

9. ON THE SLOGAN OF SOVIETS

At the present moment, after the capture of Shanghai, now that the National government possesses a territory with 200,000,000 people and large workers' centres are at its disposal, after the great workers' strikes have aroused the peasants' movement, the time has arrived when the slogan of building Soviets can and must be issued, of workers', peasants' and toilers' councils, of Soviets in which the soldiers of the National army also must have their special representation, Soviets to which the representatives of the bourgeoisie should not be admitted. The Second Congress of the Comintern (compare above) already spoke of the necessity of propagating the idea of Soviets even in the East, of creating them at the first opportunity. This moment has arrived in China. Only the building of Soviets is capable of preparing and assuring the non-capitalist road of development in China. Only the building of Soviets can create a better form for the working class leadership of the whole national liberation movement of China. Only the Soviets can shatter the old bourgeois governing apparatus and begin to create a new one, for up till now the old officials have in reality still been administering.

The present platform of the Soviets could be about as follows:

1. Nationalisation of landed property (this demand is also contained in the first programme of Sun Yat Sen. It must be interpreted in a genuinely Bolshevik sense).

2.   Genuine agrarian revolution (not mere reform) with all its consequences, that is, the complete emancipation of the poor and small peasantry from rent payments and from their debts, destruction of all vestiges of feudalism, etc. (the Kuomintang programme of recent date is extremely indefinite: (1) firm regulation of the tax rate; (2) abolition of all special taxes; (3) reorganisation of rural administration; (4) improvement of the conditions of the peasantry; (5) disbandment of all armed detachments formed against the peasants; (6) prohibition of usury; (7) establishment of maximum rent payments, etc., etc. At all events this is not the programme of an agrarian revolution).

3.   Nationalisation of the railways.

4.   Eight-hour day for the workers (and a whole series of other labour laws).

5.   Annulment of the 'unequal treaties', and also the raising of the question of foreign debts.

6.   Confiscation of the Chinese works and factories (large and medium). Nationalisation of the Chinese banks, if their owners combat the national revolution.

7.   As a perspective, the confiscation of the foreign works and factories, the concessions, as well as of plantations and other landed property, etc. The buying out of those foreigners who enter into an agreement can be permitted and the application of confiscation to those who participate in intervention.

8.   Creation of a regular and genuine Red army, that is, a workers' and peasants' army, which is led by workers and not by career officers (the latter must be drawn in and utilised in the spirit of the Russian experiences of the first years of the revolution).

9.   Arming of the workers.

10.   Emancipation of women.

11.   A series of laws that extirpate the remnants of feudalism.

The Soviets in China must of course be adapted to Chinese conditions, that is, wherever necessary 'to adapt them to pre-capitalist conditions' (Lenin). Under present conditions, the immense majority of the population can and must have access to the Chinese Soviets, above all the immense majority of the peasantry. The Soviets in China cannot be an organ of the dictatorship of the proletariat in the present period, but an organ of the dictatorship of the proletariat, the peasantry and the poor city population.

As the next slogans for the peasants we must now raise the following:

1. Abolition of rent payments or at least their immediate reduction by fifty per cent.

2. Suppression of illegal taxes and collectives.

3. Out with the gentry!

4. Disarmament of the Min Tuan.

5. Arming of the peasantry.

Necessary also is the organised arming of the revolution, that is, the creation of Soviets as real centres of the revolution (the Soviets can become the arena for the activity of the Kuomintang as well as of the Communists). The masses of the people who sympathise with the Kuomintang will support the idea of building Soviets if we follow a correct policy. Wherever we succeed in conquering city administrations the Communists must do everything possible to arm the workers and to transform the municipal organs into points of support of the revolutionary movement, and deepen the movement against the bourgeoisie and against the large landowners.

It is understood that in case of a victory of the Soviets in China, a 'Chinese' NEP would also be necessary, with even greater concessions to the petty bourgeoisie in the beginning.

The Communist Party of China must take the offensive with an open and broad propaganda for Soviets and the programme indicated above, without in any way permitting the Kuomintang to tie its hands in this regard. This would be a serious political test for the Left elements of the Kuomintang. This would also signify the attainment of the real political and organisational independence of the Communist Party of China. It would also mean a real deepening of the workers' and peasants' movement in China. A real force would be created against the imperialists and a serious guarantee that the whole present struggle would not in the end be transformed into a mere struggle between the North and the South without any deep social content.

The enormous slaughter by the British and American imperialists cannot be brought to a halt by abandoning the attempt to raise the movement to a higher stage. The imperialists will be

satisfied only if all affairs are turned over to the Right Kuomintang people, that is, to the hands of the bourgeoisie, which will
be transformed tomorrow into an agency of imperialism. The
assault of imperialism can be brought to a halt only when still
greater masses of workers and peasants are brought to their feet,
when they are armed, when Soviets are created that can organise
the resistance of tens and hundreds of millions of the Chinese
people against imperialism under the slogan: Victory or death!

10. THE FOREIGN AND DOMESTIC POSITION OF THE CHINESE REVOLUTION

The Chinese revolution is becoming the point of convergence
of international imperialism. Here is the spot, here is the
place where (for the time being to a small extent) the armed
military forces of international imperialism have gathered. Here
the possibility of a united front of the imperialists of the largest
countries is beginning to appear in outline, although it is still
far from being firmly established. The Nanking massacre shows
how bestial international imperialism becomes as soon as it perceives the first great victories of the Chinese revolution.

The complete victory of the Chinese revolution threatens the
imperialists:

(a) with direct loss of billions (concessions, etc.);

(b) with the loss of markets, particularly in an epoch when
the problem of markets is becoming decisive;

(c) with the extension of the revolutionary 'contagion' to
India, Indo-China, etc.

This also explains the fact that American imperialism, which
up till now best understood how to mask its hostility towards the
Chinese revolution by an outward benevolence, is apparently giving
up its temporising attitude.

The presence of considerable armed forces of international
imperialism in the harbours of China, in the settlement of Shanghai,
etc., creates a tremendously difficult situation for the Chinese revolution. But there is no doubt that with a correct and audacious
policy on the part of the Chinese revolution, the imperialist
brutalities will only unleash still greater forces in China, will only
lead to the disintegration of the 'reliable' sections of the im-

perialist armies, and will call forth an outbreak of indignation among the workers of Europe and America. Only thus can the united front of the imperialists be forestalled. In any case, only the leadership of the working classes can ensure success in this tense and heavy-laden atmosphere.

In April 1922, Lenin wrote:

> And India and China are seething. More than 700 million people live there. Add to them the Asiatic countries adjacent and similar to them, and they are more than half of the population of the earth. There the year 1905 is approaching, irresistibly and ever swifter, but with the essential and tremendous difference that the 1905 revolution in Russia (at least at the beginning) could pass away isolated, that is, without immediately drawing other countries into the revolution, also, whereas the revolution maturing in India and China is already being drawn now into the revolutionary struggle, into the revolutionary movement, into the international revolution. (*Works*, Volume XVIII, Part 2, page 74.)

If Lenin in 1922 was of the opinion that China was 'seething', what would he say about it now, in 1927?

The Chinese revolution can triumph only if it draws other countries into the revolution, if it draws them 'into the international revolution'.

Only when it goes over to the struggle for Soviets can the Chinese revolution get the highest degree of sympathy and support from the international proletariat. 'For the Chinese Soviets' —this appeal will meet with much more understanding and support from the international proletariat than the slogan 'For the Kuomintang'.

No matter how great may be the vacillations, as well as the attempts to shift the Right Kuomintang people to the foreground as more 'acceptable' to international imperialism as possible 'mediators', etc.—all such attempts can only destroy the cause.

The whole Northern expedition was conceived by Chiang Kai-shek not as an expedition of the revolution against the counter-revolution, but more as a strategic step that would ease the position of isolated Canton. It is no credit to Chiang Kai-shek that the powerful movement of the workers and peasants transformed this expedition, in part at least, into an expedition of the revolution against the counter-revolution. The masses themselves, millions of workers and tens of millions of peasants, infused the national struggles with a social, revolutionary content, against the leaders of the Kuomintang and in any case against the Right leaders of the Kuomintang. The events that accompanied the Northern expedition, the surging of the masses, their ebullition, show how much combustible material there is in China, what inexhaustible reservoirs of strength lie in the Chinese revolution, how great are the possibilities for deepening the Chinese revolution and giving it a tremendous impetus.

The foreign and domestic position of the Chinese revolution are closely connected.

The imperialists are extending their tactic in the present period on two fronts.

On the other hand, they are preparing a direct war against the national revolutionary movement and have already begun it in part. In all the harbours of China a war fleet is being concentrated. The strategic points are being occupied. Troops are being brought in greater numbers. The bombardment of Nanking is not merely an episode, but signifies a bloody 'beginning' which may be followed by a terrifically bloody continuation. Feverish military preparations are being made in the foreign settlements not only in Shanghai, but also in Canton. It is not out of the question that in the very next period the masks will be thrown off and foreign imperialism will undertake an open punitive expedition against the Chinese revolution, and without troubling itself about anything, will attempt to establish Chang Tso-lin and their other direct agents 'as the masters of China'.

On the other hand, the imperialists would rather come to an agreement with the 'moderate' (not merely the manifestly Right) elements of the Kuomintang, and are working towards this end not only through bribery and 'caresses' but also through intimidation, ultimatums, etc. America, Japan and France would undoubtedly prefer a 'peaceful' agreement with the 'moderates', a splitting of the national movement and a 'compromise', so that the forms of the exploitation of China, but not the essence, would be somewhat changed. This road, in the final analysis, would also be preferred by the most responsible circles of British imperialism. The imperialist armies sent to Shanghai came too late to help Sun Chuan Fang, but they can now become at the proper moment the allies of the Right Kuomintang people.

The Chinese revolution must see both of these dangers. There is only one way to overcome both these dangers: to bring to their feet all the workers and tens and hundreds of millions of peasants, to impart a clearly expressed social character to the national movement, not to be afraid of scaring away the bourgeoisie, to step forward energetically on the road to the creation of Soviets, to drive the agrarian revolution forward immediately, to proclaim the eight-hour day immediately, to bring real aid immediately to the poor population in city and country at the cost of the rich and the well-to-do, to give the whole movement the strongest impetus by beginning to break through the bourgeois bounds. Only thus can the offensive of the imperialists be repulsed. Only thus can the Rights and the 'moderate' betrayers in the camp of the Kuomintang be rendered harmless. Only thus can the Chinese revolution be saved. Only such an avalanche can halt the foreign imperialists. The endeavours to act in such a manner as 'not to scare away' the Chinese bourgeoisie, as 'not to rebuff' the Rights and the moderate Kuomintang leaders, as 'not to irritate' the foreign bourgeoisie, will only ruin everything. As soon as the imperialists see such endeavours, they will become ten times more insolent and the bourgeois sections of the Kuomintang will take the treasonable steps.

While we are doing everything for the mobilization of the international proletariat against the war danger, we must at the same time help the Chinese revolution to step forward resolutely, to rise higher, without fear of flinging the Chinese bourgeoisie into the camp of reaction.

The argument that the Chinese bourgeoisie 'cannot' betray the Chinese workers because it 'needs them for the struggle against fireign imperialism', is a Menshevik argument. The Mensheviks always said that the Russian bourgeoisie would indeed like to betray the workers but 'could not' because it 'needs them for the struggle against tsarism'. (Martinov now that he has joined the Bolshevik party, repeats the same Menshevik platitudes with regard to the Chinese revolution that he preached with regard to the Russian Revolution when he was a Menshevik.) In reality, the Chinese bourgeoisie has already begun to betray the national revolutionary movement (not to speak of the proletarian movement) as soon as it saw that the working class did not want to be only an instrument in its hands against the foreign bourgeoisie, but raised independent tasks of its own. The Chinese revolution can triumph only under the hegemony of the proletariat.

A consistent revolutionary policy against foreign imperialism presupposes a consistent revolutionary policy with regard to the leaders of the Chinese bourgeoisie, that is, the Right Kuomintang people, and vice versa.

So long as the supreme command remains in the hands of Chiang Kai-shek, so long as the most important government posts remain in the hands of the Kuomintang people, so long as these representatives of the bourgeoisie have their most serious point of support in the Central Committee of the Kuomintang, so long does the cause of the revolution continually find itself in serious danger. Betrayal from within (whether direct or indirect, rapid or slow) is under the present circumstances much more dangerous to the Chinese revolution than the bombardment of Nanking and the occupation troops of Shanghai. If the former co-fighter of Sun Yat Sen, Chiang Tsu Ming, could go over to the counter-revolution, then why should this be impossible for Chiang Kai-shek, who has already shown himself to be the emeny of the workers and the peasants, upon whom the whole imperialist press is staking, concerning whom the most influential organs of imperialism maintain that he is carrying on secret negotiations with Chang Tso-Lin? Leave the supreme command in the hands of this person (even if under supervision) and it will be such indecisiveness that it is a symptom of the greatest internal dangers. If the Communists take even the slightest political responsibility for this, they are treading a very precipitous path. They must leave it immediately.

11.   The International Situation As A Whole

The events of the recent period confirm over and over again the whole relativity of the stabilisation of international capitalism. The situation in China is as taut as a violin string. No matter how the next period may develop, the world equilibrium will in any case become ever more precarious. The perspective of a new war (or new wars) draws increasingly closer. Ever more blasting powder is accumulating in world politics.

The encirclement of the USSR becomes ever more distinct. The last note of Chamberlain is not only a 'newspaper feuilleton', is not only a 'bone thrown to the Diehards' (the differences between the two factions of the British Conservatives should in general not be exaggerated), but is undoubtedly a diplomatic preparation for more energetic steps. This note is an 'incision' whose purpose it is to permit British diplomacy at the proper moment to pass over to more sharply effective methods. This note is a link in a whole chain of policy.

The united front being prepared by American and British imperialism in China can, under certain conditions, become pregnant with great misfortune for Europe also.

A certain strengthening of the partial stabilization in Germany leads to the strengthening of the 'Western' sympathies of the German bourgeoisie. The more zealous Germany diplomacy is of late, the clearer it becomes that the moment is approaching when it may also join in the anti-Soviet front in one way or another.

Italian Fascism has entered completely into the sphere of influence of Britain (recognition of the annexation of Bessarabia by Rumania). In Lithuania a fascist *coup d'état* was carried through, without doubt with the approval of Britain. In Poland the class antagonisms are sharpening which can, all other conditions being equal, accelerate Pilsudski's adventurist designs. Under such conditions, the treaties of non-aggression concluded with Latvia and being prepared with Poland are naturally not the slightest serious security for the USSR, although they do have a certain positive significance for the USSR.

The attacks upon the institutions of the USSR in Peking and the other large cities of China were undoubtedly organised by England and also enjoyed in part the support of America. They are links in a whole chain of a deliberate policy of provocations with which, of course, the USSR neither has had nor will have anything to do. The Peking *coup* was counted on to provoke sharp measures by the Soviet government in Manchuria, and thereby to draw Japan into the struggle against the USSR and free the hands of Britain and America. But among other things it is also counted on to facilitate the work of the Right elements in the Kuomintang and above all to frighten the most moderate leaders of the Kuomintang. It is also not impossible that Chamberlain, by referring to 'documents' which are being forged after the raids and the arrests of our comrades by the Northern troops, will take a new step in the struggle against us, will contrive a campaign in the whole bourgeois press of the world, and will perhaps go to the length of breaking off diplomatic relations with the USSR.

This will be all the easier for Chamberlain, since the General Council of the Trade Unions is obviously ready for any baseness.

The day after the 'cordial' deliberations of the Anglo-Russian Committee in Berlin, the General Council, together with the Central Committee of the Labour Party, declared that it deplored the 'insult to the British flag in China' and proposed to submit the 'conflict' with the National government to the League of Nations, that is, for the same Chamberlain to decide.

Our answer to the action of the imperialists in Peking must be twofold: (1) on the one hand, not to fall into the trap, to answer the provocation with calmness, restraint, and the continuation of the policy of peace; and (2) at the same time to do everything in China itself to deepen the mass movement, to arouse ever-broader sections of the toilers against the imperialists, against their lackeys in the North and against the Right Kuomintang.

By and large, the international situation is becoming tenser than it has been for a long time.

The Chinese question is becoming the main question of the immediate destiny of the world revolution. It may exercise a direct influence on the immediate destiny of the USSR. It is right now that the moment is arriving which Lenin foresaw when he wrote in his political testament:

> To ensure our existence until the next military conflict between the counter-revolutionary imperialist West and the revolutionary and nationalist East, between the most civilised countries of the world and the Orientally backward countries, which, however, account for the majority must become civilised. We, too, lack sufficient civilisation to enable us to pass straight on to socialism, although we have the political requisites for this.

Whether we get 'a second respite' (Lenin, *ibid.*), whether the new crusade against the USSR will fail, as it 'broke down owing to the antagonisms in the camp . . . of the Eastern and Western exploiters, in the camp of Japan and America'—those are the things to which Lenin attached decisive significance.

That is why the very greatest responsibility now rests upon our party and the whole Comintern.

The tactical problem of the present moment consists essentially of this:

1. Along with rendering assistance from every point of view to the Chinese revolution, we must at the same time do everything possible to prevent the extension of an open intervention of international imperialism against the South.

2.   The USSR must pursue, as before, a policy of peace, calling upon the toilers of every country to aid in defending the cause of peace which now finds itself in very serious danger.

3.   At the same time, everything possible must be done to drive the Chinese revolution forward as far as possible and to exert all forces so that it will not only have a merely national, but also a deep social character.

4.   To this end, we must endeavour to create genuine centres of the revolutionary movement of the workers and peasant masses of China, namely, Soviets.

5.   The Communist Party of China must be assisted to achieve real political and organisational independence at all costs. Everything must be destroyed that binds and limits the independence of the Communist Party of China.

*   *   *

This disarming of the workers of Shanghai, the shootings of the Shanghai workers by the commanders of the National Armies, the arrest of the chairman of the Shanghai Trade Union Council, the disarming of the workers in other cities of China—all these are events of the greatest significance.

The present leaders of the Kuomintang are directly taking over the role of Chinese Cavaignacs. The shootings and disarming of the workers in Shanghai are leading directly, from an international viewpoint, to the embracing of the foreign imperialists. The latest events confirm completely the line that is developed in the accompanying document.

G. ZINOVIEV.

Moscow, April 14, 1927.

Speech of Vuyo Vuyovich
DELIVERED AT THE EIGHTH PLENUM OF THE ECCI

COMRADE BUKHARIN began his speech with a historical presentation. Permit me to carry his historical exposition further from where he broke off, for the history of the great revolutionary movement in China does not end on the eve of the march to the North, on the contrary, it is precisely here that its most important phase begins.

First of all, however, a few words on our policy in China up to the Sixth enlarged Plenum of the Communist International, that is, up to the spring of 1926. Yesterday, comrade Petrov, basing himself on numerous quotations, demonstrated here that the principal decisions and the policy of the Chinese party as well as the decisions drawn up by the ECCI before and after the Sixth Plenum were correct.

I am very thankful to comrade Petrov for proving, on the basis of quotations, not only that comrade Zinoviev participated actively in the establishment of the political line in China up to the spring of 1926, but also that all the decisions of principle of the Chinese party and the Communist International at that time were correct.*

That is the best answer to the contentions of comrade Bukharin.

It is highly gratifying that comrade Petrov wants to share the responsibility for the policy in China before the Sixth Plenum of the CI but he exaggerates when he asks that comrade Zinoviev assume the responsibility for the policy that was carried out in

---

* Vuyovich, former secretary of the Young Communist International, was a supporter of the Zinovievist section of the united Opposition Bloc and as such sought to present Zinoviev's whole preceding course as correct. However, this view was not in harmony with the facts. Zinoviev's position on the problems of the Chinese revolution was not only incorrect—and quite in harmony with Stalin's and Bukharin's—prior to 1927, but was extremely weak during the period of the Bloc. As can be seen from his theses, he actually defended a semi-Centrist position even at the time he was delivering a telling criticism of the official line. In their speeches and articles of that period, the apparatus supporters made much of the contrast they revealed between Zinoviev's position and that of Trotsky.—Tr.

China since the Sixth Enlarged Plenum of the ECCI, that is, since the march to the North; for it is a notorious fact that all the decisions on the political independence of the Communist Party of China, on the necessity of preserving its own physiognomy, were practically trampled under foot only in order to maintain the bloc with Chiang Kai-shek at any price.

Comrade Petrov even went so far as to adduce here quotations from the decisions of the Plenum of the Central Committee of the Communist Party of China in July 1926, in order to show that the Communist Party of China always had the intention of preserving its independence and an independent policy. Petrov, or perhaps comrade Martinov, submitted the decisions of this Plenum to a severe criticism in Number 11 of *die Kommunistische Internationale*. The official organ of the ECCI condemned these decisions and proposed to the next congress of the Communist Party of China to revise them. Now, after the *coup d'état* of Chiang Kai-shek, comrade Petrov comes along and bases himself upon the decision whose revision he had asked for, and he wants to prove thereby that the Communist Party of China had a correct policy. Surely, there is no greater hypocrisy than this.

We said in our theses, and we repeat it here: the Chinese Communist Party repeatedly endeavoured to correct its line and to leave the bloc-at-any-price with Chiang Kai-shek, and we proposed in our theses to send a telegram instantly to the Central Committee of the Communist Party of China, saying that the decisions of the July Plenum were correct in essence and that their realisation must be begun immediately. Unfortunately, all the attempts of the Chinese party to correct its political line and its false tactics, encountered the formal opposition of comrade Borodin and the representative of the ECCI in China.

If you want to know what the practical execution of these decisions looked like, the decisions which comrade Petrov condemned two months ago but praised here yesterday, then have the letter of the three comrades from Shanghai laid before you and you will get a vivid picture of what went on in China and continues to go on. You will then grasp much more easily how the *coup d'état* of Chiang Kai-shek was possible.

But let us return to history. It was said here that the Opposition remained silent up to the *coup d'état* of Chiang Kai-shek and that it is now endeavouring to utilise this *coup d'état* for its 'factional' purposes. How do matters really stand?

After the Sixth Plenum of the ECCI, comrade Radek sent his first communication to the Political Bureau of the Communist Party of the Soviet Union in July 1926 and asked for an answer to a series of questions that were arising in China, so that he could bring his activity as rector of the Sun Yat Sen University into harmony with the political line of the party. This letter remained without an answer. In view of the great events that were taking place in China, comrade Radek, at the beginning of the school year, sent a second letter to the Political Bureau with the request for enlightenment, the essential points of which were as follows:

These are questions that require an answer:

1. The establishment of a military dictatorship of Chiang Kai-shek after March 20, 1926 and our attitude toward this dictatorship. The difficulty of this question lies in the fact that Chiang Kai-shek is the leader of the Kuomintang and that Borodin supports him formally. Our intervention against Chiang Kai-shek has a very great political significance here.

2. The results of the work of the Kuomintang among the peasants.

3. The demand of the Kuomintang that the Communists renounce their criticism of Sun Yat Senism.

4. Should the Kuomintang work among the proletariat?

5. How should we support the Left elements of the Kuomintang?

6. The question of the semi-Menshevik tone of the last manifesto of the Plenum of the Executive Committee of the Party of China, in which it says: we must carry on a minimum of class struggle and when the policy of the Communist party is designated as Bolshevik, it is not a matter of Bolshevism but of Bolshevism in the interests of the whole nation.

I consider it my duty to raise these questions and beg you to call upon me to make a report.

After comrade Radek had sent the second letter in July 1926, he took up all these important questions again in September 1926. Absolute silence was the only answer of the Political Bureau.

In January 1927, comrade Radek again took up the most important questions of the Chinese revolution in a series of lectures which he gave in the Sverdlov University in accordance with instructions. But the course of events was so rapid and the dangerous mistakes had accumulated to such an extent, that after the Hankow crisis, comrade Radek considered it his duty to raise these questions openly. Only then did he finally speak in the Communist Academy, where he posed the questions in the following manner:

> The conclusive fate of the Chinese revolution will be decided in Hankow and not in Shanghai. Not the immediate military successes are decisive for the progress of the revolution but the issue of the class struggle inside the national revolutionary movement. Chiang Kai-shek's generals are shooting the workers and peasants almost everywhere and are mobilising for the decisive struggle. The Left Kuomintang and the Communist Party have to muster the courage and the necessary forces to drive away the Right wing and to take over the leadership of the movement. To this end, the workers and peasants must be armed immediately, workers' and peasants' detachments must be formed in the army, the agrarian revolution must be consummated, the social questions must be solved by fulfilling the demands of the workers and above all the organisational independence of the Communist Party must be established, for this independence does not exist in reality and we must fight for the achievement of real homogeneity in the national-revolutionary movement.

What was the answer of the historian Bukharin and of the other comrades of the majority who 'foresaw everything and whose prognoses were confirmed by the facts'?

Instead of examining seriously the questions raised by comrade Radek, they raised a cry about panic, and since just at that time there followed the settlement of the conflict with Chiang Kai-shek, his 'submission' and his declaration of loyalty towards the Central Committee of the Kuomintang, a great shout of victory was raised. But they forgot that in the revolution, as in every other thing, the bourgeoisie never submits to resolutions, but only to armed power.

A few days later Shanghai was taken and a new shout of victory was raised.

In the meantime, the development of events showed that Chiang Kai-shek's march on Shanghai was not a march against the imperialists but a march towards the imperialists in order to establish contact with the imperialist armies stationed in Shanghai, in order to provide himself with a rear guard, and in this way to prepare the execution of the *coup d'état* that had ended in failure a month previously.

Why did they raise a cry about panic, instead of adopting immediately the necessary measures for the dispatch of the enemy in our ranks? Because of the false evaluation of the events in China, because of the underestimation of the bourgeoisie and the role it plays in the Chinese revolution. What were the most characteristic answers?

1. The bourgeoisie would already like to fight against the workers and peasants, but it cannot do it, because it is above all anti-imperialistic and it needs the workers and peasants for its struggle against the imperialists (Martinov).

2. The big bourgeoisie wants to eliminate feudalism in China in order to create the economic foundation for the development of industry. Therefore, it marches against the feudal militarists of the North and against the imperialists who support the remnants of feudalism (Bukharin).

3. The bourgeoisie is a minority in the revolutionary parliament which is constituted by the Kuomintang. It subordinates itself to the majority composed of the Left wing and the Communists. It can do us no harm, we have all the means to utilise it in our own interests and then to cast it aside (Stalin).

In my opinion, there is no essential difference between these three viewpoints which, unfortunately, I have not the time to analyse.

But since I have assumed the role of historian, I would like to bring a really historic speech to your attention, which might otherwise remain unknown to history. That is the speech of comrade Stalin to the party workers of Moscow on April 6, 1927, that is, almost at the very moment when workers' blood flowed in streams in the streets of Shanghai. I take the risk of being accused of lack of loyalty, or of making personal attacks, for comrade Stalin did not touch upon the question yesterday, since he probably counts it among the personal questions. Nevertheless, I made exact notes and hope to render the content of this speech faithfully enough to preserve my calling as a former translator at congresses of the Comintern. Comrade Stalin will always have the opportunity of rectifying unintentional inaccuracies by laying his stenogram before us. What did comrade Stalin say? (I touch only upon the most important questions.)

The Chinese revolution differs from the Russian revolution of 1905 by the fact that it is primarily anti-imperialistic. The essential error of comrade Radek consists of not comprehending that the tempo of development of the revolution in China cannot be so rapid as he would wish. He is impatient; he would like the events to develop rapidly, he does not comprehend that the Russian revolution of 1917 had many difficulties to overcome although the imperialists were divided into two camps at that time which strove against each other; the Chinese revolution will have still greater difficulties, for the imperialists are making a united front in China. That is why the tempo of development will be slower. Radek appears here with very revolutionary slogans: Break with the Right Kuomintang, drive away the Right—a few more of such r-r-revolutionary slogans and the Chinese revolution is lost. Out of the false estimation of the international situation, of the Chinese revolution and its tempo of development, result all the other mistakes of Radek. The Kuomintang is a bloc, a sort of revolutionary parliament with the Right, the Left and the Communists. Why make a *coup d'état*? Why drive away the Right, when we have the majority and when the Right listens to us?

The peasant needs an old worn-out jade as long as she is necessary. He does not drive her away. So it is with us. When the Right is of no more use to us, we will drive it away. At present, we need the Right. It has capable people, who still direct the army and lead it against the imperialists. Chiang Kai-shek has perhaps no sympathy for the revolution, but he is leading the army and cannot do otherwise than lead it against the imperialists.

Besides this, the people of the Right have relations with the generals of Chang Tso-lin and understand very well how to demoralise them and to induce them to pass over to the side of the revolution, bag and baggage, without striking a blow. Also, they have connections with the rich merchants and can raise money from them. So they have to be utilised to the end, squeezed out like a lemon and then flung away.

This, mind you, was said three days before the *coup d'état*.

The Chinese revolution is being led by a broad revolutionary party, whose Central Committee forms a sort of revolutionary parliament. The hegemony belongs to the Communists. If the Communists provoke the Kuomintang, they will be beaten and the hegemony will be transferred to the Right, etc.

In what manner did comrade Stalin view the massacres of workers and peasants by the generals of the national armies, these 'individual questions' with which comrade Bukharin cannot occupy himself from Moscow? Comrade Stalin said: There have been such and there will be more of them. It would be ridiculous to think that a revolution which has lasted two years already could proceed without that. Do we conceal this? No, that is not true. We do not conceal this, but we do not want to exaggerate it in our press, and Stalin concluded with the assurance that there are ways, other than those proposed by Radek, to achieve our aim, not so swift it is true, but more certain.

This speech was delivered a few days before the *coup d'état*. It was never made public. We protest against the confiscation of the articles of the Opposition, against the silence imposed upon us, but we are democratic enough to protest also against the silence that comrade Stalin has imposed upon himself, against this self-confiscation, which in all likelihood is to replace self-criticism. And after all this our new historian, comrade Bukharin, appears here and becomes indignant that comrade Zinoviev in 1925 did not foresee the course of events in 1927 and allowed Hu Han Min to speak before the enlarged Executive in 1926. But comrade Bukharin forgets to read the very next paragraph of comrade Zinoviev's pamphlet, in which Zinoviev, already in 1925, launched the slogan of the arming of the workers and peasants, a slogan that could not be carried out by you, because you wanted to maintain the bloc with Chiang Kai-shek at any price. If you had armed the workers and peasants of China at the right time, the course of the revolution would have been quite different and the *coup d'état* of Chiang Kai-shek would have been made impossible.

To be sure, the secret directions of the Political Bureau of March 3 were quoted here. If these directions actually signified a change of the political line in China, why did it not have any effect at all upon the attitude of our press and upon the content of the speeches which comrade Stalin and comrade Bukharin made a month later to the Moscow party workers? If it was really understood that the line was false, that it must be changed, that another attitude must be adopted towards the big bourgeoisie and Chiang Kai-shek, why was confusion sown in the ranks of all our parties, why was there such a fear to admit the mistakes committed? The directions of March 3 only make the political responsibility of the majority and the responsible organs of the Comintern greater, for this body concerned itself with the Chinese questions, at any rate not the Presidium.

Instead of that, comrade Stalin, on April 6, 1927, accused comrade Radek of understanding nothing about the Chinese revolution, which was above all anti-imperialistic. The principal task consisted of triumphing over the militarists of the North; to break with the Right prematurely would signify the destruction of the revolution. We need not hurry, we need not insist, for the big bourgeoisie is obedient, and we are utilising them. A remark in passing: it was not we who utilised the big bourgeoisie, but they who utilised us, by hastening to occupy more than half the territory that the Kuomintang held at that time and to slaughtter thousands of proletarians so as to carry through the *coup d'état* of Chiang Kai-shek.

Up to now, all the mistakes committed in China have been justified by saying that this was 'a special tactic', corresponding to the 'special conditions' and due to the role of imperialism in China. Today, imperialism has completely disappeared from the presentation of comrade Stalin. Not a word on imperialism in China. The agrarian revolution has stepped into the place of imperialism. In its name, the attempt is now made to justify an equally false policy, in the same way that the false policy before the *coup d'état* of Chiang Kai-shek was justified by the role of imperialism in China.

But where was the agrarian question before the *coup d'état* of Chiang Kai-shek? Was not the agrarian revolution an essential point of the whole national revolution? Because before the *coup d'état* you had postponed the solution of the agrarian question, the completion of the agrarian revolution on the land and, in like manner, the arming of the workers and peasants, only in order to maintain the bloc with the bourgeoisie, which, according to Bukharin, was thoroughly anti-feudal and anti-imperialistic. Formerly, you wanted to use the bourgeoisie in order to beat the militarists of the North and to exterminate the feudal remnants. We have seen the successes. It was demonstrated that the Chinese big bourgeoisie can fight against the remnants of feudalism just as well as the big bourgeoisie of other countries who have achieved the same level of capitalist development.

Now, comrades, you say that the agrarian revolution in China stands on the order of the day, and you contend that the Hankow government has been appointed to complete the agrarian revolution and to direct it. Formerly you said: Chiang Kai-shek must not be driven away, he will not betray us. We, on the contrary, told you that the militarists of the North and the imperialists can be beaten only by removing the big bourgeoisie and Chiang Kai-shek from the leadership of the Kuomintang army. This time, you are repeating the same mistake with the Hankow government, by contending that the petty bourgeoisie has been appointed and is in a position to carry through the agrarian revolution in China. You say 'no Soviets before the agrarian revolution'! Only after the left Kuomintang has completed the agrarian revolution, only when we have utilised them in this sense, will we be able to build Soviets in China. We answer you and appeal to the Chinese workers and peasants: You will never have the agrarian revolution under the leadership of the petty bourgeoisie. You are continuing the same false and criminal policy that prepares a repetition of the *coup d'état* of Chiang Kai-shek, and this time a *coup d'état* of the vacillating Left leaders of the Kuomintang and the generals of the national army of Hankow.

The government of Hankow will be able to accomplish the agrarian revolution only when the hegemony of the proletariat is guaranteed on this territory. And the only means of achieving the hegemony of the proletariat in the Hankow government and in the left Kuomintang does not lie in making concessions to the petty bourgeoisie, for it swings continuously to and fro between the proletariat and the big bourgeoisie and will finally go over to the stronger side; the only means lies in the organisation of the forces of the proletariat and the peasantry and in investing it with an organisational form—the Soviets—that will not only make it possible for us to mobilise the broad masses, but also to conquer the leadership of these masses for the Communist party, in the Soviets as well as in the Kuomintang.

Comrades, what you are doing in this case is only a continuation of the policy of concessions, but this time to the petty bourgeoisie. Comrade Bukharin could not cite a single concrete fact to show what the Hankow government has done, since the last session of the Central Committee of the party, or at least since the *coup d'état* of Chiang Kai-shek, really to arm the workers and peasants and to help the peasants take possession of the land.

(*Heinz Neumann:* The Hankow government has defeated the militarists of North China!)

Comrade Neumann, Chiang Kai-shek also defeated the militarists of the North. We greet these victories with all our heart. But we repeat to you once more: the most essential thing is not the overthrow of the militarists of the North in general, but their defeat by the national armies, by the national movement, whose direction lies in the hands of the only class that is really in a position to accomplish the agrarian revolution, namely, in the hands of the proletariat.

We do not know what surprises the present generals of the Hankow government, Tan Shen Shi and Feng Yu-hsiang, are preparing for us tomorrow. You do not know, either. The former is a real feudal lord, and the latter entered the Kuomintang only recently. The last number of the *Manchester Guardian* carries the report that Feng Yu-hsiang is sending telegrams to Chiang Kai-shek in Shanghai to keep him informed on his military victories.

The only possible organisation at present is the Soviet which mobilises the masses of the workers and peasants and guarantees the hegemony of the Communist party in the Kuomintang and on the territory of the national revolutionary movement.

(*Semard:* That is full of contradictions-)

There is no contradiction here. If the Hankow government is revolutionary, as you contend, if it is in a position to accomplish the agrarian revolution, then why should this Hankow government be against Soviets and against the revolutionary organisation of the workers and peasants? It is against them, because it will only help to accomplish the agrarian revolution when we are strong enough to consolidate the armed workers and peasants in Soviets under the leadership of the Communist Party. Only in this case will the petty bourgeoisie be able to accomplish the agrarian revolution. In the contrary case, however, it will finish by running over to the side of the big bourgeoisie.

I conclude my speech with the remark that the Chinese comrade was right when he said today that the Chinese revolution will triumph only under the banner of Lenin. That is true, comrades; it is not under the banner of the Kuomintang, so dear to our comrade Bukharin, that the revolution in China, even the agrarian revolution, will triumph, but only under the red banner of the Soviets and under the banner of Leninism.

V. VUYOVICH.

Moscow, May 1927

The Letter from Shanghai

THE EVENTS OF recent months and especially the last events in Shanghai have finally convinced us that the present leadership of the Communist Party of China is incapable of conducting a firm Communist policy, a policy which is all the more necessary in political conditions that have become most complicated. In the leadership of the party there is a group which is determinedly driving the party to the Right on the path of liquidation, and this group and its policy are supported by the representative of the ECCI. The further this goes the deeper and more extensive will become the crisis that has risen in the party, and if the ECCI does not intervene immediately, it may have grave consequences for the party as well as for the Chinese revolution. The reason for the crisis must be sought in the fact that the leaders of the Chinese party have considered and still consider the Chinese revolution as the bourgeois revolution from which nothing more than democratic liberties and a slight improvement in the economic situation can be expected. They do not believe in the socialist path of development of the Chinese revolution, just as they do not believe either in the Chinese proletariat or in the peasantry, in the masses or in mass action. The conception of the leading kernel was approximately this: China is living through its national revolution, which is directed against the imperialists and the feudal militarists. In this revolution all classes are participating, among them also the national bourgeoisie, the well-off gentry and the landowners, and that is why class peace must be maintained as the guarantee for the victory of the revolution. We give only one example of how this conception was transformed in practice into the worst kind of opportunism. The resolution on the report of the CC at its Plenum of December 13, 1926 speaks of dangerous tendencies in the national revolutionary movement and declares:

> The greatest danger is that the mass movement is developing towards the Left, while the political and military authorities, seeing the swift growth of the mass movement, are seized with panic, and begin to incline to the Right. Should these *extreme tendencies* continue to develop in the future, the cleavage between the masses and the government will deepen, and in the end the Red united front will be demolished and the whole national movement will be endangered.

The natural conclusion from this is: the mass movement must be limited, the wave of the workers' and peasants' movements, rising with an elemental force, dammed up.

> In the practical struggle of the workers and peasants [the resolution further declares] we must avoid illusions (exorbitant demands of the artisans and the workers, participation of the workers' guard in administrative affairs, seizure of land by the peasants, etc.), so as to eradicate the infantile disease of Leftism.

The leading circle of the party does not understand the mass movement; still more, it is afraid of it, it considers it as something out of place, at any rate, as an untimely phenomenon that hampers the united front with the bourgeoisie. It therefore subordinates the interests of the working class and the peasantry to the interests of the bourgeoisie and trots along at the heels of the bourgeoisie; therefore, on the one hand, it curbs the mass movement and, on the other hand, enters into all sorts of combinations at the top, sinking into bargaining over crumbs, and to horse-trading, which, under revolutionary conditions, are equivalent to Menshevism. Since it regards itself solely in a secondary rôle of assistance in the Chinese revolution, it effaces itself, the party and the mass movement, and thus plays into the hands of the Right. The last four months brought a great deal that is new into the Chinese revolution. The growth of the revolutionary movement, and the sharpening of the inner contradictions based on this growth, have created an extremely complicated situation. The struggle for the hegemony of the proletariat in the Chinese revolution is actually the task of the day. We are of the opinion that it is just in these last months that the leadership of the Chinese party has shown that it can lead the party and the working class only to defeat and capitulation.

Recent months, that is, the period beginning about the end of November, are characterised by the following facts: 1. The national revolutionary army has won a decisive victory by defeating Sun Chuan Fang; 2. In connection with this victory, a certain flirting of the imperialists with the Nationalist government and the Right Kuomintang has begun; 3. The mass movement has embraced ever new strata and has swung to a height never before attained; 4. The accentuated inner contradictions have led to an acute conflict between the Left and the Right Kuomintang. This period is marked by four features. 1. The reaction in Hankow;

2. The occupation of the concessions in Hankow; 3. The conflict between the CC of the Kuomintang and Chiang Kai-shek on the question of the seat of government; and 4. The uprising in Shanghai. Now, what were the tactics of our party in this period?

CANTON

Since the departure of the government for Wuhan, the Rights, who remained in Canton, with Li Ti Sin at their head, and with the approval of Chiang Kai-shek, have inaugurated a rabid campaign against the Communists. It was said that since the Northern Expedition had won a decisive victory in Kiangsi, Canton was therefore outside of the war zone and a certain stabilisation had to be established, which demanded 'normal' conditions. The first step towards creating these 'normal' conditions was the removal of the police chief for his amicable relations with the Communists, the dispersal of the Kuomintang committee and the replacement of the Left by the Right, the decree forbidding strikes in the large public utilities, the prohibition of picketing in strikes, the disarming of the workers' guard, etc. The new Provincial Committee of the Kuomintang decided to prevent strikes, to give strike-breakers a free field, and it pronounced itself against the decreasing of rental payments by twenty-five per cent. Then began the arrests of workers, the persecution of workers among the peasantry, anti-British demonstrations were forbidden and the gentry in the villages were encouraged. The government began to subsidise and to arm the Right-Wing labour organisation, the Mechanics' Union, and the Workers' Federation of Kwangtung, and incited them against the left-wing labour organisations.

This 'stabilisation' mood infected the Kuomintang people not only in Canton, but also in the North. In Hankow, the organised bourgeoisie came out against the workers' demands. The government wanted to follow the example of Canton and introduce compulsory arbitration. Finally, the notorious Right Kuomintang speech of comrade Borodin also runs in this groove and was inspired by the same 'stabilisation' mood. Now, how did our party respond to the reaction that began in Canton and spread all over the country? In general, not at all, so far as one can speak of measures of struggle against the reaction. The resolution on the Kwangtung question adopted by the Central Committee says literally as follows:

> The reason for the recent joint attack against the Communists and
> the elements of the Left who stand close to them, by the Centre,
> Right and Left is, first, that the Provincial Committee of our party
> in Kwangtung does not recognise the Left wing, and second, that
> it underestimates the influence of the Left leaders.

And the CC proposes to wait until Wang Chin Wei returns.
. . . We do not want to justify the standpoint of the Canton Left
who, thanks to Borodin's influence, actually underestimated the
Left, but we cannot understand how the leading organ of the party
can throw the responsibility for the activities of the reactionaries,
which are to be explained by the growth of the mass movement, on
the local party organisation without adopting the standpoint that
this mass movement must be emasculated. The CC of our party
has showed itself helpless to begin the struggle against the reaction.
The proletariat of Hankow undertook this struggle over the head
of the Kuomintang, and over the head of our party and its leading
organs, when it occupied the British concessions on January 3,
stimulated a new upsurge of the anti-imperialist movement, and
struck the heaviest blow at internal reaction at the same time.

HANKOW

Nobody foresaw the events of January 3. The occupation of
the concessions by the Hankow workers took place spontaneously,
without any leadership or instigation either from the government,
from the Kuomintang, or from our party. They were all confronted by an accomplished fact, by a spontaneous act of the
masses, and all of them had to reckon with it. The events in
Hankow were of exceptional significance. Britain had its ears
boxed. The masses and the party organisations, which had suc-
cumbed to disillusionment, were again aroused, the Right wing
of the Kuomintang received a blow, and the national anti-imperialist
movement overflowed the whole country and forced even such
reactionaries as Chang Tso-lin to begin speaking a pseudo-
nationalist language, to demand the return of the concessions, etc.
Besides this, the events in Hankow had a great revolutionising
effect upon the government and upon Borodin: against their will,
they turned to the Left under the pressure and the influence of

this spontaneous action of the masses; the December moods were in a certain sense destroyed and when, two weeks afterward, the conflict arose with Chiang Kai-shek over the question of the seat of government, the members of the government and Borodin adopted a Left position, which would most likely have been unthinkable without the events of January 3. The Left wing, which, as many believed, hardly existed any longer, consolidated itself, and this was accomplished by a certain crystallisation of the Right wing around Chiang Kai-shek in Nanking, which led to the conflict between Nanking and Hankow.

Now, how did the CC of the Communist Party of China react to the events in Hankow? *At first, it did not want to react at all.* When the question was presented at the conference of the CC and the Russian comrades, comrade Chen Du-Siu exclaimed: *'Why should we clamour over it and what kind of agitation should we develop when the aggressors were not the British but the Chinese?'* This was already on January 12 or 13. Only two or three weeks after the events did the CC issue an appeal on them. At the same time it sent a letter to the Hupeh Committee, and accused our comrades of responsibility for the fact that the workers' guard had maintained order from the first day of the occupation of the concessions. The CC was of the opinion that the foreigners and the petty bourgeoisie should not have been incensed.

NANKING-WUHAN

In January began the conflict over the question of the seat of government. The Wuhan group, the majority of the CC of the Kuomintang and of the government, insisted that in conformity with a decision that had been adopted back in Canton, the government should be transferred to Wuhan. The Nanking group, however, with Chiang Kai-shek at its head, insisted that the seat of government 'be left' at Nanking. Naturally, this dispute was not a simple dispute over the seat of the government. The question was whether the national revolutionary movement would go with the masses and the Communist Party, or with the dictator Chiang Kai-shek, who was already steering towards a compromise with Japan and Mukden. The dispute was and is concerned with the two paths of development of the Chinese revolution. The conflict assumed an extremely sharp character. For two months already there have actually existed two governments, two Central Committees and two Political Bureaux of the Kuomintang, two armies. Nanking has become the Right wing centre. The Kuomintang committee of Shansi, composed of a majority of Communists, was dispersed and replaced by a new one composed of seven Rights, one Centrist and one ex-Communist. Chiang Kai-shek entered into negotiations with Yeng Yui Tin (of Mukden) without the Kuomintang knowing a thing about it. Through politcians like the former minister Tuan Tsi-Chui, through Huan Fu, or Tai Tsi Tao, and also directly, he carried on secret negotiations with the Japanese. The same is being done by his creature, Ho Yin-Tsin, in Fuchang. Without daring to stand up openly against the USSR and the CI, Chiang Kai-shek began a struggle against Borodin, Galen and others, and endeavoured to invest the conflict with a personal character.

Very characteristic is the following declaration by Chiang Kai-shek* to the Commander of the Sixth Army Corps, Chen Chin:

> I am not at all opposed to the Russian Communists, I am only against the Right wing of the CPSU at whose head stands Stalin, but I know that a Left wing also exists in the CPSU, led by Trotsky and Zinoviev. I am ready to work together with them because the Left is for the complete support of the national revolution in China and for the withdrawal of the Communists from the Kuomintang, while the Right wing, represented by Borodin, Galen and others, though also for supporting the national revolution, are, however, against the withdrawal of the Communists from the Kuomintang. If they would send Radek or Karakhan here, I would be able to work with them.

While Chiang Kai-shek disguises himself as a 'Russian Left Communist' (as Chen Chin expresses it), he has conducted a rabid hunt against the Communists, and finally came forward on February 21 with a veritable pogrom speech against the Communist Party of China.

What did the CC of our party do on this occasion? One would think that it should have launched the broadest mass campaign under the slogan of support to the Wuhan government and with the demand that the Nanking group submit to the decision of the majority of the CC; one would think that the party would expose the real motives behind this conflict, uncover the Right

---

* It is to this alleged statement by Chiang Kai-shek that Trotsky refers in his reply to Stalin's theses. See page 65.—Tr.

intriguers surrounding Chiang Kai-shek and vigorously push the government and Borodin so that they would drop the personal tinge they imparted to this conflict and come forward before the masses with a political platform of social reforms, primarily of agrarian reform, and force Chiang Kai-shek (if he would) to take up the struggle on the basis of a definite political platform, which would have created the greatest difficulties for him. But the CC of the Communist Party of China and the representative of the ECCI simply 'did not notice' this conflict for a long time and took no position towards it. Even up to the middle of February, that is, when the conflict had already come to an unusually sharp pass, nobody in Hankow knew what was the position of the CC of our party. Upon our energetic proposals to the representative of the ECCI and the CC to move immediately to Hankow so as to direct from there the party and the government of the Wuhan group, we were met with nothing but evasions. Neither the representative of the ECCI, nor the CC, wanted to participate in the struggle against the internal reaction, which the Left and Borodin (probably against his will) wanted to begin, and they were of the opinion that we can and must make concessions to Chiang Kai-shek, even though they didn't say so openly. This line, if it can be called a line at all, was not so much the course of the CC as it was of comrade V.* This can be seen, for example, from the fact that, after he had left for Hankow and seen Chiang Kai-shek, he made the request of Moscow to recall Borodin and supplemented this request ambiguously with the remark that otherwise Chiang Kai-shek would not make any serious concessions. During his absence, however, the CC adopted a more correct standpoint, when it declared that it was a question of the struggle of the proletariat for hegemony, and that any concession in the form of a recall of Borodin would be equivalent to a complete capitulation.

We do not entertain the slightest illusions about Borodin. As a Communist, we regard Borodin as one who is greatly similar to a Left Kuomintang man; and like every petty bourgeois revolutionist, he is subject to very great vacillations. After March 20,

---

* The reference is evidently to Voitinsky, one of the apparatus 'experts' on the Far East who represented the Communist International at that time in China.—Tr.

1926*, he was for withdrawing from the Kuomintang, denied the significance of the Left wing and even denied its very existence. By this, he lent support to that nihilism towards the Left Kuomintang which is prevalent among the Kwangtung comrades. Then, this denial of the Left wing led him remorselessly to the Right, to that capitulationist and laggard's position which found expression in his speech of December 12, and in his idea of 'buying back the land'. In January, he oscillated towards the Left, came forward at a banquet with a speech against personal dictatorship, that is, against Chiang Kai-shek, and thus became the involuntary instigator of a struggle from which he himself immediately recoiled in fright. In the middle of February, he himself confessed to comrade F.† :

> I am afraid I made a mistake in this question. My standing up against Chiang Kai-shek was provoked by the pressure of public opinion, and I do not know if I acted correctly. We will get as far as Peking with Chiang Kai-shek, but hardly with the party [i.e., with the Kuomintang].

With this, Borodin characterised himself excellently, and one can hardly speak of a principled difference between the position of the Right group in the CC of the CPC, of comrade V. and of Borodin.

But we are of the opinion that to recall Borodin under the present political circumstances, would be to put ourselves at the mercies of Chiang Kai-shek, because just as Chiang Kai-Shek has by force of circumstances become the banner of reaction, so Borodin has become the banner of the revolutionary elements of the national movement and the banner of the USSR. With all his shortcomings, with all his wretchedness and lack of principle, Borodin today nevertheless personifies the Left wing of the Kuomintang on the one hand, and the USSR on the other. This accounts for our position on this question. But the position of the representative of the ECCI cannot be explained by any principled motives. Since he disregards the principled content of the struggle, he has slipped down, here as everywhere else, into a combinationism which is pernicious and dangerous for the whole revolutionary movement.

---

* The date of Chiang Kai-Shek's first reactionary coup in Canton, which was carefully hushed up in the international Communist press.
† The initial apparently stands for Fokine, one of the signatories to this document.—Tr.

We repeat: in the Nanking-Wuhan conflict, the leading core of the party took no steps for a period of two months, and if we do not count the last telegrams about Borodin, adopted on the insistence of a group of 'Left' comrades, the CC has only concealed itself and evaded an answer to the questions posed before it by the situation.

The local party organisation in Hupeh developed a campaign on its own responsibility on this question without waiting for the decision of the CC.

But the question of Borodin has become one of the main questions in this conflict. Chiang Kai-shek and the Right Kuomintang people have come out openly against the Communists. Our party should have answered openly every accusation brought against it with a clear and distinct political declaration. It did not do this. The Right Kuomintang and the bourgeois and imperialist press conducted a rabid campaign on this occasion and the Communist Party of China was silent, hoping to liquidate the conflict by all sorts of combinations, agreements and dickering.

Under the conditions of struggle between the Right and Left wings of the Kuomintang, the Shanghai question assumes special importance. Chiang Kai-shek needs Shanghai as a base for his further struggle against the Left wing and the Communists, as well as for his negotiations with the North and the imperialists; Chiang Kai-shek marched against Shanghai with the idea in mind that its occupation would give him an incontestable preponderance in the struggle with the Left for the leadership of the Kuomintang. Through Chiang Kai-shek, the Chinese bourgeoisie aspires to assure its hegemony in the national revolution. There could be and there were three tactics in this connection. One group of comrades, especially the Russians and Borodin, were of the opinion that it would not hurt for Chiang Kai-shek to break his neck on Shanghai and Chekiang, and they egged him on; comrade Galen was of the opinion that the march on Shanghai was a hopeless military undertaking and did not participate in it. These comrades failed to take into consideration that not only Chiang Kai-shek, but also the Chinese national revolution was conducting the struggle in Chekiang, and that a victory for Chiang Kai-shek would at the same time be a victory for the revolution, while a defeat would be shared by Chiang Kai-shek and the revolution.

The second tactic consisted of supporting, unconditionally and without circumlocution, Chiang Kai-shek's march on Shanghai, of uniting with his representative in Shanghai itself to prepare an uprising, and thereby to help the troops of the national revolutionary army to march into Shanghai. This group of comrades, representing the Right wing of the CC and the Shanghai Committee, failed to consider that Chiang Kai-shek would create a Right-wing government in Shanghai and would seek to convert Shanghai into a fortress of the Right wing of the Kuomintang. Whether consciously or not, these comrades consented to hand over power to Chiang Kai-shek in Shanghai, that is, to help the bourgeoisie entrench itself there.

The third tactic, which we and a part of the Chinese comrades supported, consisted, on the one hand, of supporting with all means the capture of Shanghai by the people's revolutionary army and, on the other hand, by unleashing of a mass movement in Shanghai as a counterpoise to the Right wing, of creating a democratic people's power so that the democratic factor would predominate over the military factor and the occupation of Shanghai would simultaneously result in the victory of the national revolution, of the anti-imperialist movement, and in the defeat of Chiang Kai-shek as the representative of the bourgeois Right wing of the Kuomintang. We were of the opinion that Shanghai had become the point at which the question of the hegemony of the proletariat would be decided. Moreover, the uprising of the Shanghai proletariat from February 19 to February 24 was objectively an attempt to assure its hegemony.

With the first reports of the defeat of Sun Chuan Fang*, the atmosphere in Shanghai became red-hot and in a couple of days a spontaneous strike of 300,000 workers broke out which just as spontaneously changed into an armed uprising and, lacking leadership, vanished into nothing.

In a previous letter, we have dwelled in detail upon the tactic of our party during the events in Shanghai. We therefore want only to underscore here the principal points.

The Canton advance guard is twenty-five to thirty miles from Shanghai. The troops of Sun Chuan Fang, absolutely demoralised, begin pillaging and dispersing homewards. In the city, sections of

---

*   Chinese mercenary general whose defeat in the Shanghai territory finally made possible the occupation of the city by Chiang Kai-Shek's troops.—Tr.

the military forces waver, the fleet comes over to our side. Three hundred thousand workers go out on strike and pass over to armed struggle. The military commander executes dozens of workers. A part of the petty bourgeoisie already comes out in sympathy with the workers, intervenes in the struggle and shuts up shop. At the same time, the CC of our party, which was taken completely unawares by the strike, even though it participated in its preparation, reflects on whether the uprising should be made or not, at the very moment when the uprising is already taking place. Neither the workers, the soldiers, nor the petty bourgeoisie receive as much as a single suggestion about what is to be done. The party confines itself to the bare slogan: 'Down with Sun Chuan Fang' and 'Hail the Northern Expedition' (in some places even simply 'Hail Chiang Kai-shek'). The anti-imperialist slogans disappear completely. One of the appeals to the workers, for example, declares:

'Sun Chuan Fang was far more cruel than the imperialists who committed the bloody massacre of May 30.'

By the very separation of the struggle against Sun Chuan Fang from the struggle against the imperialists, the party cooled the ardour of the masses. Instead of speaking with the masses, the party representatives spoke with the representatives of the bourgeoisie, waited for them, put their hopes in them. The slogan of the democratic national assembly, which we had advanced shortly before the strike, was conceived of as a new means of combinations at the top, and was not launched among the masses. As a result, we let slip by an exceptionally favourable historical moment, a rare combination of circumstances, where power lay in the streets but the party did not know how to take it. Worse yet, it didn't want to take it; it was afraid to.

Thus, the Right tendency, which has already contaminated the party for a year, found a crass and consummate expression during the Shanghai events, which can only be compared to the tactics of the German Central Committee in 1923 and of the Mensheviks during the December uprising in 1905. Yet there is a difference. It lies in the fact that in Shanghai the proletariat had considerably more forces and chances on its side and with an energetic intervention, it could have won Shanghai for the revolution and changed the relationship of forces within the Kuomintang.

It is not by accident that the leadership of the Chinese Communist Party committeed these errors. They flowed from the right-wing conception of the revolution, the lack of understanding of the mass movement and the complete lack of attention towards it.

THE PARTY AND THE MASSES

The upper strata of the Communist Party of China are not in touch with the masses. This is explained historically by the fact that three years ago the party was still only a small circle of intellectuals, and that the party leadership found it hard to understand that it had long ago ceased to be a circle and had been transformed into a party with 30,000 members, which enjoys influence over millions of workers and peasants and is the most powerful organised force of the Chinese revolution. Instead of hastening the liquidation of this detestable spirit of a small circle, the representative of the ECCI encouraged it and gave it his blessing.

The leadership of the party, of the organisations of the workers and peasants, consists everywhere of intellectuals, students, who with all their good qualities are very little connected with the masses and do not always understand their needs. This condition persisted up to now, not, it is true, because there were no workers capable of participating in the leadership, but because the upper circles of the party organisations do not want to admit the workers into leadership. Only a short time ago, in the middle of February, a party conference took place in Shanghai. As is known, seventy per cent of the Shanghai organisation consists of workers, but in the newly-elected party committee, sixteen were chosen, among whom there was not a single worker; three workers did get through as candidates. The attitude of the party leaders towards workers and peasants was best formulated by the member of the Central Committee, comrade Petrov*, when the question of selecting students for a special course at the Communist University for the Toilers of the East was being considered. According to the arrangements, 175 workers and 100 peasants were to be named. Comrade Petrov explained to us that the CC decided to send only intellectuals and students, and motivated the decision with the following arguments:

---

* Despite the Slavic name, in all probability a Chinese Communist, a number of whom adopted similar pseudonyms.—Tr.

1. The workers cannot read, cannot write, cannot speak and cannot understand anything. Where shall we find 175 workers for the course?

2. The workers and peasants, should they get the chance for a special course in Russia, will live under favourable conditions. This will have a demoralising effect upon them and upon their return to China they will not want to work for the party.

The students, on the contrary, according to comrade Petrov's opinion, are not afflicted with this defect. What was necessary was not Communist workers and peasants, but non-party people who could read and write very little, or illiterates. When we insisted on this, the CC, even if unwillingly, accepted our plan, but the attitude of the leaders of a workers' party towards the masses is very characteristic in this case. The attitude of the CC to the workers' guard in Hankow was about the same. The Old Man* said to us that the workers' guard in Hankow must be disbanded because it consisted of petty bourgeois and artisans, and partly of non-industrial workers. He was of the opinion that the workers' guard must consist of a small number of 'honest, class-conscious, irreproachable' workers (it was a question of the workers' guard of Hankow).

When we looked into the matter, it appeared that the reference to the petty bourgeois nature of the workers' guard in Hankow was simply a slander, which the representative of the ECCI had picked up. The workers' guard in Hankow consists of workers, mostly of non-industrial workers, it is true, but to call it an 'armed power of the petty bourgeoisie' is not at all correct.

The attitude of the right-wing group in the CC towards a people's representative assembly in Shanghai is also accounted for by this lack of faith in the masses and lack of understanding of them. When we proposed to carry through the elections to this popular national assembly in the factories and the streets, the

---

* Chen Du-Siu, secretary, founder and acknowledged leader of the Chinese Communist Party during the whole revolutionary period. A respected figure in the Chinese revolutionary movement, he faithfully executed the policies of Stalin and Bukharin during 1925-1927. In 1929, he published a letter to the Chinese Communists announcing his support of the Left Opposition led by Trotsky and explaining his own part in the defeat of the Chinese revolution as well as the part played by Stalin and Bukharin under whose direction he had worked.—Tr.

leading comrades could not understand it for a long time. They decided to substitute representatives of organisations instead of elected delegates, in connection with which the Old Man said: 'Otherwise the workers may elect the devil knows whom'.

According to the conception of the leading core of the party, the workers and peasants are a dull, dumb mass, unconscious and inactive; this mass must be led by the Communists along a road which they themselves outline, without consulting these masses. The party leadership declares, for example, that the peasants do not want land. Still more, they would not even demand the reduction of rent payments, had not the Communists incited them to it with their agitation. In Shanghai, the leaders declared at the very moment when the workers were in an uprising, that the workers want no uprising, and that the people of Shanghai do not want to take power. The idea of a people's representative assembly is called by the secretary of the Shanghai Committee, Bukharov,* an 'exotic idea'. This complete lack of understanding of the needs, the demands, and the struggle of the masses, this disdainful and arrogant attitude leads to this: that all mass movements take place spontaneously, without the party and outside of it. It has already reached a point where events are ascertained *post factum* and then 'acknowledged'. The struggle of the peasants against the gentry, the struggle for the reduction of rent payments and the price of land, took place and still takes place spontaneously. The Hankow proletariat occupied the English concessions spontaneously. The strike in Shanghai arose and went on almost spontaneously. The right-wing group of party leaders, however, stubbornly persist in its disbelief in the masses. At best, the party creeps along at the tail of events, is in no position to direct them, not because its influence has been organisationally insufficiently strong, but because the heads of the party are sinking into opportunism and tail-end-ism.

THE PEASANTS' MOVEMENT

Disbelief in the masses is reflected above all in the lack of attention to the mass movement and also in the curbing of this movement.

---

* See footnote at the bottom of page 413.—Tr.

Up to October 1926, the question of the peasantry, the question of the struggle of the peasantry, was never raised in a more or less serious form either by the representative of the ECCI or by the CC, if the decisions of the June Plenum of the CC are excepted which completely hushed up the peasants' struggle and appealed for a bloc with the 'good gentry' and the big landlords. In October, a programme of peasants' demands was worked out, but the representative of the ECCI, as well as the party leaders, considered it only as a programme for the party congress. For a period of three to four months, this programme did not pass beyond the walls of the CC and only in January was it sent out to the local organinsations. But up till now, nothing has been essentially changed in the tactics of the party in the peasant question. The old line of curbing the struggle in the village and applying the brakes to the peasants' movement as a whole, still prevails. Despite the fact that the curbing of the peasants' movement was already condemned in November and December in the report of Bukharin to the Plenum, in his speech, and furthermore, at the Plenum and in the resolution, the party has not revised this tactic to this day and has not recognised its mistakes. One should not even expect it to recognise them when the representative of the ECCI already declared in January at the session of the CC:

> So far as I know (I have not any official documents yet), we were attacked a bit in the ECCI because the party has not bestowed sufficient attention upon the peasant question. There is not a kernel of truth in that. . . .

The fear of the peasants' movement has existed and still remains in the party. The realisation of peasant possession of the land (that is, the occupation of the land by the peasants) is called by the CC 'a dangerous infantile disease of Leftism'. It continues to speak of 'the united front with the good gentry and the small and middle landlord against the bad gentry and the blackguards' (report from Hunan of December 30). The expression: 'good gentry', is found to this day in all party documents, in articles by leading comrades. This replacement of social categories by moral categories is essentially a suspension of the revolutionary movement in the village.

At the December Plenum of the CC, a resolution on the peasant question was adopted with the participation of the representative of the ECCI. Not a word is to be found in this resolution on an agrarian programme and on the struggle of the peasantry. The resolution does not answer a single one of the most burning questions of the day; the question of the peasants' power is answered negatively. It says, the slogan of a peasants' power must not be raised so as not to frighten away the petty bourgeoisie. From the neglect of the peasants' revolution springs the suspension by the leading party organs of the arming of the peasantry. When Tan Shen Shi made a proposal to our comrades in Wuhan to recruit volunteers and members of the Peasants' Leagues for his army, the Wuhan Committee rejected it. The comrades are of the opinion that the peasants do not need to arm themselves. Typical is the declaration of the Old Man at the December Plenum where the question came up of arming the peasants in Hunan. In the villages of Hunan a genuine civil war is in progress; the gentry are murdering the peasants by the dozens and hundreds, but the Old Man says:

> If the peasants do not need arms now, then we are not opposed to the government keeping the arms. If neither the Min Tuan nor the peasants have weapons, then the latter will win even though the struggle should be kindled.

THE WORKERS' MOVEMENT

The tactic of the party in the workers' movement is no different from its tactic in the peasants' movement. Above all, there is an absolute underestimation and lack of attention to it. The CC has no trade union department. More than a million organised workers have no guiding centre. The trade unions are separated from the masses and remain to a large degree organisations at the top. The political and organisational work is replaced everywhere by compulsion, but the main thing is that reformist tendencies are growing inside as well as outside the revolutionary trade union movement.

The continual hobnobbing with employers, sharing in profits, restriction of production, participation in the raising of labour productivity, the submission of the trade unions to the employers and masters, are common phenomena.

On the other hand, there occur refusals to support and defend the economic demands of the workers. Out of fear of the elementary growth of the labour movement, the party in Canton consented to compulsory arbitration, then it did the same thing in Hankow (the idea of compulsory arbitration itself comes from Borodin). Especially great is the fear of the party leaders of the movement of non-industrial workers. Incidentally, the overwhelming majority of the organised workers in China consists of non-industrial workers.

The report of the CC at the December Plenum says:

> It is unusually difficult for us to decide our tactics in relation to the middle and petty bourgeoisie, since the strikes of non-industrial and office workers are only conflicts within the petty-bourgeoisie themselves. Both sides [i.e., the employers and the workers] being necessary for the national united front, we can support none of the two sides, neither can we be neutral. . . The employees in concerns producing vital necessities (rice, salt, coal, fuel, etc.) must never resort to strikes if there is the slightest possibility of attaining concessions in a peaceful manner.

Thus, the party abandons the defence and support of the non-industrial workers, i.e., of the majority of the Chinese working class, and covers it up with the necessity of the united front with the petty bourgeoisie. Incidentally, it is quite clear that it is not so much a question of the petty bourgeoisie, especially of the artisans, as of the commercial middle bourgeoisie.

In the telegram elucidating the resolution of the CC, adopted and signed as it was even by the representative of the ECCI, and Borodin, the checking of the struggle of the non-industrial workers is spoken of. Therein is concealed the checking of the workers' struggle in general, since the few industrial establishments existing in Central China are either closed or else belong to the state or to joint stock corporations, and as is well known, strike struggles must not be started in state establishments.

The party leadership also fears the arming of the workers. We have already spoken of the slander spread against the Hankow workers' guard and of the attitude of the CC towards the worker pickets who participated in the occupation of the concessions in Hankow. One solitary time was the question of arming the workers raised in the CC, and even here it was decided that a part of the pickets must be disarmed because they are petty bourgeois elements. Even in the days when the uprising in Shanghai was in process, some party organisations would not so much as permit that the workers be furnished with common bamboo sticks. The party never spoke to the workers about arms or armed struggle. That is how the collapse of the Shanghai uprising came about. The Right group in the party, especially the leaders of the Shanghai organisation, pictured the uprising as an action of purely military forces, as a putsch. That is how the uprising of October 23 and February 22 was carried through.

THE ARMY

A characterisation of the party attitude towards the army was given by Comrade Chou En Lai in his report. He said to the party members: 'Go into this national revolutionary army, strengthen it, raise its fighting ability, but do not carry on any independent work there.' Up to recently there were no nuclei in the army. Our comrades who were political advisors, occupied themselves exclusively with military and political work for the Kuomintang.

The CC of the party staked everything on the commanding staff, not on the commanding staff coming forward from the ranks but on the old staff. With the aid of all sorts of combinations, oppositions, etc., our comrades hoped to maintain a balance of forces in the army, but it never occurred to them to capture it. In the opinion of the party leaders and the representative of the ECCI, the Canton army is not the armed people but a mercenary army in which it is impossible to do any political work. With particular ardour does the representative of the ECCI deny the possibility of political work in the army. The December Plenum of the CC adopted a decision to build nuclei in the army (*only of commanders, to be sure, with the prohibition against taking in soldiers*) and in January of this year, when the other Russian comrades (not for the first time) raised the question of work in the army, Comrade V. already expressed himself sharply against the organisation of nuclei. In the beginning he said (to Comrade Mandalyan*) that Moscow has decided against the organisation of nuclei, then he showed the impossibility of organising them: first, because the military command, especially Chiang Kai-shek, would

---

* A representative of the Russian Communist Party in China. His agreement with the views expressed in this document, among others by Nassonov, who represented the Russian Young Communist League in China, caused them both to be recalled to Moscow by Stalin.—Tr.

see in it the machinations of the Communists, which would strain
the relations; second, because the Cantonese Army was not sus-
ceptible to influence from below. When it was proposed to draw
workers and Communists into the army on a mass scale (very
great unemployment happened to be prevalent among the industrial workers, there were a few thousand trained worker pickets
in Canton as well as in Hankow), as well as peasants and members of the Peasants' Leagues, he laid it aside with pretexts, declaring that nobody would take them into the army anyway,
nothing would ever come of it, there is no recruiting going on
now, etc. And since he did not dare to appear as an opponent
in principle in the question of arming the workers, he discovered
a thousand difficulties, and showed that the arming of the workers is absolutely unthinkable, that we can't get weapons anywhere,
etc.

Besides, there are dozens of company commanders and a few
regimental commanders who are Communists and have a colossal
influence, there is a Communist regiment, and through all these
channels an enormous work could be conducted. But out of the
fear of revolutionising the army which pervades some party leaders,
the various comrades working in the army become detached from
the party, are transformed into 'individual' Communist commanders, and, as one of the Russian comrades in charge of military
work in the CC declared: 'they probably refuse to take workers
into their sections of the army, because the workers constitute a
turbulent element.'

Despite the fact that the representative of the ECCI after a
long resistance admitted to us that the work of the party in the
army must be reorganised, he subsequently did nothing to carry
through this reorganisation. We do not even know if he spoke
about it to the CC.

The Petty Bourgeoisie

The lack of faith in and understanding of the masses leads
quite naturally to the fact that some party leaders regard the
party as something between circle and clique, much like the other
cliques existing in China. From this comes a special passion for
negotiations at the top with military leaders and with the big
bourgeoisie. The whole tactic of our party in Shanghai consisted

for half a year in continuous meetings with the national bourgeoisie and its representatives. Besides, these meetings are covered
up with the formula of the necessity of a bloc with the petty
bourgeoisie. The bogey of the petty bourgeoisie runs to the grotesque. No peasants' power can be organised, for it will frighten
away the petty bourgeoisie. No demands must be raised for the
workers, for they will scare away the petty bourgeoisie. No strike
movement must be developed, else the petty bourgeoisie will fall
away. No Communist Party must be developed, for it will frighten
the petty bourgeoisie. No actions should be taken so long as the
petty bourgeoisie has not taken any. In reality, however, the party
leadership interests itself very little in the petty bourgeoisie,
especially in the artisans and the home workers among the petty
bourgeoisie, who run into the millions, if not tens of millions. The
party has never applied itself to this stratum, has conducted no
work there, has not attempted to make connections with them.
It occupies itself only with parleys at the top with representatives
of the small and middle commercial bourgeoisie, representatives
who are closely bound up with the big bourgeoisie. By this alone,
the party has sanctioned the subordination of the petty bourgeoisie
to the big bourgeoisie.

The petty bourgeoisie has in reality lost and is still losing
more than the other sections of the population who participate in
the revolution. That is just why one would think that the Communist party would have to lend its attention especially to the
fact that the petty bourgeoisie should not be ruined by the infla-
tion, the high taxes, by an insane tax system, by usury, etc. But
here the party proceeds mainly along the line of restricting the
demands of the workers. In the political report of the CC on
January 8, it says:

> We must raise the slogan: 'Discharge of the bad and greedy officials',
> 'honesty with the people's money', etc., but not 'Reduce the bur-
> dens of the people'—especially not in the period of the war with
> Mukden.

When it is a question of immediately necessary social reforms
in the sense of lightening the tax burdens which fall chiefly upon
the peasantry and the petty bourgeoisie, and the shifting of these
burdens on to the possessing classes, the party shows a fear
which, to call a spade a spade, is a fear not of the small bourgeoisie,
but of the big bourgeoisie and the landed aristocracy.

In the days of the Shanghai general strike, when a part of the petty bourgeoisie had already joined the strike, and another part awaited a signal and a call, the Right wing in the party sought to procure the support of the big bourgeoisie under the pretext of the passivity of the petty bourgeoisie. We speak of this in our letter on the Shanghai uprising and in the letter of Tsiu Tsiu Bo.

THE PARTY, THE KUOMINTANG AND THE GOVERNMENT

The tactic of the party in the peasants' and workers' movement, as well as in the army, is really a covert support of the bourgeois wing of the national revolutionary movement. This is an inevitable consequence of the disdainful and arrogant attitude towards the masses and the purely bourgeois conception of the revolution which the Right wing of the party possesses. Not for nothing do we frequently encounter such designations as a 'Chiang Kai-shek Communist', a 'Tan Shen Shi Communist', etc. and when this tactic is accompanied by the fear of raising big political questions, byt the fear of perspectives, the party must fall into a narrow, business practicalism which is not far removed from reformism. Comrades Petrov and Bukharov are the most typical representatives of this Right tendency. It is with them that this petty business spirit is mostly manifested, this striving to reduce a principled question to trifles, to technical difficulties. It is not surprising that with such a conception, the struggle of Chiang Kai-shek against the Left elements around Wang Chin Wei appeared to many comrades less as a struggle of two tendencies than as a struggle between two cliques (Comrade V. furnished the 'theoretical' foundation for this). From this also followed the attitude towards the return of Wang Chin Wei as the salvation from all evil, the neglect of the social content of the struggle and of the necessity of mobilising the mass movement. In the political report of the CC of January 8, it says:

> In our opinion the most important task that stands before us is re-establish good relations between Wang Chin Wei, Chiang Kai-shek, and the other generals. If we cannot solve this task then the whole national movement will be absolutely destroyed.

It is now more than half a year since this campaign has been conducted and Wang Chin Wei has not returned and probably never will return; in the meantime our party has bound up all its work within the national revolutionary movement with the return of Wang Chin Wei.

All talk of the Left Kuomintang, of connections with the Left Kuomintang, leads in the end to Wang Chin Wei. In the meantime, the Hankow events of January 3 have shown that the Leftward developments of the Kuomintang and the formation of a Left wing is only possible on the basis of a rise of the mass movement, not only a movement of the petty bourgeoisie but also of the workers and peasants. The CC, on the contrary, and the ECCI representative have sought the Left Kuomintang at the other extreme occupying themselves with fishing for Left leaders from above. In conformity with this policy, there was a theory that these Left leaders must be given a part of the masses over whom the Communists had acquired the monopoly of influence.

In the resolution on the report of the CC at the December Plenum, it says:

> In the mass movement, we must cling to every possibility to collaborate with the Left and help them to win the masses (the peasants and the urban petty bourgeoisie).

It will appear then that it is not the masses who must push the leaders of the Kuomintang to the Left, but that the latter must win the masses.

In the question of the government, the position of the party was ambiguous. Locally, the Communists told the workers and peasants that the government is a people's government, something very close to a workers' and peasants' government; the CC, on the contrary, is of the opinion that the government is not yet a people's government, that the people are not yet free. Proceeding from this, it is against the entry of Communists into the governmental organs even on a local scale. When some Communists were made magistrates (that is, district chiefs) in Kiangsi, the CC wrote a letter on December 2 to the party committee in Kiangsi:

> The comrades are of the opinion that the government is already a people's government, that the people are already free. Further, they forget that our party is not yet the party in power, that we must not in any way enter a government in order to take up any kind of posts. Can we, if we receive the posts of two or three district chiefs, carry through the tactic of our party? Everyone knows that this is absolutely impossible. This would only mean that we would lose the positions from which we can now speak to the masses, that we would lose the confidence the masses have in us. The party

committee must immediately correct this serious and erroneous deviation. All these comrades must immediately be ordered to resign or leave the party.

This standpoint, was also supported by Comrade V. who, in October 1926, on the proposal that the posts of certain district chiefs in Hupeh and Honan be given to Communists, declared that this would be tantamount to covering up the Right wing policy of Tan Shen Shi, and that the Communists would take over the responsibility before the masses for this policy.

The CC, as well as Comrade V., were still more opposed to Communists entering the Canton central government, not because Communist principles would thereby be soiled, as the letter of the CC asserted, but because they were afraid of colliding with the Right government, for entry into a government organ would have obligated them to a struggle against the Right bourgeois tendency. It is characteristic that there was no essential difference here between the positions of Borodin and Comrade V., even though Borodin was *for* entering the government. *In reality, the latter regarded this entry as a cover for the Right policy, as a capitulation to the Right.*

THE INDEPENDENCE OF THE PARTY

Since the right-wing leadership feared the government as well as the masses and showed extraordinary caution wherever it was a question of extending and deepening the mass movement, it also came to the point of minimizing the role and the significance of our party. The party concealed itself, went deep into the underground, without daring to show its face to the masses. Yet there was no one at all from whom the party had to hide, so far as the Right and the reactionaries were concerned, for Chiang Kai-shek as well as Feng Yu-hsiang, Tan Shen Shi and even Wu Pei Fu were in correspondence with the CC of the Communist Party of China through the intermediary of the Old Man. A party of 30,000 members is fed by a little weekly sheet which, moreover, fails to appear for weeks at a time. The party is afraid to legalise itself and gives as its motive that this would surely frighten the petty bourgeoisie. In Honan, the party organisation decided not to extend its work and to close its books to new members in order not to scare the petty bourgeoisie. The party leadership says:

> So far as the political problems on the field of the national government are concerned, we must elucidate the practical political events, but we must not conduct propaganda or raise our propaganda and agitation to the level of the Kuomintang propaganda.

The Honan Committee says in a letter on December 30:

> Our anti-imperialist propaganda is still too far advanced, it is more advanced that that of the Kuomintang, which is a big mistake. We have a Left deviation. Everywhere we hear: 'Long live the Communist International!', 'Long live the Communist party!' . . .

That is the tactic of the party, more correctly, of its Right leaders. The revolutionary movement is rising to a higher plane, the class antagonisms grow sharper. The bourgeoisie and the possessing classes in the village are conducting, together with a part of the militarists, an active struggle against the democratic tendencies. This struggle proceeds along four basic lines: 1. Restriction of anti-imperialist propaganda; 2. Restriction of the peasants' movement through armed repressions; 3. Restriction of the workers' movement by direct military and administrative pressure as well as by compulsory arbitration; 4. Creation of a bureaucratic government supporting itself on the army. And the Communist Party of China is yielding its positions along all these four lines. The struggle for the democratizing of the government was not conducted by the party up to the recent events in Shanghai. Even now, the party leadership has not sufficiently understood the necessity of this struggle.

It would, however, be false to draw the conclusion from this letter that our whole party is infested with opportunism. The party masses and many of the lower organisations are, on the contrary, more than healthy. But the replacement of the leading circles, or more correctly, the Right wing, is an urgent necessity. Without this replacement and the adjustment of its tactical line, the recovery of the party is unthinkable.

The responsibility for all this lies equally with the Right wing of the leadership and the representative of the ECCI. In tactical questions in the past he cannot be separated from the CC; on the contrary, every time that the party hesitated and began to seek new paths, he forced it back into the old swamp of petty combinations, tricks, of political jugglery, which have nothing in common with revolutionary tactics. Completely lacking in principle, he adapted himself to the party and frequently excelled the other leaders in his zeal. Thus, infected with a capitulationist mood, he proposed after March 20, 1926 (together with Borodin) that the Communists withdraw from the Kuomintang. While he declared to us that Petrov and Bukharov were opportunists, and that Ho Sun-Lin, the chairman of the Shanghai Trade Union Council, was an adventurer, he not only made no effort to help the other Chinese comrades to remove them from leadership, but on the contrary he supported them. Despite the fact that he saw many shortcomings in the party, which were to be explained simply by ailments of growth (for example, its narrow 'circle' character, its organisational formlessness thanks to which decisions adopted by the party remain on paper), he not only made no attempt to correct them, but sanctified them by reference to 'specific Chinese conditions'. He sent Moscow bastardised information, held back material, and concealed the real situation in the party from the ECCI. Without principles, as well as without political courage, he viewed everything as a functionary and did not stop at pushing the CC into absurd decisions. For example, when the telegram arrived from Moscow saying that the Northwestern army must return to Mongolia, that is, must traverse some 660 miles, the Central Committee and its military collaborators were of the opinion that this was absolutely impossible to realise. But Comrade V. brought this decision (from Moscow) before the CC, without deciding to show Moscow the absurdity of such an operation. But a week later, Moscow itself reported that this decision had been adopted without a knowledge of the real situation and that it had been revised after the receipt of supplementary information.

In December, Comrade V. came out against participation in the government. After receiving the resolution, he declared that it was possible to enter the government, only not right away, and when the resolution was being considered together with the CC, he announced that we had indeed always been supporters of participation in the government, which made the Old Man indignant.

Such a representative of the ECCI can only ruin the work. Were he not here to cover up the right-wing elements with the authority of the ECCI, the party would perhaps be able to fight the right wing successfully with its own forces. Now even this will be difficult. It is not only necessary to recall Comrade V., but to send here a much stronger worker who is capable at the same time of representing the ECCI and of directing Borodin.

In the Central Committee itself, which now really consists of three people, Petrov constitutes the right wing, Tsio Tsiu Bo the Left and the Old Man the Centre. We believe that by isolating Petrov and Comrade V., and by letting some fresh air into the CC by the introduction of a certain number of workers, the Old Man who, in spite of all his defects, is a much stronger man than Comrade V. and enjoys an enormous authority, could continue to be one of the party leaders. But outside of all this, it is necessary that the ECCI should once more confirm and concretise the tactical line presented in the Plenum resolution. It is necessary that our leading comrades accord China more attention than they have up to now.

Shanghai, March 17, 1927.

N.Nassonov.
N. Fokine.
A. Albrecht.

GLOSSARY

Anglo-Russian Trade Union Committee: founded in 1925 to unite British trade union 'lefts' with Soviet trade union leaders. Provided a 'left' cover for the TUC General Council in its betrayal of the General Strike.

Baldwin, Stanley (1867-1947): British Tory politician. Prime Minister, 1924-1929 and 1935-1937.

Bauer, Otto (1882-1938): Austrian Social Democrat. Developed his own form of revisionism, 'Austro-Marxism'.

Black Hundreds: name given to the 'Union of the Russian People', an extreme monarchist, ultra-reactionary organisation founded by the Tsar in 1905 to foment pogroms and murder revolutionaries.

Blanc, Louis (1811-1882): French utopian socialist, rejected class struggle and violence. Head of the Labour Commission set up by the revolutionary government in 1848, but opponent of the Paris Commune of 1871.

Blanqui, Louis-Auguste (1805-1881): French revolutionist. Advocated dictatorship of the proletariat by insurrection of resolute minority. Spent most of his life in prison.

Blum, Leon (1872-1950): Right-wing leader of the French Socialist Party before World War II. Premier in the Popular Front government of 1936.

Borodin, Mikhail (1884-1953): Comintern functionary, former Bundist. Emigrated to USA, 1908-1918. Joined Bolsheviks on his return. Comintern representative in China, accredited to Chiang Kai Shek. Loyal Stalinist.

Boxer Rebellion: nationalist, anti-imperialist uprising 1900-1901, led by secret society called 'The fists of righteous harmony', hence 'Boxers'. Brutally crushed by the imperialists.

Brest-Litovsk: Polish city. Site of the talks between the Soviets and the Central Powers leading to the signing of the Brest-Litovsk treaty in 1918.

Browder, Earl R. (1891-): American member of Comintern delegation to China, 1927. Later leader of US Communist Party from which he was expelled in 1946.

Bubnov, Andrei (1883-19): Bolshevik from 1903. Central Committee member, August 1917. Member of the Military Revolutionary Committee. In Bukharin's 'Left Communist' group, 1918. One of the organisers of the Chinese Communist Party. Later Commissar for Education. Disappeared in 1938, released and rehabilitated in 1956, after 18 years in prison.

Bukharin, Nikolai (1888-1938): Bolshevik from 1906. Close collaborator of Lenin, assuming ultra-left position on important issues. Leader of the right wing of CPSU after Lenin's death, joined with Stalin against Trotsky. President of the Comintern, 1926-1929. Eliminated from the leadership in 1929, capitulated to Stalin. Executed after third Moscow Trial.

Cachin, Marcel (1869-1958): leading French Stalinist. Social patriot during World War I. Took part in formation of French CP. Later distinguished for his slavish worship of Stalin.

Cadets: Name given to the Constitutional Democrat party in Russia. Organisation of liberal capitalists and landowners.

Cavaignac, Louis-Eugene (1802-1857): reactionary French general, notorious for his slaughter of thousands of workers after the July revolution in 1848.

Chamberlain, Austen (1863-1937): Tory foreign secretary in 1924 Baldwin government. Won Nobel Peace Prize for negotiating the Locarno Pact.

Chang Tso Lin: warlord of Manchuria from 1911 to 1928, later operating from Peking. Ultra-reactionary agent of Japanese imperialism. Killed by a bomb placed under his train. His son, Chang Hseuh-Liang, captured Chiang Kai Shek in the famous 'Sian incident', 1936.

Chen Du Siu (1879-1942): founder of the Chinese Communist Party. As Dean of Letters at Peking University Chen was a major influence on Chinese youth. General Secretary of the Party until 1927, he was made a scapegoat for Stalin's betrayal of the Revolution and expelled. Later he became a leading Trotskyist and was executed by Chiang Kai Shek.

Chen, Eugene (1878-1944): born in Trinidad. Foreign Minister of Canton Nationalist government up to 1927. Later joined Madame Sun's short-lived Wuhan government, a 'revolutionary centre' according to the Comintern.

Chernishevsky, Nikolai (1829-1889): called by Marx the 'greatest Russian scholar and critic'. Materialist philosopher, utopian socialist, tirelessly engaged all his life in enlightening the people. Enormous influence on 19th century Russian intellectuals.

Chiang Kai Shek (1887-): Generalissimo of the Nationalist Army. 'Associate member' of Comintern executive, 1926. Butcher of the first Chinese revolution, and military dictator. Driven out of China in 1949 by the victorious Chinese Red Army, now dictator of Formosa.

Chicherin, George (1872-1936): old Menshevik, joined Bolsheviks in 1917. Commissar for External Affairs, 1921-1930.

Chu Teh (1886-): former communist officer in the Kuomintang army. Later one of Mao Tse Tung's most able generals. Led the Fourth Route Army on the Long March. Now one of the leaders of the Chinese Red Army.

Citrine, Walter (1887-): notorious right-wing British trade union leader, one of the heads of the Anglo-Russian Committee, later ennobled.

Commune: workers' dictatorship established in Paris after the uprising of March 18, 1871. Crushed with hitherto unparalleled savagery 72 days later.

Compradors: that section of Chinese capitalists most closely tied to foreign capitalism.

Control Commission: body inside Bolshevik party for settling inner-party disputes, etc. Later used by Stalin as an instrument of internal repression.

Dai Tshi Tao: developed theory of an independent capitalist road for China. Principal theoretical inspirer of Chiang Kai Shek.

Dan, Theodore (1871-1947): Menshevik leader, opponent of Bolshevism. Banished from the Soviet Union in 1922, remained a virulent enemy of the Soviet regime.

Duma: Russian parliament under the Tsar, with little power and elected by very restricted suffrage, granted only after the 1905 Revolution.

Entente: name given to the alliance during World War I of Britain, France, Italy and Russia.

Fabianism: opportunist, reformist tendency in the Labour Party. Named after the Fabian Society, which believes in gradual reform of capitalism.

Feng Yu Hsiang (1881-1948): Northern warlord, known as the 'Christian General', who drove Wu Pei Fu from Peking in 1924. Later allied himself with Chiang Kai Shek, and was counted on by Stalin to carry out the 'democratic dictatorship of workers and peasants'. From 1927 to 1947, Feng alternately fought and 'co-operated' with Chiang Kai Shek. Went to USA in 1947, and publicly attacked Chiang. On his way back to China via Moscow, according to the official story, he was killed in a fire on board ship.

Galen: pseudonym for **Vassili Blucher (1889-1938):** Siberian metal-worker who became one of the leaders of the Red Army in the Civil War. Later commander of the Soviet Far Eastern Armies, and adviser to Chiang Kai Shek. Shot in 1938 after the trial of Tuchachevsky, over which he presided.

Gallifet, Marquis de (1830-1909): General of the Versailles troops notorious for his brutal butchery of revolutionists after the Commune.

Haase, Hugo (1863-1919): leader of the German Social Democratic Party, follower of Kautsky during World War I. Helped found the Independent Social Democratic Party. Murdered in 1919 by fascists.

Heller, Leo: Far-Eastern representative of the Red International of Trade Unions (Profintern).

Herriot, Edouard (1872-1957): pre-war leader of French Radical Party.

Herzen, Alexander (1812-1870): Russian writer, father of Russian populist movement. Agitated from exile in London and Geneva against Tsarism and for the liberation of the peasantry.

Hicks, George (1879-1954): British 'left' trade union leader of the 1920s, secretary of the National Federation of Building Trades Operatives. Labour MP for E. Woolwich, 1931-1950. Leading light on the Anglo-Russian Trade Union Committee, took part in the betrayal of the General Strike.

Ho Lun (1895-): Chinese Communist general, leader of guerrilla detachments in South China. Now vice-chairman of the Military Affairs Committee of the Chinese Red Army, and a Marshal.

Hu Han Min (1884-1936): leader of Kuomintang right wing. Implicated in 1925 in murder of Liao Chung Kai, leader of the KKMT left wing. Persuaded by Borodin to go to Russia so as to avoid scandal, he was acclaimed at the Sixth Plenum of the ECCI and elected to the leadership of the Peasant International. Played a major part in suppressing the Chinese Revolution.

International Press Correspondence: periodical of the Comintern, otherwise known as 'Inprecorr'.

Jordania, Noah (1870-1953): old Menshevik, head of the independent Georgian Menshevik government until its overthrow.

Kalinin, Mikhail (1875-1945): leading Stalinist, official head of state of USSR for many years. Old Bolshevik. Succeeded Sverdlov as Chairman of the Soviet Central Executive Committee in 1919. Member of the Political Bureau of the CPSU.

Kamenev, Leon B. (1883-1936): old Bolshevik and close collaborator of Lenin. Editor of 'Pravda' before 1914, again in 1917. Opposed the seizure of power. Member of the Political Bureau from 1919-1927. Lined up with Stalin against Trotsky 1923-1925. Collaborated with Trotsky in the Unified Opposition for a short time, then capitulated to Stalin in 1928. Executed after the first Moscow Trial.

Kautsky, Karl (1854-1937): leading theoretician of the Second International. Outstanding Marxist scholar before World War I, later leader of the anti-Marxist Centrist tendency. Opponent of the Russian Revolution.

Kemal Pasha (Kemal Ataturk) (1880-1938): Turkish nationalist dictator after the 1919 'Young Turk' revolution.

Kerensky, Alexander (1881-): Social Revolutionist lawyer, prominent in the Provisional Government after the March 1917 Russian Revolution. Became premier after the July Days. Overthrown by the Bolsheviks. Now lives in the USA.

Kolchak, Admiral Alexander (1874-1920): leader of the White counter-revolutionary armies in Siberia during the Civil War.

Kornilov, General Lavr (1870-1920): Tsarist military officer who attempted unsuccessful coup in 1917. After the Revolution, commanded White detachments against the Red Army.

Kuomintang: literally 'People's Party', Chinese nationalist party founded in 1911 by Sun Yat Sen. Later led by Chiang Kai Shek, it was the chief counter-revolutionary party in China after 1925. The Kuomintang government was overthrown by the Red Army in 1949. Now the ruling party in Formosa.

Kuusinen, Ottomar (1881-1964): leading Stalinist. Former Finnish social-democratic leader, fled to Moscow after the failure of the Finnish revolution of 1918, for which he bore considerable responsibility. Later became a Comintern functionary, noted for his supple adaptation to all the twists of Stalinist policy.

Ledru-Rollin, Alexander (1808-1874): petty-bourgeois democrat in the 1848 French revolution. Member of the provisional government of 1848, led troops against the workers. Leader of the right wing of the democrats after July 1848.

L'Humanité: official organ of the French Communist Party.

Li Ti Sin: Reactionary Kuomintang general in Canton who seized power there in 1927.

Lominadze, G.: Stalinist functionary, elected to the CPSU Central Committee in 1924, sent to China, 1927. Leader of an opposition of discontented Stalinists in 1931. Disappeared during the purges.

Losovsky, Solomon (1878-1952): loyal Stalinist. Bolshevik 1903-1909, later a conciliator. President of the Red International of Trade Unions, 1921-1927, then Vicecommissar for External Affairs. Purged in 1949. Died in prison.

Lvov, Prince (1861-1925): Russian bourgeois politician and land-owner. Minister in the provisional government from March to July 1917.

Makhno, Nestor (1884-1934): Ukrainian anarchist guerrilla leader. Opponent of Soviet power. Escaped when his bands were smashed by the Red Army, and died in exile in Paris.

Manuilsky, Dmitry (1883-1952): loyal Stalinist. Bolshevik from 1903, worked with Trotsky during World War I. Elected to the Central Committee in 1922, became an official of the Comintern. Held various leading positions in the Stalinised Comintern, was secretary from 1929-1934. Later represented the Ukraine at the United Nations.

Martynov, Alexander (1865-1935): former right-wing Menshevik, joined Communist Party only in 1923. Promptly became a leading campaigner against 'Trotskyism', specialising in distorted quotations from Lenin. Chief theoretician of the 'bloc of four classes' in China, which he defended against the Opposition.

Maslov, Arkadi (?-1941): leader of ultra-left wing of German Communist Party. Opposed Brandler after the failure of the March Action of 1923 and gained the majority at the Frankfurt Conference of 1924. Opposed the Left Opposition while still in the leadership, flirted with Trotskyism after his expulsion from the Comintern, but rapidly went over to its enemies.

Ministerialism: opportunist tendency in socialist movement advocating participation in capitalist cabinets.

Min Tuan: armed bandits organised and maintained by Chinese landowners and capitalists.

Molotov, Viatcheslav (1890-): notorious Stalinist, for many years Stalin's right-hand man. An old Bolshevik, he headed the Comintern from 1930-1931. Vice-president of the Supreme Soviet in 1953 after Stalin's death, he was relegated to a diplomatic post in Mongolia in 1957.

Monmousseau, Gaston (1883-1960): French Stalinist trade union leader.

Neumann, Heinz ( ): one of the leaders of the German Communist Party after the defeat of the Maslow-Fischer group. Comintern representative in Canton during the 1927 insurrection. Murdered during Stalin's purge in 1937.

New Economic Policy (NEP): policy adopted by Soviet government in 1921, which allowed a free market in grain, and commercial concessions to small capitalists, encouraging the recovery of the war-shattered economy.

Northern armies: troops of the reactionary northern warlords.

Paper tigers: movement of compradors and capitalists in Canton during 1924 against the Nationalist government. Quickly defeated.

Pepper, John (1886-1939): pseudonym of the Hungarian adventurer and Comintern functionary, **Pogany**. A counter-revolutionary during the Hungarian revolution of 1918, headed the 'ultra-left' opposition to Lenin and Trotsky at the Third Congress of the Comintern. Expelled for factionalism from the Hungarian party, and sent to the USA, where he became a leading supporter of Bukharin.

Piatakov, Yuri (1890-1937): Bolshevik from 1910, later in exile in Japan. Organised clandestine struggle against the Whites in the Ukraine, 1918. Considered by Lenin as one of the most promising of the younger Bolsheviks. Left oppositionist from 1924 to 1927, deported then capitulated. Later organised development of heavy industry. Executed after the second Moscow Trial.

Pilsudsky, Joseph (1867-1935): extreme Polish reactionary. Socialist before World War I, later leader of Polish White armies. Dictator after coup in 1926.

Pokrovsky, M. N. (1868-1932): prominent Bolshevik historian.

Poincaré, Raymond (1860-1934): reactionary French imperialist politician.

Populists: petit-bourgeois movement in Russia, turning to peasantry for action against Tsarism.

Purcell, A. A. (1872-1935): British trade union 'left', former member of the Communist Party. Labour MP, 1923-1929. A leading light in the Anglo-Russian Trade Union Committee, he helped betray the General Strike in 1926.

Radek, Karl (1885-1945?): Polish Lithuanian Social Democrat, later leading Bolshevik, founder-member of the German Communist Party. From 1923, Comintern delegate to the German CP. Oppositionist from 1923, capitulated in 1929, and vilified Trotsky. Later a journalist on 'Pravda', and Stalin's adviser on German affairs. Sentenced to 10 years' imprisonment at the Second Moscow Trial. Reported to have been killed by a fellow-prisoner after World War II.

Rafes, M. (   ): former member of the Jewish Bund and opponent of Bolshevism. Supported Petliura against the Red Army. Later joined the Communist Party and became one of the chief architects of Stalin's policy in China.

Rakovsky, Christian (1873-1942?): Bulgarian leader of Rumanian, Bulgarian and Russian socialist movements. A revolutionist from the age of 16, he worked with almost all the leading figures of the European revolutionary movement. Member of the Bolshevik Central Committee from 1919-1925. A left oppositionist from the inception, he was expelled from the Party and deported to Astrakhan in 1928. He was one of the last to capitulate, in 1934, after six years under terrible conditions. Sentenced to a long period of imprisonment in the Third Moscow Trial. Died in prison.

Raskolnikov, Feodor (1892-1939): Bolshevik from 1910, one of the military leaders of the revolution. Leaned towards the Left Opposition for a time in 1923. Directed the Eastern work of the Comintern for a period, carrying out Stalin's policies. Denounced Stalin's crimes in 1938 while abroad and refused to return to Russia.

Remmele, Herman (   ): Stalinist, one of the secretaries of the German Communist Party and its representative in Stalin's International. Murdered in the purge of 1937.

Renaudel, Pierre (1871-1935): leader of the right wing of the French Socialist Party. Journalist on 'L'Humanité' during World War I, when he was a notorious chauvinist.

Romanov, Grand Duke Michael (1878-1918): Russian royal duke, regent for a short period after the abdication of Nicholas II.

Rudzutak, Jan (1887-1938): Bolshevik in 1906, served 10 years' hard labour before the revolution. President of the Central Asian Bureau of the CPSU, 1921-1924. Faithful supporter of Stalin until his arrest in 1937, possibly for attempting to oppose the purges.

Rykov, Alexis (1881-1938): Bolshevik from 1903, always on right of the party. Joined Bukharin's faction after Lenin's death, and became prominent in the 'anti-Trotskyist' campaign. Expelled along with other 'rightists' in 1929, but allowed back after self-criticism. Tried with Bukharin in the Third Moscow Trial, condemned to death and executed.

Safarov, George (1891-1938): old Bolshevik, with Lenin in Switzerland, returned after February revolution in the 'sealed train'. Specialist in Eastern questions, carried out a number of missions for the Comintern. Member of the Comintern EC. A Zinovievist, he was sent to China and then to Turkey where he carried on secret oppositional activity. Disappeared during the purges.

Scheidemann, Phillip (1865-1939): extreme right-wing German Social Democrat. Notorious for his role in the crushing of the German revolution in 1919.

Smeral, Bohumir: Czech Stalinist, formerly an Austrian social-chauvinist.

Smilga, Ivan (1892-1937?): old Bolshevik, active in revolutionary movement from 1907. One of the military leaders of the Russian Revolution. Later a member of the Supreme Economic Council. Joined the Unified Opposition, then the Left Opposition. Capitulated in 1929. Arrested in 1932, given five years' imprisonment. Disappeared in the purges.

Stolypin, Peter (1862-1911): Tsarist prime minister from 1906, attempted agricultural reform with the aim of destroying village communes and opening up capitalist farming. Assassinated by a police spy.

Sun Chuan Fang (1885-1935): warlord of Shanghai, supported by the British. Overthrown by Nationalist forces in 1926.

Sun Yat Sen (1866-1925): Chinese Nationalist leader and founder of the Kuomintang. Provisional president of Chinese Republic in 1911. Head of Canton Nationalist government until his death.

Svinhufvund, Peter (1861-1944): Finnish Nationalist leader and extreme reactionary.

Thaelmann, Ernest (1886-1944): Stalinist leader of German Communist Party. Carried out Stalin's German policy faithfully right up to Hitler's seizure of power. Imprisoned by Nazis and murdered in 1944 at Buchenwald Concentration Camp.

Tomsky, Mikhail (1880-1936): leader of the Soviet trade union movement until 1929. Bolshevik from 1904, several times imprisoned. On the right wing of the party with Bukharin, eliminated from the leadership in 1929. Committed suicide in 1936 to avoid trial. Condemned posthumously by the Stalinists as 'an enemy of the people'.

Tseretelli, Irakly (1882-1959): Georgian Menshevik, former hard-labour convict. Minister of Posts in 1917 provisional government. Remained anti-Bolshevik in emigration.

Ustraliov, N.: bourgeois professor and Cadet. Was for intervention against Soviets, but finally became reconciled to working for them, although still hoping for restoration of capitalism. Supported Stalin as a step in that direction.

Voroshilov, Klimenti (1881-): leading Stalinist. Bolshevik from 1903. Representative of petty-bourgeois, anti-centralist tendency in Red Army during the Civil War, intrigued with Stalin at Tsaritsin against Trotsky, becoming one of Stalin's closest collaborators, he was largely responsible for the great military purge of 1938. Held high office after Stalin's death.

Vuyovitch, Vuyo (-1938): Serb socialist, Zinovievist and secretary of the Young Communist International. Expelled in 1927, capitulated 1928. Arrested 1935. Expelled from Yugoslav C.P. in 1939. Disappeared during the purges in 1938.

Wang Chin Wei (1883-1944): intimate collaborator of Sun Yat Sen. Head of the short-lived 1927 Hankow government. Leader of various abortive attempts to form a 'left' Nationalist alternative to Chiang, he finally joined Chiang's government in 1932. Became a Japanese puppet in 1937 and died, still a Japanese stooge, in 1944.

Wilson, Joseph Havelock (1858-1929): ultra-reactionary strike-breaking head of the National Union of Seamen from 1911 to 1929.

Yeh Tin: Chinese Communist leader of guerrilla troops from the late 1920s onwards. Eventually became Commander of the New Fourth Army, and was captured by Kuomintang troops in 1941. Held prisoner until the end of the war, he was released from prison in 1946. Shortly afterwards he was killed with a number of other Chinese Red Army officers when a US plane taking them to Chunking crashed.

Yuan Shi Kai (1859-1916): Nationalist general. Adviser to the Empress Kuang Hsu (1898). Provisional president of Chinese Republic, 1912, and compelled the Manchu emperor to abdicate. Made himself Emperor by a coup, December, 1915. Overthrown by Sun Yat Sen, 1916.

Zetkin, Clara (1857-1933): close associate of Rosa Luxemburg before World War I. Collaborated in foundation of Spartacus League. Leading figure in the Comintern, supported Brandler after 1923.

Zinoviev, Grigori (1883-1936): Bolshevik from 1903. Lenin's closest comrade during the period before the revolution. Opposed the seizure of power, 1917. One of the most prominent Bolshevik leaders after the Revolution. Formed one of the 'troika' directed against Trotsky after Lenin's death. Later broke with Stalin and formed Unified Opposition with Trotsky and Kamenev. Expelled late in 1927, capitulated in 1928. Sentenced to 10 years' imprisonment in 1935. Condemned to death and executed after the first Moscow Trial.

Witte, Count Sergei (1849-1915): 'liberal' Tsarist minister, influenced the Tsar to issue the famous manifesto promising liberty and a Duma.

Wu Pei Fu (1873-1939): Northern Chinese warlord in the pay of the British imperialists.

Yaroslavsky, Emilian (1878-1943): notorious Stalinist hatchet-man. Bolshevik from 1903, deported from 1908 to 1917. Elected to the Central Committee 1919-1922. Later on the Central Control Commission, where he led fight against the opposition. Author of an official party history. In disgrace from 1932 onwards.

CHRONOLOGY

1520. Pires, representative of Albuquerque arrives in Peking.

1557: Portuguese settlement set up in Macao.

1638: Manchu dynasty installed at Mukden. Jesuit influence at that court.

1757-1842: Foreign maritime trade restricted to Canton.

1784: US enters China trade.

1821: Transfer of opium trade to Lintin island.

1839: Chinese destroy opium imports.

1840: Opium Wars. British seize Hong Kong, Canton, Amoy, Foochow, Ningpo. Shanghai opened to British trade. China forced to pay 21 million dollars in indemnities.

1844: US gains extra-territorial jurisdictional rights for its subjects. French secure toleration of Roman Catholicism.

1850-1864: Taiping Rebellion.

1857: Anglo-French seizure of Canton. US and Russia impose treaty of Tientsin opening 11 more ports, giving access to Christian missions, conceding maritime customs control, legalizing opium trade, ceding north bank of the Amur to Russia.

1860: British sack Peking, demand further indemnities, French secure right of catholics to own land, Russians annex Maritime Province.

1863-1908: Capitalist development of China. Christian missions increase from 200 to 1,300.

1872-81: First group of students go abroad to study.

1876: another 10 ports forced by Britain.

1879: Russians take port of Ili to return it later.

1881-5: French despoil Chinese tributary states in Annam.

1888: First imperial railway, coal mines, steel works opened up.

1894: Sun Yat Sen organizes first secret revolutionary society.

1895: Japan takes Korea, Formosa, Pescadores, Liaotung, opens four more ports.

1895-6: French, German and Russian loans for industrial development.

1897-9: Germans seize Kiachow, precipitate scramble for concessions. Britain gets extensive right to Yangtse, a British Inspector General of Customs, Kowloon; Germany gets exclusive rights to Shantung; Russia secures southern portion of Liaotung province, Dairen, Port Arthur; France takes Kwangchow; Japan gets Fukien, but Italian designs on Chekiang rebuffed.

1899: 'Boxer' rebellion against imperialism. German and other foreign armies defeat the 'boxers' and Manchus to obtain indemnity of 738 million dollars.

1904-5: Russia returns Manchuria by Treaty of Portsmouth. Chinese resistance to imperialism increases. British reduce opium quota, loans extended, US remit half Boxer indemnities.

1908: Draft Constitution.

1911

Wuchang garrison uprising precipitates the Revolution led by Sun Yat Sen.

1912

Yuan Shi Kai overthrows the Manchu dynasty and is sponsored for President by Sun.

1912-1913

Earliest socialist, working-class and Marxist ideas percolate into China. Coup of Yuan Shi Kai dissolving parliament, banning Kuomintang and installing his dictatorship.

1913-1916

'New Youth Movement' founded in Peking by Chen Du Siu and Li Ta Chao. Yuan Shi Kai dies.

1916-1919

China prey to warlords. Sun Yat Sen in the Canton Government of June 1917. First World War and the Russian Revolution. Turbulent rise of trade unionism. Li Ta Chao forms Marxist Study Groups in Peking. Mao Tse-tung forms Study and Work organization in Hunan.

1919

March 2-6: First Congress of the Communist International. May 4: the May 4 Movement launched against Japanese imperialism: for a cultural renaissance; struggle against imperialism; social reform. The Second Congress of the Communist International. Warlords seize Peking. The Canton government forced to flee.

1920

Voitinsky, representative of the Communist International in China. Communist groups formed in France and the 'Young Socialists' in China. September: Shanghai Conference of Marxists, to prepare for the Chinese Communist Party.

1921

May: Sun Yat Sen elected President of Republic. First peasant unions set up. June 22-July 12: third Congress of the Communist International. July: founding Congress of the Chinese Communist Party where Maring (Sneevliet) and delegation represent CI.

1922

January: Moscow Conference of Toilers of the East. CPC represented. January-March: protracted but successful strike of seamen in Hong Kong. April-May: Canton Government's expedition to the North is halted. May 1-6: first pan-Chinese Congress of workers, representing 300,000 workers and inspiring a surge forward in organization. May-June: Second Congress of the CPC which proposes anti-imperialist united front with the KMT which is rejected by Sun. August: extraordinary meeting of the CC of the CPC which accepts the CI proposal that CP members join the KMT as individual members. November-December: Fourth Congress of the CI. Radek defends the CPC-KMT alliance.

1923

January: joint statement of Sun and Joffe (CI) on Sino-Soviet and CPC-KMT relations. February: murderous suppression of the great railway strike throws back the advance of the workers' movement. CPC driven into illegality. Sun retakes Canton. June: Third Congress of the CPC decides that members join KMT on individual basis. August: CC of CPC declares that workers' movement must not dissolve itself inside the KMT. September: Borodin and Soviet generals arrive in Canton as advisers to Sun. Chiang sends envoy to Moscow. October: failure of the German Revolution, the debate on the New Course, Trotsky in opposition.

1924

January: First KMT Congress; alliance with the USSR, and the CPC, support for workers and peasants. Some CPers elected to the EC. Death of Lenin. May: Whampoa military academy founded, staffed by Soviet officers, commanded by Chiang and with Chou En Lai as Political Commissar. June 7-July 8: Fifth Congress of the CI, a setback for the Opposition and the initiation of the 'bolshevization' of the affiliated parties. June-August: Canton-Hong Kong general strike. August-October: workers' militia and Whampoa cadets defeat armed bands of the bourgeois-British imperialist 'Merchant Volunteers'. 'Christian' general Feng Yu Hsiang takes Peking. Sun advances idea of a National Convention.

1925

January: Fourth Congress of the CPC. Old leadership re-elected and Workers' Secretariat disbanded. February: victorious strike of Shanghai cotton workers led by Li Li San. March 12: death of Sun Yat Sen. A background of battles between the warlords. March 21-April 6: Fifth Enlarged Plenum of the ECCI in Moscow. May 1-7: Second pan-Chinese Congress of Workers (500,000 members). May 30: British massacre 30 demonstrators in Shanghai. Wave of strikes and demonstrations in response. Massive three-month strike movement in Shanghai by new general Union. May 30 marks a new period of worker-peasant resurgence. CPC membership grows from 900 to 20,000. June 25 shooting by British police provokes great strike-boycott of Canton-Hong Kong which assumes dual-power characteristics (militia, courts, etc.). Leaders of the KMT Right decide to destroy the Communists. October: CC meeting of CPC. Chen Du-Siu proposes party pulls out of the KMT and prepares to fight counter revolution. But the party follows the CI and decides to remain inside.

1926

January: 'Left' wing of KMT predominates at 2nd Congress. 'Christian' general Feng feted and given arms by Moscow. March 6: Plenum of ECCI in Moscow: KMT defined as 'the revolutionary bloc of workers, peasants, intellectuals and the urban democracy ("bloc of four classes")'. The KMT admitted to the CI as a 'sympathizing party', and Chiang elected a member of honour of the Presidium against Trotsky's dissentient vote at the Politburo. March 20: Chiang proclaims martial law, shuts down branches of the Canton workers' organizations, disarms pickets, arrests CPers. Soviet press denies news. Soviet advisers refuse 5,000 rifles to workers and peasants. CI slaps down CPC proposals to form left factions in the KMT. April-May: Feng's army ejected from Hunan-Zhili by warlords who begin white terror. May 1: Third Congress of Labour. Chiang guest of honour at this Communist-dominated Congress representing half China's workers. Reference to the coup of March 20 suppressed. Instead, a decision to reinforce the Canton government. May 15: KMT excludes Communists from all responsible positions. CPC and Borodin accept this. July 7: Chiang's Northern expedition to clear out the warlords meets with popular response, but on July 19 Chiang declares martial law, forbids strikes. August: Feng joins KMT. September: Hankow falls to Chiang. October: army suppresses Canton-Hong Kong strike-boycott. October 26: telegram of the ECCI instructs CPC not to embarrass Chiang with peasant struggles. November 29-December: Seventh enlarged Plenum of the ECCI. Tang Ping Shan criticizes these policies as subordination to the KMT and calls for preparation of a fight against the KMT right wing. But the Stalin-Bukharin formula of reinforcing the bloc prevails. M. N. Roy becomes CI representative in China. November-December: the Wang Chin Wei-Chiang conflict ('Left vs. Right' of KMT).

1927

January 3: Spontaneous mass occupation of British concessions in Hankow. Chiang's army slows down advance to North to allow warlords to massacre workers and peasants. Shanghai armed uprising treated similarly. Communists as ministers in Wuhan government. March 17: Letter from Shanghai from young Comintern representatives in China. March 21: Uprising in Shanghai which opens the gates to Chiang who promptly gangs up with imperialists, bourgeois and underworld. April: Communists arrested. Trotsky warns of danger of a coup by Chiang and calls for independence of the CPC. April 5: Chen Du Siu and Wang Chin Wei confirm the alliance between CPC and KMT. Stalin tells Moscow Communists that a coup by Chiang is impossible. April 6: Chang So Lin in alliance with Chiang arrests Communists including Li Ta Chao, who are later garrotted. April 12: Chiang with the support of the reactionaries commences a sustained massacre of the Chinese workers. M. N. Roy and Doriot telegraph Chiang asking him not to take unilateral action. April 21: the CI admits Chiang's betrayal but Stalin declares events to have confirmed line of the CI. April 27: Fifth Congress of the CPC switches support to Wuhan government of Wang Chin Wei. Soviet embassy attacked by Chiang. May 18: Trotsky predicts that Wang Chin Wei will line up with Chiang. May: Wang Chin Wei attacks workers. May 20-26: Eighth Plenum of the ECCI. Trotsky attacks pro-Wuhan policy, calls for Soviets in China. Stalin says: not while the KMT exists and not with Wuhan as 'revolutionary centre'. May 21: veritable massacre of Changsha workers and peasants. Peasant agitation grows. June: CPC proposes anti-Chiang front to Wuhan which replies with a savage onslaught on the workers and the CPC. July 13: CPC ministers in Wuhan government resign. July 15: ECCI denounces CPC leadership as responsible for the defeat but insists they still stay in the KMT. End of the Wuhan government. Borodin and M. N. Roy leave China to be replaced by Lominadze, Stalin's representative. August 1: rising of troops at Nanchang under communist influence (Ho Lung and Yeh Ting). August 7: extraordinary conference of CPC with Lominadze. Chen Du Siu, condemned as opportunist, is scapegoat. Likewise Tang Pin San with the peasants. Qui Qui Bai, general secretary along with a new leadership. September: Platform of Left Opposition criticizes CI policy in China. Hunan peasant uprising led by Mao Tse Tung. October: Soviets in Shensi. Trotsky and Zinoviev expelled from the CPSU. Decision taken to stage a rising in Canton to coincide with the 15th Congress of the CPSU. December 11-14: Canton Commune uprising instigated by Lominadze and Neumann, CI representatives. Holocaust follows. December 2-9: All the Left Opposition expelled.

1928

January: Trotsky and Oppositionists deported. May: formation of the 4th Red Army in Hunan. July-September: Sixth Congress of the CPC held in Moscow. Qui Qui Bai condemned for Putschism. New leadership of Li Li San and Chou En Lai.

1929

August: Peasant Soviets of Mao in Shensi. November: Chen Du Siu expelled from the CPC.

1930

May: Mif arrives in China with a team of militants trained in Moscow. August-September: Li Li San condemned for Putschism.

INDEX